Whether you are a world-renowned neurosurgeon, a CEO, or a teacher, this book applies to anyone who ever wondered about the difference between the pacesetters and those who struggle to keep up. It is the pacesetters who *Take the Risk*, and this book explains when and why to take risks to empower everyone to become a trailblazer rather than a mere spectator. For anyone who wants to rise above mediocrity, this book is a must-read.

ARMSTRONG WILLIAMS, author and radio host,
The Armstrong Williams Show

Dr. Carson continues to use the lessons he has learned in his rich and well-examined life to empower others to live and dream to their fullest potential. The risks he takes convey not only his willingness to face the unknown, but a deep faith that is both inspirational and intrinsic to his success.

SHEILA DIXON, mayor of Baltimore

There's a difference between taking risk ... and gambling. That's why corporate America uses a process called "due diligence". Ben Carson persuades me that taking risk ain't always a gamble. Great read.

GENERAL TOMMY FRANKS, United States Army

TAKE THE RISK

Learning to Identify, Choose,
and Live with Acceptable Risk

BEN CARSON MD

with Gregg Lewis

ZONDERVAN

Take the Risk
Copyright © 2008 by Benjamin Carson

This title is also available in a Zondervan audio edition.
Visit www.zondervan.fm.

Requests for information should be addressed to:
Zondervan, 3900 *Sparks Dr. SE, Grand Rapids, Michigan 49546*

This edition: ISBN 978-0-310-34183-3 (softcover)

Library of Congress Cataloging-in-Publication Data

Carson, Ben.
    Take the risk / Ben Carson, with Gregg Lewis.
        p.   cm.
    Includes bibliographical references and index [if applicable].
    ISBN 978-0-310-25973-2 (hardcover)
    1. Risk-taking (Psychology). I. Lewis, Gregg, 1951– II. Title.
  BF637.R57 .C37
    302'.12 — dc22   2007010480

Interior design: Beth Shagene

First printing 2008 / Printed in the United States of America

Contents

I

Introduction

PEOPLE WHO BECOME SURGEONS — PARTICULARLY NEUROSURGEONS — tend to be risk-takers. You don't go into a field that requires cracking people's heads open or operating on something as delicate as the spinal cord unless you are comfortable with taking risks.

Every day I make critical, split-second decisions that affect the longevity and the quality of other people's lives. Taking such risks gives me pause. It forces me to think about my own life and the risks I face. Those experiences enable me to move forward and avoid becoming paralyzed by fear. As a result, I probably do a lot of things that more cautious people would never attempt.

On September 10, 2003, the interviewer on National Public Radio asked me how, as a doctor and as a human being, I could take so many risks — such as separating conjoined twins, girls joined at their heads.

"Why *risk?*" I responded. "It should be, why *not* risk?"

That's what this book is all about — risk.

In our culture, security has become an obsession. It dictates everything from public policy to Madison Avenue's commercial appeals, from medical care to education and personal and family life. We buy every kind of insurance — from life insurance to replacement policies for our cell phones — to provide us with the security we think we need. We pay extra for warranties on our computers and appliances. We read safety test results in *Consumer Reports* before buying an automobile. We purchase safety seats to keep our children secure and safety helmets for them to wear on their bike rides around the block.

We buy flame-retardant pajamas for our kids and wouldn't think of purchasing Tylenol or aspirin (or any other medicine) that didn't come in a tamperproof container. We go on low-cholesterol diets, exercise regularly, and make sure we get regular dental and medical checkups to protect our health. We invest in low-risk mutual funds in an attempt to ensure a comfortable retirement. Our nation spends billions of dollars on equipment and manpower to keep airports and air travel as safe as possible.

What we're buying and what everyone is selling us is the promise of "security." And yet the only thing we can be sure of is that someday every one of us will die.

Could this fact have something to say about our view of risk-taking? And how might that impact our vocations, our personal lives and relationships, or our faith?

Anyone who refuses to test his limits, anyone unwilling to move out of her comfort zone, is destined to live life inside the envelope. The most important developments in science, history, technology, and the arts came from taking risks. In the chapters ahead, we'll look at the downside of not taking risks. We'll examine the case for risk-taking and look at some of the personal characteristics, attitudes, and resources required to be a risk-taker. We'll also consider some of the common barriers to risk.

In the process I'll share some of the risks I've taken in my life—and some others that I live with every day—not just as a neurosurgeon, but as a man, husband, father, and son. Not everything I write on the subject is drawn from personal experience, however. I've thought a lot about the ramifications of risk in the lives of some familiar and less-familiar people. By doing so, I hope to shake up your thinking and inspire you to take appropriate risks.

Not long ago, in an after-dinner conversation with best-selling author Tom Clancy, we shared some of our professional experiences. He flattered me by saying, "I don't understand how you can take so many risks. But I admire that."

As part of my response, I explained a simple risk analysis exercise I use whenever I face an uncertain situation—in my professional or personal life. It's a quick and practical guide that can help anyone answer these questions: "*When* should I take a risk?" and "*What* should I risk?" (This exercise is outlined in chapters 8 and 9.)

I'm going to risk right now, here in this book, by thinking big about this subject.

I hope you'll take the risk of reading it and thinking through the topic with me.

Risking
Their Lives

BALTIMORE TO LONDON TO SINGAPORE ...

I had no time to rest and recover after my twenty-hour journey. As soon as I arrived at the airport, I was whisked through customs, ushered into the backseat of a waiting Mercedes, and driven directly to Singapore's new and prestigious Raffles Hospital for a lengthy introductory meeting and then a light lunch with my surgical colleague hosts.

After these preliminaries, I was ready for my first appointment—the long-anticipated encounter with our special patients. It promised to be one of the most fascinating and unusual interviews of my life. I don't recall what my fellow neurosurgeon Dr. Keith Goh said to me as the entourage of physicians, nurses, and medical administrators rounded the corner in that hospital corridor—but I will never forget my first sight of Ladan and Laleh Bijani.

The young women waited to greet me in the hallway outside the suite of rooms that had been converted into a small apartment. They had lived there for a number of months while an army of medical doctors, specialists, and technicians examined them and conducted test after test after test. The Bijani twins wore the traditional Iranian attire of their homeland—long skirts, long-sleeved tops, muted colors, nothing over their faces, but a large scarflike cloth covering the thick, dark brown hair on their heads. Their warm and welcoming smiles struck me immediately.

Dr. Goh, a short, dark-haired Asian in his forties, quickly introduced me to the women. The Bijanis' English, which I'd been informed they had learned since arriving in Singapore seven months before, was broken and stilted but more than adequate for simple conversation.

After shaking hands with and greeting the first twin, I stepped around to greet the other one—a semi-awkward little side step necessary because Ladan and Laleh could not face me at the same time. Indeed, the twenty-nine-year-old sisters were a true medical rarity: identical twins conjoined at the head, their two skulls fused above and behind their ears so that their faces turned permanently away from each other at about a 130-degree angle.

The connection of their skulls held their heads nearly straight up and down. But with their ears touching and their shoulders and arms constantly rubbing, they were forced to lean their upper bodies toward one another and drop their inside shoulders to simultaneously create room to maneuver and maintain the balance necessary to move and stand together.

The result of a single fertilized egg that divides but never completely separates in the womb, conjoined twins (meaning they are attached at some point of their bodies) occur only once in every 200,000 births. All but a few are stillborn or die shortly after birth. Live craniopagus (from the Greek *cranio*, meaning "helmet," and *pagus*, meaning "fixed") twins are attached at the head and are the rarest of all—perhaps one in two million births. The odds of such twins living to two years of age are much, much slimmer—which made Ladan and Laleh's survival into adulthood a remarkable thing indeed.

Even more astounding is the fact that these young women had done far more than survive. Adopted by a compassionate Iranian medical doctor when their birth family couldn't care for them, Ladan and Laleh were given every possible opportunity to adapt and live as normal a life as possible. And adapt they did.

They attended elementary school with their peers. In time they grew, graduated from secondary school, and went on to university, where they studied journalism and pre-law. The two graduated from law school and were now fully qualified attorneys—which had recently precipitated a crisis resulting in added tensions between the sisters. Only Ladan wished to pursue a legal career, while Laleh had decided she wanted to go into journalism. Their physical bodies bound them together in a mutually shared existence, even as their two distinct personalities° and now two very different life dreams—pulled them in different directions.

For years Ladan and Laleh had searched the world over for a neurosurgeon who would agree to operate and give them at least a chance of achieving their lifelong dream of pursuing two normal, individual, and distinctively different lives. Expert after expert refused to consider their request. Every doctor willing to examine their records told them that surgery would be too risky, that at least one of them—and probably both—would die. Their case was just too complex, they were too old, and the odds of a positive outcome were too low.

But the Bijanis refused to give up. When they read that Dr. Goh and his team had successfully separated eleven-month-old Nepalese craniopagus twins a couple of years before, they contacted him. After studying their medical records and concluding that a successful surgery just might be possible, he contacted me to ask if I'd be willing to help.

I had consulted and worked long-distance with Keith Goh on the Nepalese babies through the use of our virtual workstation at Johns Hopkins. I had also served as one of the primary surgeons for the first successful separation of occipital craniopagus twins (the Bender boys at Johns Hopkins in 1987). Ten years later, at the Medical University of South Africa, I was primary surgeon for the Zambian brothers Joseph and Luka Banda during the first separation of Type 2 vertical craniopagus twins in which both not only survived, but remained neurologically intact. Because of all those experiences, Dr. Goh wanted me to work with him on the surgery, and the Bijani twins themselves had also requested that I join their case.

I had actually declined their invitation when I'd first been contacted months before. The very fact that these young women had adapted so well and had already survived to the age of twenty-nine seemed to me reason enough to recommend against surgery. In an attempt to dissuade them, I had suggested to Dr. Goh that he remind the Bijanis of the case of Chang and Eng Bunker, the original "Siamese twins." Born in Siam (now Thailand) back in 1811, these brothers achieved celebrity, traveling the world as the headline attraction of P. T. Barnum's circus before retiring from show business, purchasing adjacent properties in North Carolina, and becoming successful farmers. They married sisters, fathered a total of twenty-one children between them, and lived healthy lives to the age of sixty-three.

If ever I'd heard of another set of conjoined twins who I thought rivaled the Bunkers' adaptability and who just might match or exceed their amazing longevity, it was these remarkable young women who had already survived and accomplished so much. The idea of separating them at the age of twenty-nine just didn't make sense, and after examining their records and studying the initial CAT scans Dr. Goh had sent me, I was convinced the risks were just too high.

Yet now, months later in Singapore, standing face-to-face with these two determined, obviously bright, and outgoing young women — who just happened to be attached at the head — I found myself incredibly impressed and thoroughly charmed.

Ladan and Laleh smiled shyly and even giggled at the commotion of the people who'd come with me to meet them. I was amazed by how at ease they seemed to be with all the attention. Dr. Goh had told me the twins had become quite the celebrities since their arrival in Singapore. Every time they'd ventured outside the hospital — to eat, shop, or just sightsee — the Bijanis had attracted media and crowds of curious well-wishers who clamored for pictures and autographs or simply wanted to shake their hands. So far, according to Dr. Goh, the young women seemed to find the attention more amusing than troubling.

The crowd gathered in that hospital hallway that afternoon, however, was logistically awkward, so the Bijanis invited me (along with Dr. Goh and a couple of others) into their living quarters to continue our conversation. As they led the way, I could see they had mobility down to a science. I followed, watching with interest and marveling at the smooth, almost subconscious choreography required just to turn and walk, slip through a doorway, and then gracefully seat themselves on the short couch that dominated a sitting room just inside the living area.

I sat in a chair directly across the room, a coffee table between us. From there I would be able to lean a little left to talk with one sister and then just tilt my head and lean a little right to speak to the other.

Not only did I want to be able to respect their individuality by speaking to each of them separately and making eye contact as I did so, but I wanted to be able to read the expressions on their faces and the looks in their eyes as they answered my questions.

We made pleasant small talk for a short time — about their stay in Singapore, the ease with which they had picked up conversational English, and all the media attention they'd experienced. At that point I lightheartedly "warned" them that all the attention they had received so far would seem like a drop in the bucket compared to the media frenzy that would result from a successful surgery. "The queen, the king, and everyone else will want to meet you," I said. They laughed at the prospect but didn't seemed at all troubled.

As we talked, I noted that Ladan was decidedly the more outgoing and talkative of the two. Laleh seemed, if not exactly shy, at least more reserved and pensive.

When the discussion moved on to the impending surgery, the twins became a bit more somber. As they talked honestly about some of the difficulties they had faced in life, I realized even the simplest and most routine movements — from getting in and out of a car to bending over and picking a pencil up off the floor or fixing a snack — required complex choreography and complete cooperation between the two of them. Every life choice — from what classes to take in school, to which friends to spend time with, to when to go to the bathroom — was a committee decision demanding unanimous consent.

But the longer I spent in their presence, the less I found myself trying to imagine all of the challenges they had overcome. Instead, I tried to picture how different things would be for them if a successful operation were to free them to live separate lives. After twenty-nine years of perpetual and involuntary attachment to another human being, the abstract idea of privacy would be very appealing — but what would it really feel like to be wholly alone for the first time in your life?

One of the primary reasons I had declined the Bijanis' case when I'd first been approached was that I feared the psychological ramifications of separating conjoined twins after twenty-nine years. What if separation proved more emotionally damaging than remaining attached? My thinking began to shift, however, as I learned more about their situation, their conflicting aspirations, and their determination to pursue the operation. I knew they had undergone extensive psychological counseling in recent months, but still, I needed to hear their own responses to my concerns about the formidable psychological adjustments they would face if they were separated. So I asked them to tell me what they thought about the issue.

They assured me that they knew a successful separation would not bring an end to the many challenges they faced. They acknowledged that some of their lifelong emotional bonds might be hard to sever. But again they expressed their determination to press ahead with the operation. They were determined.

When I asked if I could feel their heads, they readily agreed. As I ran my fingers over the top, side, and back of their skulls, I explained that after many hours spent studying their CAT scans, I had a good idea of what their brains looked like. Still, before surgery the next day, I told them, "I want to get a sense of the junction of your skulls."

The examination only took a few seconds, but it was long enough to remind me just how complex this surgery promised to be. It was one thing to look at film on a lighted board or to hold a life-size plastic model of their conjoined heads and try to visualize the challenge this surgery would present. It was another thing entirely, however, to run my fingertips through their hair, tracing the extent of the solid, bony juncture of their two skulls. The attachment covered an area that was almost half the size of a head — from above and in front of the ears on the side of the head, then over the ears and down to almost the base of their skulls in the back.

I knew that Dr. Goh had explained to them the various steps and procedures involved in the surgery, but I wanted to know for myself that they understood the risks. "I have to tell you," I said to them, "what I believe you already know — that this will be an extremely complex and risky surgery." To make certain they understood, I waited for their translator to repeat what I said in Farsi. "Based on my experience and my study of your case, and despite the excellent resources available to your fine surgical team here at Raffle Hospital, I still think there is at least a 50 percent chance this surgery could result in death or serious brain damage for one or both of you. I need to make certain you both understand that."

At Johns Hopkins my colleagues and I routinely perform some of the most complex neurosurgical procedures in the world. Any operation with as much as a 10 percent chance of mortality would be considered an extraordinarily dangerous procedure—a sky-high risk. So a 50 percent risk is truly stratospheric. I wanted to be sure that Ladan and Laleh understood the stakes.

Both women assured me again that Dr. Goh had been very honest with them. They understood the challenges. But most convincing for me was hearing the emotion and conviction in their voices as they insisted, "We would rather die than not pursue this if there is any chance we could be free to live our own separate lives. Death would be better than continuing to live like this!"

Because we put such a premium on life, it was startling to hear two healthy, vivacious young women state such feelings in a straightforward manner just hours before an operation. Most of us, even those of us who deal with life-and-death issues every day, don't often stop and think seriously about what quality of life means to us. But as we spoke, I had a growing awareness that these women had thought long and hard about the subject and that it would be extremely difficult for anyone not in their situation to even begin to understand how they felt.

I had already heard from the Singaporean medical team, who had learned it from one of the twins' caretakers, that the tension between the women had escalated in recent months. Some arguments had even led to physical altercations. I could only imagine how awful it would be to experience serious conflict with someone you could never walk away from.

Most people can easily understand why someone who is enslaved or imprisoned would risk death to escape and experience freedom. For Ladan and Laleh, their state was very much the same thing. They desperately wanted to escape what was for them an untenable situation. The hope of freedom was worth any risk. As I began to understand that, I also began to feel better about embarking on such a potentially dangerous course of action.

Meeting these young women—and hearing the determination in their voices, recognizing the desperation in their lives, and seeing the hope and resolve in their eyes—sealed the deal for me. By the time our conversation began to wind down, I was thinking, *Let's get these women separated so they can get on with their lives!*

Even though I had assured Ladan and Laleh during our interview that I cared about their well-being, before leaving their apartment, I looked them both in the eyes once again and acknowledged that we were about to embark on a long, arduous, and extremely dangerous operation. That while the odds were not good and I could not promise them a successful outcome, I did feel optimistic enough to think there was reason to hope. I said, "There are a lot of things in life beyond our human ability, knowledge, and control. But there is nothing beyond God."

As I stood and shook hands with them and bid them good-bye—until I saw them in the operating room the next morning—I told Ladan and Laleh what I tell all of my patients during my final pre-op exams: "I've never known a case yet where worry helped. So I'm going to say my prayers tonight before I go to sleep. I hope you'll do the same. I believe if we do that, we'll all have less to worry about tomorrow."

As I turned and walked out of that room, I believed beyond a shadow of any doubt that both Ladan and Laleh Bijani truly understood what they faced. They were approaching this dangerous and unprecedented surgery with much the same spirit of determination they had shown in tackling so many challenges in their lives.

Most of all, they had convinced me that they understood the risks.

To Risk or Not to Risk?

MY FIRST PRIORITY, AND THAT OF THE ENTIRE MEDICAL TEAM, WAS to do everything possible, even before the surgery, to reduce the risks facing Ladan and Laleh. So we went straight from that half-hour interview with the Bijanis to a planning conference, where the whole team—twenty-eight physicians and approximately one hundred additional nurses, technicians, and assistants—sat down to talk. Every person in that room would play an important role in the marathon operation, which was expected to last two or three days, perhaps even more.

Most of the team had already walked and talked their way through our step-by-step plans for the surgery itself, the organization and coordination of the various experts, and the actual setup, positioning, and staging of the patients and the thirty to forty medical staff who would need to be in the operating room at any given time. Every person needed to be clear about who would be where and when and what they would be doing.

I was impressed by Dr. Goh's meticulous attention to detail, his organizational skills, and the impressive team of experts he'd assembled from Singapore, the United States, France, Japan, Switzerland, and Nepal. He reviewed the plans with us until everything had been covered—and much of it more than once. Finally, there was nothing left for me to do but check into my nearby hotel and try to combat my jet lag with a good night's sleep.

Before crawling into bed, I did what I'd promised Ladan and Laleh I would do. I prayed. I prayed for them, for the operation, for myself, and for the rest of the surgical team—that God would grant all of us wisdom, calm, and peace, that his presence would be in that operating room, and that his will might be done.

It was not the first time I had prayed about the case.

As I said, not only had I originally turned down Dr. Goh's invitation to join him on the Bijani case, but I had actually advised him against the operation altogether. Several weeks after that, I learned my evaluation had been presented to the twins—and they had decided to proceed with the operation anyway. A team was being assembled, and Dr. Goh contacted me again. Would I please reconsider?

Again my inclination was to say, No, *if you foolishly want to pursue this, go ahead without me. I don't want to be involved.* Although two out of three craniopagus surgeries I'd taken part in had been successful, the odds for this one just didn't look good.

But the more I thought about it, the more my reaction felt like a copout. I realized that my decision not to participate had been based on personal batting averages and success rates—and that's not who I am or the kind of person I want to be. So I prayed, "Lord, if you really want me to get involved, I will."

Since the Bijani twins were determined to move ahead with or without my help, I had to ask myself, *If things do go badly, will I wonder for the rest of my life what I might have done to help?* I didn't want to find out. Since I had more experience with craniopagus twins than any other neurosurgeon in the world, I knew there was a real possibility that I could be of help.

One of my neurosurgical colleagues at Johns Hopkins, a valued friend, came to me when he learned I was rethinking my decision. He warned me, "Participating in this case could hurt your reputation, Ben. There's just not a high likelihood of success. You really need to think this through before getting involved."

My friend was genuinely concerned. I knew that and understood what he was saying about the risk to my professional reputation. So I seriously considered his warning ... for about two seconds. That's all it took for me to realize, *This should not be all about my reputation.* My "risk" was insignificant compared to the high risk of death or debilitation that the twins faced. All of the real risks were theirs.

That was a major factor in my decision, as was the realization that God had provided me with certain abilities and experience and had put two people before me who might benefit from them. I needed to do my utmost to see if something could be done for them.

Whenever I face a hard decision or a risky situation in life (personally or professionally), all my thinking, all my analysis, all my planning can be boiled down to four simple questions:

- What is the best thing that can happen if I do this?
- What is the worst thing that can happen if I do this?
- What is the best thing that can happen if I don't do it?
- What is the worst thing that can happen if I don't do it?

By the time I've thought through those four questions (which we'll examine in more detail in chapter 9 and in the last half of this book), I've usually analyzed the risks thoroughly enough to make a reasoned decision.

After all my thinking and praying, my decision came down to the fact that I felt obligated to do everything I could to help. Once Ladan and Laleh had made their decision, I didn't really have any other choice. That's why I had flown halfway around the globe on a Fourth of July weekend to take part in what I now expected to be the most publicized craniopagus twin surgery in the history of medicine.

As I made my inspection of the OR/ICU/angiogram suite early Sunday morning, the twins, lying on a standard hospital bed, arrived for their final pre-op procedures. They warmly greeted everyone they rolled past, smiling while they first offered cheery good mornings and then expressed grateful good-byes. Struck yet again by their courage, I walked over to them, took their hands in mine, and promised we would do the very best we could to care for them. As they thanked me, I sensed Ladan and Laleh were at peace with whatever lay ahead.

Despite the uncertainties I felt, one distinct certainty about this first-ever attempt to separate adult craniopagus twins was apparent.

Unlike any of the conjoined twins I'd operated on previously—in fact, unlike any of my pediatric neurosurgical patients—the Bijanis were able to give their own "informed consent." What's more, given the fact that they were both lawyers, that doctor after doctor had attempted to talk them out of this surgery for years, and that they remained adamantly determined to proceed, I doubted there had ever been another operation with as much "informed consent."

But that knowledge, like the twins' courageous and optimistic spirits, provided only small comfort to me that morning. Nothing could change the odds that their surgery might be the most challenging and risky in my twenty-plus years as a neurosurgeon.

Because the twins had complained in recent weeks about severe headaches, we assumed they were suffering from elevated intracranial pressure. If so, it should ease once we separated them and gave them added room for their brains. But just to be sure we had all of the information before we began, we took one more pre-op angiogram to look one final time at the Bijanis' circulatory patterns.

Then, while some world-class neuroradiologists, who had flown in from France, interpreted that film, the twins were anesthetized, their heads shaved, and two small burr holes drilled in the anterior part of their skulls so that pressure monitors could be inserted. The monitors confirmed our suspicions—intracranial pressure was significantly elevated. But the angiogram revealed no surprises.

It was time to begin.

I wasn't in the OR for stage one. Instead, I watched the proceedings on a closed-circuit television from a nearby room, which had been converted into a doctors' conference, lunch, and break room. I followed the progress of the vascular surgeons as they harvested a large vein from Ladan's thigh. That piece, several inches long and almost as thick as my little finger, would soon be needed for what everyone anticipated would be the single most critical step in the entire operation.

Indeed, the most troubling aspect of the Bijanis' case was the fact that much of the blood circulating through the women's brains passed through a single draining vein in the back of their heads. Years before, a group of German doctors, the first medical team to examine the twins, had deemed the operation "too dangerous" for that reason alone. But with encouraging progress and recent technological advances in the field of vascular transplants, Dr. Goh's team had determined it would be possible to divide and reroute the circulation by retaining the current drain for Laleh and grafting in a transplanted vein to create a new drain for Ladan. Such a procedure had never been tried before, but it seemed feasible. A top neurovascular team from Japan would tackle that challenge — but not before our neurosurgical team took our first turn in the operating room.

By the time that happened, we were already well into Sunday afternoon. Once the surgeons had successfully acquired the vessel — an eight-inch-long segment — they had to close the leg. Then it was a matter of getting both women repositioned, prepped, and draped for the cranial part of the operation. That setup alone took hours.

Unlike the many infants I'd separated, adult patients couldn't simply be flipped around to give the surgeons a better angle. Ladan and Laleh had to be positioned on a custom-designed operating table that could be pulled apart once we separated them. They also had to be propped up on pillows and held in place with special braces at nearly a forty-five-degree angle. That one fixed position had to provide us surgeons access to the entire operating field — from the top and front of their heads, which we would have to reach by standing on stools and leaning in toward and above them from the side, to the very base of their skulls' junction, which we could see and reach only while sitting on stools, bending low, and looking up from the end of the table.

Once we completed the prep work, the plastic surgeons moved in to separate the scalp from the skull and turn it back in large flaps, which we would use to help close the wound once surgery was done. This was another significant difference from the previous separation surgeries I'd done. Weeks before separating babies, plastic surgeons would insert balloonlike scalp expanders, which they would gradually inflate to stretch the scalp and force the bodies to grow enough additional skin to cover the exposed area on both babies' heads. None of that was necessary with the Bijanis. Because they were adults, we would be able to harvest enough skin grafts from other parts of their bodies to completely cover any area still exposed when we finished the operation.

Once the plastic surgeons exposed the bone, they backed out, and our neurosurgical team moved in to begin the tedious process of opening a bone window, which would give the neurovascular team access to the brain itself.

Six neurosurgeons worked in shifts—usually two at a time—for almost twenty-four hours as we encountered a couple of unanticipated issues. The primary problem confronting us was the thickness of the skulls themselves. Naturally we had allowed for the fact that adult skulls are much harder and thicker to cut through than those of young children. But no one was prepared for the fact that the posterior juncture (near the base of the two skulls) had continued growing together over the years until that whole rear portion of the twins' shared skull was literally as thick as a brick—and a lot harder.

That created the second challenge: the location of that thickest portion of skull (low and in the back of the head, behind and below the ears) was the most difficult place for the surgeons to access. With our patients propped and tilted back at a angle, we had to reach into a very narrow triangular tunnel between their overlapping shoulders and ears. It was exhausting, muscle-cramping, and nerve-racking to aim, maneuver, and control our high-speed drills and saws to carve, cut, and punch through so much bone in such a confined space.

The whole physically awkward and emotionally taxing procedure was made even more so by our painstaking awareness that just beneath that section of incredibly hard and thick skull we were exerting all our strength drilling and sawing through—adjacent to that bone on the very surface of the brain itself—were large blood sinuses. These extensive venous lakes run through the layers of the dura (the thin leatherlike material that covers the brain) and help drain normal blood flow out of the organ. One slip of a saw, one drill bit poking through a fraction of a millimeter too far, could mean the sudden and disastrous end to the surgery before we even started to separate our patients.

Those were the conditions we faced as we chipped, ground, and sliced away, bit by bit, a six-by-six-inch section of the thickest part of the skull to provide the neurovascular team room to see and reach a wide enough field to graft in the new bypass drainage vein for Ladan. With that mission finally accomplished, I retreated to the break room to watch the critical next step.

Working meticulously, a renowned Japanese surgeon, an expert in vascular grafts, began tying in one of the pieces of leg vein they'd harvested the previous morning. As the hours passed, everything seemed to be working as planned. When he finished and the rerouted blood began to flow through the bypass, spirits soared throughout the entire surgical department of Raffles Hospital. Each woman now had a working drain. We thought we'd surmounted our most serious threat; that troubling and sinister shared vascular structure no longer seemed to pose a problem.

But we were about to be proven wrong.

For more than a day, the thoughts and prayers and energies of the 125 members of our medical team were so focused on that crowded OR suite that the remainder of the world seemed to fade away. It was easy to forget that a surprising amount of the world's attention was attuned to our history-making efforts. An army of reporters gathered in and around the hospital as the story of the Bijani twins made headlines in papers and news broadcasts around the globe.

In its Monday coverage, *China Daily* led with the headline "Conjoined Iranian Twins Begin Surgery in Singapore," and the article, which drew from various news agencies, said, "An unprecedented, high-risk operation to separate adult Iranian twin sisters joined at the head began in Singapore on Sunday.... Law graduates Laleh and Ladan Bijani, 29, have undergone tests and counseling since November and say they are willing to risk death for the chance to lead separate lives."

The article reported that the operation, headed by Dr. Goh, was expected to last at least forty-eight hours. It gave some background on conjoined twins and cited Dr. Goh's success in separating the eleven-month-old Nepalese babies Jamuna and Ganga Shrestha in a four-day operation a couple of years before. The article went on to list the principal surgeons: "Goh is being assisted by Dr. Walter Tan, a plastic surgeon, and Dr. Ben Carson, director of pediatric neurosurgery at

Johns Hopkins in Baltimore." The article cited my experience separating conjoined twins and also quoted one of our surgical team members, French radiologist Pierre Lasjaunias from the Center Hospitalier de Bicetre, who, the day before the surgery, had expressed his opinion that "all steps" to provide for the twins' safety had been taken. "Most of the security that could be achieved has been achieved," he had said. "Now the journey has to go on."

The article concluded by raising the specter of controversy over this kind of surgery. It quoted the head of medical ethics at Imperial College in London, Dr. Richard Ashcroft, who expressed his opinion that because the twins were not in any immediate at risk of dying without this high-risk surgery, the decision to proceed was a controversial one. "It's a genuine moral dilemma," said Dr. Ashcroft. "And where you have a dilemma, people will make different decisions because there is no obvious answer what the right thing to do is."

Before our neurosurgical team could get started with the next phase of the operation, a crisis arose. A blood clot blocked Ladan's graft, and the blood stopped draining out the new route. Worried that such a major blockage could trigger a severe stroke or send the patients' blood pressure skyrocketing, and also realizing that any significant loss of blood could result in irrevocable damage to affected brain tissue, the vascular team desperately worked to clear the blockage and restore normal blood flow through the transplanted vein.

Again the neurosurgeons began their work. But then the vein hardened and backed up a second time as another clot closed off the newly installed drainage vessel. What was happening?

Alarmed and concerned that the most crucial step of the whole operation may have been an inexplicable failure, I studied the bypass intently and felt all around the exposed brain tissue. Despite the obvious blockage, the entire segment of brain that I could see maintained its healthy pink color. Obviously it continued to receive oxygen. The tissue itself pulsed and remained pliable and soft—without swelling or rigidity, which would indicate the sort of dangerous pressure buildup you would expect from such a blockage. Amazingly both women's vital signs remained stable.

I quickly verbalized my observations to Dr. Goh and the other doctors. "The circulatory paths have clearly changed. The blood has found somewhere else to flow. We have no idea where. The patients are stable. This might be a good time to stop and rethink our strategy."

Dr. Goh agreed to take a few moments to continue the discussion outside the OR. So I followed him and the administrative chairman of Raffles Hospital, Dr. Loo Choon Yong, out into an adjacent corridor.

"Things have obviously changed—significantly," I argued. "The blood has found another place to go and another way to get there. Which means we no longer know what we're doing because we don't know what's going on inside the women's brains. They seem to be fine. Everything is stable right now. But I recommend we call a halt right now, sew the patients up, and move them into ICU.

"If we wait a few weeks to go back in," I continued, "that might give the new circulation channels time to develop and get stronger. We can take more scans and have a chance to study the new vascular landscape. The women would have the chance to regain their strength and heal from what we've done thus far. The medical team is already exhausted; it would allow us to come back and continue fresh."

Dr. Goh agreed. My suggestion, he said, made a certain amount of sense, but his boss, the administrator, intimated it might not be possible. That's when he told me (the first I'd heard anything about it) that the Bijanis had insisted that he and Dr. Goh promise them that once the surgery had started, there would be no turning back. The operation would not be stopped until the separation was complete—no matter what!

"But things have significantly changed!" I argued. There was no doubt in my mind that our best chance—and the Bijanis' best chance—for a positive outcome was to halt the operation and try to find out what was going on.

The young brains of the infants I had separated in previous operations had spontaneously formed new and drastically different circulatory channels. That never surprised me much because the immature brains of infants and even older children exhibit a remarkable adaptability. Indeed, when Dr. Goh had consulted with me before he operated on the Nepalese twins back in 2001, I had emphasized the value of taking things slowly enough to allow some of those collateral circulation pathways to develop naturally and establish themselves. He had evidently taken my advice to heart at that time because the successful operation to separate the Nepalese babies had lasted more than ninety-six hours.

"Surely there's some way we can stop now," I continued to argue. "Then we could restudy the situation, restabilize the patients' heads with plates and screws, and come back armed with knowledge of the new circulation. We wouldn't require nearly as much time for the next surgery. Plus we'd know better what we are doing, which would improve our chances of success!

"I understand your promise to the patients," I added finally, "but there must be someone we can talk to, some chance they might relent...."

Dr. Loo looked from me to Dr. Goh before he responded in a somewhat doubtful tone. "I would have to speak to the twins' appointed guardian. With this new information we could see if she'd be willing to overrule the Bijanis' stipulation."

Dr. Goh and I quickly followed Dr. Loo down the hall. We stood a short distance off, watching and waiting, as he spoke quietly with a middle-aged Iranian woman to whom Ladan and Laleh had signed over legal guardianship. The woman listened intently and seemed to be asking questions. But then she shook her head before giving what looked like an intense and emotional response.

Dr. Loo nodded, said something more to her, then turned and walked back to give us the final verdict. The guardian had said she understood that things had changed, but Ladan and Laleh had made her promise, as they had made the doctors promise, that the surgery would go on, no matter what. They had been very clear on that—they would wake up separate or they wouldn't wake up at all. The promise had been made and the guardian insisted she could not go back on it. She refused to grant us permission to stop; the surgery needed to go on.

My heart sank. It wasn't until that point I fully experienced another significant difference between the Bijani case and earlier separation surgeries I'd taken part in. That is, the ultimate decision wasn't mine this time. No matter how strong my convictions or professional opinions, Dr. Goh and Dr. Loo were in charge. I was merely one member of their team, one person whose help they had to count on despite how I felt about the decision to continue.

We were thirty-two hours into the operation. The die had been cast. The end was not yet in sight, but we would not turn back.

We spent the next several hours drilling and sawing an inch-wide channel through the bone around the perimeter of our operating field to actually separate the two skulls at their juncture. In effect, we had to work our way completely around a large ring, roughly the diameter of an average-size head. To do so, we again had to reach in from every direction and elevation to cut the two women apart, inch by inch. But even after the skulls were almost entirely separated, we were far from done.

Ladan and Laleh didn't share any brain structure or tissue; each of their organs was distinct and complete. But because their brains had grown and been squeezed together over their lifetime, they were extensively attached—as if someone had spread superglue over the surface of their brains, pressed them tightly together, and let them dry for twenty-nine years.

There was no area of freedom. Approximately one hundred square inches of brain surface had bonded so tightly that we had to tease them apart, millimeter by millimeter, careful not to tear the tissue or rip loose any of the surface blood vessels that had grown out like a network of tentacles and become entangled over the years.

For much of this stage, all six neurosurgeons operated at once, two on stools high above us working on the anterior portion of the women's brains, two working on the brain section they could reach standing next to the operating table, and the other two seated on stools below so they could see to operate on the brains at the rear and base of the skulls.

Soft strains of classical music ebbed and flowed through the operating room for hours as we continued—gently lifting and pulling the brains apart, carefully slicing between the outer layers of adhered tissue, gently snipping and then clamping off or cauterizing tiny blood vessels as we went. Progress, though tedious, remained steady. Everything still seemed under control. So even as the hours passed and incredible exhaustion descended on our physical bodies, our spirits began to soar.

Slowly but surely we were separating Ladan's and Laleh's brains.

My hands and fingers began to cramp, and I could feel the muscles tighten across the back of my neck and shoulders. But as the operation approached the fifty-hour mark, I could see a promising light at the end of the tunnel—a happy ending indeed for two special and brave young women.

We'd had to sacrifice some vessels, but the patients were still stable. We had separated about 90 percent of the brain surfaces. Some of the last bits to clip and cut were located in the hardest place to reach—in the back, down below the ears, near where we'd also left one final bit of fused bone to stabilize the bases of their skulls and hold the women together.

Unfortunately, the difficult angle wasn't the only problem we encountered there.

We found where all the blood had gone. Every time we'd clip off one bleeder in the area, a new one would start.

I couldn't help thinking that if we had stopped the operation earlier, all that blood might have gradually found other places to go rather than pooling and building up pressure at the base of the skull. As it was, we fought furiously for the next two hours just trying to stem the tide. We managed to locate and control one bleeder after another after another—until it looked like we were gaining and might actually win the battle.

But right about that time, the anesthesiologist announced that Ladan had arrested. I was frustrated that we'd had no warning. It seemed impossible that she would reach such a crisis point without some prior indication that her condition was deteriorating.

Such a precipitous development left us with few options. Fortunately, we were close enough to the finish line that it made sense to hurriedly clip through the last remaining tissue and sever the final bit of bone. So that's what we did—taking less than five more minutes to completely separate the twins. Then the two halves of the special operating table could be unhooked and pulled apart so that each woman could be worked on separately.

Dr. Goh and I fought to control Laleh's continued bleeding while the other team tried desperately to resuscitate her sister. Some doctors did chest compressions and administered CPR to Ladan. Others tried to stop the bleeding in her head. They did everything they could possibly do for thirty minutes before acknowledging their efforts were in vain.

Ladan died at 2:30 p.m. on Tuesday.

Sadness settled over one side of the OR.

But those of us still working on Laleh didn't have time to grieve. Most neurosurgeons have developed the ability to isolate bad things. We have to. If you're thinking negative thoughts about what just happened, you're not going to be able to concentrate on what needs to happen next.

We were in yet another life-and-death battle with Laleh's bleeding. We could see where it was coming from, so we'd tamponade the area—holding cotton balls over it—while trying to locate the base of the vessel to coagulate it. But we'd no sooner get one spot under control than another one would break loose with another little red fountain of blood. By this time there was so much pressure in the system, the blood was simply looking for places to escape.

Thirty minutes rushed by. An hour. We worked desperately, fighting to keep from losing another battle. Finally, just as we gained enough stability to begin hoping that Laleh's bleeding might be under control, she arrested as well. Ninety minutes after her twin sister, Laleh Bijani also died from uncontrollable blood loss.

The music stopped in the OR. A somber numbness permeated our entire medical team. Tears flowed. After fifty-three hours, with only three or four one-hour-long catnaps, I wasn't sure which sensation cut deeper, my sadness or my fatigue. I just knew it was a horrible feeling I never wanted to experience again.

When *Is* Risk Worth It?

Not until the following day did I get a sense of the worldwide fascination with the Bijani twins and their quest to live separate lives. Reporters and news crews from around the globe packed the press conference at Raffles Hospital. Most of the doctors who took part in the surgery were there, facing the crowd of questioners who were assembled behind their cluster of cameras and an even greater mass of microphones.

Only a handful of queries were directed at me. Briefly I described my motivation for getting involved in such a dangerous procedure, my expectations going into the operation, my role during the surgery, and my reaction to the loss of our patients. Dr. Goh fielded most of the questions with the help of Dr. Loo, the chairman and administrator of Raffles Hospital.

The tone of the extensive question-and-answer session was reflected in a summary article in the *China Daily* published under the headline "Iranian Twins Die in Separation Surgery":

> Fifty grueling hours into an unprecedented operation to separate adult twins conjoined at the head, Dr. Keith Goh's heart sank. He was working furiously Tuesday to save Laleh Bijani, who began bleeding profusely the moment surgeons made the final cut to separate her from her sister.... Then Goh glanced over at Ladan. She was losing blood even faster. The twenty-nine-year-old twins died shortly thereafter, Ladan at 2:30 pm, and Laleh ninety minutes later. Both were still under anesthesia....

In their homeland, Iranians cried out in shock or wept as state television announced the deaths of the twins from a poor family who touched the world with their determination to lead separate lives—and to see each other face-to-face, rather than in a mirror.

The article described the family's grief back in Iran even as diplomatic arrangements were being made to transport their bodies home—in separate caskets—for burial. Based largely on Dr. Goh's explanations, the article summarized the challenges encountered during the operation and described how the unexpected and unpredictable changes in blood flow led to the women's deaths. The article even cited the dilemma we had faced at the thirty-two-hour mark, whether to stop and leave the Bijanis attached or, as Dr. Loo said in the press conference, to "continue with the final stage of the surgery, which we knew would be very, very risky." Dr. Loo explained, "The team wanted to know once again, 'What are the wishes of Ladan and Laleh?' We were told that Ladan and Laleh's wishes were to be separated under all circumstances."

Dr. Goh assured the assembled press that everyone, including the twins, had realized the risks involved. Even he had tried to talk them out of it. Now that they had both died, he expected people to question the wisdom of trying. "The decision to go ahead with the surgery, which seems so impossible to do, was a difficult one to make," he admitted. "But having seen and understood how these women suffered over their last twenty-nine years, I and many other world-renowned experts decided to contribute our time and skills to trying to give these women some measure of a decent, normal life."

In support of my colleague, I told the press, "These were individuals who were absolutely determined to be separated. The reason I felt compelled to become involved is because I wanted to make sure they had their best chance."

Dr. Loo revealed that final preoperative tests had shown that the intracranial pressure was double what it should have been: "The implication was that the twins would get into trouble sooner or later if nothing was done," he said.

After the press conference and a postmortem wrap-up with Dr. Goh and a number of the doctors on the surgical team, I headed to the airport. Only four days had passed since I'd arrived in Singapore. It seemed much longer. So did the long, sad flight home.

Still, I wasn't nearly as discouraged now as I had been after the South African Makwaeba twins died during an attempt to separate them back in 1994. Not until we had separated those infants did we discover that only one of them had adequate heart function to sustain life, and she had been dependent on the kidney function of her weaker twin. Their health had been deteriorating so quickly that separation seemed to be their only hope of survival, but once we got them apart, neither had the physical resources to survive on her own. With or without the surgery, they had little chance of survival.

After the Makwaeba surgery, I asked God a lot of "why" questions.

Why did you let me get involved in a situation in which there was never any possibility of success?

Is there anything else we could have done to achieve a positive outcome?

Why would you provide an opportunity like this only to allow us to fail?

For a long time I received no answers. The whole unfortunate episode made no sense.

Then, three years later, I was invited back to South Africa, to the same hospital, to work with many of the same medical team members to operate on the Banda twins. Before that experience was over—the most successful craniopagus separation in history up to that point—I realized we never would have achieved such positive results without the experience we had gained through the pain and disappointment of our earlier "failure" with the Makwaebas.

So I had a different mind-set flying home after the Bijani case. I may have had a deeper sense of sadness at the loss of Ladan and Laleh, if only because I'd been able to interact with them as adults and had gotten to know them personally. Again I had some unanswered "why" questions. But I'd learned some important lessons over the past nine or ten years. I now had enough faith not only to believe there were answers, but to feel certain that those answers would become apparent at some point in the future.

Already we had gained some surprising and encouraging new insights into the amazing potential of the human brain. The spontaneous circulatory changes we saw with the Bijanis would not have surprised us in a pair of infants, but their degree of adaptability was not only unexpected in adult brains, but unprecedented. That was a lesson that would serve us well if we ever had another occasion to operate on older twins. I was confident that something good would come out of yet another difficult and disappointing case.

More immediately, however, I was in desperate need of a couple of long nights of sleep—although that would have to wait. The day after I returned to Baltimore, so many media outlets wanted to talk to me that the public relations staff at Johns Hopkins set up a personal press conference. The last thing I felt like doing was facing another roomful of reporters, but I'd come to realize that the Bijani twins' case had become a major human-interest story around the world. I knew I would be pestered about it until I answered some questions about my role. So I agreed to have one big press conference—letting everyone ask whatever they wanted—so that we could all move on. It seemed like a good idea. It was and it worked.

That Friday afternoon, I faced a crowd of local and national radio and television news outlets and newspaper reporters, and I did an exclusive interview for ABC's *Nightline*. At first, the questions focused on my decision to get involved in the Bijani case, the wisdom of performing such a dangerous and unprecedented operation on two such seemingly healthy patients, why the decision had been made to proceed with, rather than stop, the surgery after we encountered unexpected developments, and whether I thought the tragic outcome might have been avoided.

I suppose the questions could have become adversarial, but I tried to avoid being defensive. I just told the truth—about my own interaction with Ladan and Laleh; about their feelings; about my own feelings and thoughts before, during, and after the operation; about what the doctors did and what happened at each stage of the surgery. I reported that the family friend and guardian had been adamant that the surgery continue. I also mentioned my reaction when I found out at such a critical juncture that the doctors also had promised the operation would be completed no matter what. "At that point," I said, "I must say I felt like a person heading into a dark jungle to face a hungry tiger with no gun."

I described how the new vein kept clotting, but the brain tissue remained soft, indicating that blood continued to circulate through other channels. But because we did not know exactly how or where the blood was flowing, I had suggested stopping the surgery to study what was happening and revise the surgical plan accordingly.

I explained that we eventually found that the blood had flowed through the thin brain covering called the dura, which in the twins' case was swollen with blood at its base and about ten times as thick as it should have been, and that when we tried to cut the last of the dura apart, the result was uncontrollable bleeding that led to the young women's deaths.

I admitted our medical team still didn't know why the blood began flowing through the dura instead of the new vein but that if I were to perform a similar operation in the future, this experience with Ladan and Laleh had taught me that the procedure should be done in two or more stages, some weeks apart. That would give new circulation patterns time to establish and would enable doctors to understand what needed to be done to keep the blood in controllable channels.

Asked how I felt about the "failure" of the operation, I acknowledged my feelings of respect and affection for the Bijani twins and my great sadness about their deaths. But I also added, "It's a failure only if you don't get anything out of it. Thomas Edison said he knew 999 ways that a lightbulb did not work; yet we have lights today. I think a day will come when twins such as these can have a normal life and a safe separation. And I think Ladan and Laleh will have contributed significantly to those individuals in the future who will be able to enjoy what the aspiration of these two courageous young ladies was."

I assured my questioners that the sisters had been fully aware of the risks. They knew the odds were fifty-fifty. Still, they were determined and unflinching in their conviction that death was preferable to living joined at the head.

More than once I expressed my great respect for the twins' courageous spirit. "They were amazingly cheerful and optimistic going into surgery. They knew they would either come out separated or they probably wouldn't suffer anymore—and that made them happy."

By the time we finished, I thought we'd covered most of the major topics, and my questioners seemed satisfied. At least the tone of their questions had changed—from queries attempting to get at my motivation or elicit judgments about the wisdom of the operation to more accepting, curious, even respectful questions aimed at better understanding the facts of the case and focusing on the human-interest angle of two remarkably brave young women and their quest for freedom and independence.

The continued level of interest in the Bijani twins amazed me. My press conference and *Nightline* comments were picked up all over the world, as illustrated in this wire service follow-up report out of Iran a couple of days later:

> Lohrasb, Iran—Iranian twins Ladan and Laleh Bijani were buried side by side, but in different graves on Saturday as thousands mourned the conjoined sisters, whose determination to lead separate lives touched people around the world.
>
> Mourners lined the hillsides and beat their chests as a Muslim cleric read verses from the Koran and the bodies were carried aloft to the graveyard close to their parents' mud-brick home in a remote valley in southern Iran.
>
> Born joined at the head, the sisters died on the operating table in Singapore on Tuesday in the final stages of a lengthy and risky attempt to separate them....
>
> Dr. Ben Carson said ... [he and other] members of the surgical team that operated on the women made "a great deal of effort" to try to talk them out of it beforehand.... "They absolutely could not be dissuaded," Carson, director of pediatric neurosurgery at Johns Hopkins University Hospital in Baltimore, said in a television interview. "I think even if one minute before surgery, they had said, 'We've changed our minds,' we all would have been extremely happy," he said of the surgical team....

Even a month and a half later, fascination with the case remained so high that National Public Radio booked me for its *Morning Edition* program. Co-host Renee Montagne began her extensive interview with the following introduction:

> The most famous brain surgeon in America has a middle name he says proves the Lord has a sense of humor. Ben Solomon Carson made his name as the first doctor to successfully separate infant twins joined together at the head. Among the other dramatic procedures he's pioneered—hemispherectomies, removing half a brain to prevent devastating seizures. Most recently Dr. Carson was part of the international team that attempted to separate adult twins joined at the head. The Iranian Bijani twins died, putting Dr. Carson on one side of the debate over extremely risky surgery.

After a few minutes of conversation, our interview went like this:

RENEE MONTAGNE: What we really want to sit down and talk to you about today ... [is] treatments that may appear to be worse than the disease—or at least are quite risky and have that potential.... Can I take you back to just earlier this summer? You joined the team in Singapore that separated the two young Iranian women, twenty-nine years old. They were joined at the head. They were basically healthy.

But they themselves wanted to be separated, and it was a tricky operation.... Their chances of surviving were put at something like fifty-fifty.

ME: Right, no better than fifty-fifty.

MONTAGNE: Tell us how tricky it was, and then why you agreed to participate.

ME: Okay.... Extraordinarily tricky, number one, because no one had ever tried to do that before with adults. So we weren't exactly sure what we would encounter. Number two, because of the vascular anatomy, we knew they shared some very major draining systems.

MONTAGNE: And a single vein.

ME: Right.

MONTAGNE: A single critical vein.

ME: Exactly.... There were a number of very, very hazardous things that we were going to have to deal with. Why did I decide to participate?

Because I felt that having had ... as much experience with these as anybody in the world, I would probably be negligent to turn my back and say, "No, I'm not going to participate. You guys are on your own."

MONTAGNE: This surgery, it brought up an ethical question that has come up over and over again with risky surgery and experimental surgery: do you do what the patient wants? ... Other doctors, other very skilled doctors ... had turned down these twins.

ME: But they were going to eventually get it done. That became very clear to me. Now I must say ... going into it, I felt like many other people — *Being stuck together, it's not that bad. It's not the worst thing that could possibly happen to somebody. Yeah, you can get by. Come on, get over it.* But after I met them, I understood. I mean, they were extremely vivacious, very intelligent, but had been quite depressed. And it became clear as I talked to them the reason for the depression. They had very, very different aspirations in terms of where their lives would go, and yet they couldn't get there because they were stuck together, because every decision was a committee decision, even going to the bathroom.

When I talked to them and I understood that and they said to me they couldn't stand it and that they'd rather die than to spend another day attached, I felt a little better about my decision to participate ... still recognizing that it was going to be an extraordinarily difficult and challenging situation.

MONTAGNE: Where do you think you came by this ability to really not just take a risk but embrace risk? And there's obviously a negative side to that.

Then we talked for a minute or so about my background and some experiences that influenced my life and thinking. The interview wasn't long enough for me to elaborate on the subject of risk, and at that point I'm not sure what I would have said anyway.

But it got me thinking.

And evidently I wasn't the only one.

Someone at Zondervan, the publishing house that had issued my first three books, heard that National Public Radio interview and took the idea to the editorial team. A month later I received a phone call from the editor-in-chief, who asked if I'd consider writing a book—about risk.

I told my publishing friend, "It's interesting that you should ask. After fielding so many questions about risk in recent interviews, I've been thinking about what more I would like to say about the subject."

So here we are!

Since then I've thought a lot about the subject. Invariably, whenever I mentioned to people that I was working on a book on risk, they were immediately intrigued.

Perhaps I shouldn't be surprised that in our post 9/11 world, with its whole new level of obsession with security, the topic of risk is a hot button. Scientists regularly make headlines with warnings about such new risks as bird-flu pandemics and flesh-eating bacteria and old risks like category 5 hurricanes and earthquake-triggered tsunamis. We live in a world where risk-benefit analysis has become a recognized science, where "risk management" is a popular college major that prepares more and more young professionals to work in all manner of industries—from banking and insurance to manufacturing and retail.

But no matter what safety steps we take or what security precautions we adopt, our risk of death is not approximately—but *exacly*—100 percent. There is no margin of error on that statistic. As we humans put more of our trust in technology, I wonder whether we lose the sense of wonder and mystery that marked past cultures.

And what impact does such security-mindedness have on our willingness to take risks?

Life Itself
Is a Risky Business

THE BIJANI CASE WAS NOT THE FIRST TIME I WEIGHED THE RISKS OF performing a ground-breaking surgery that made headlines around the world. My first experience involved a beautiful, brown-haired, four-year-old girl named Maranda Francisco.

Maranda had suffered her first grand mal seizure at eighteen months. Her second came two weeks later. By her fourth birthday they had become much more frequent and seemed to affect only one side of her body. She didn't pass out during the seizures, but they left her weak on her right side and sometimes unable to talk for hours at a time.

By the time she came to Johns Hopkins, she was experiencing as many as a hundred seizures a day, sometimes only three minutes apart. Curiously, she was seizure-free whenever she slept. As one newspaper article reported, she "lived her life in brief intervals between convulsions." Because the seizures came on so quickly, the danger of choking was too great to allow her to eat. So she took nourishment through a nasogastric tube.

According to her mother, Maranda had been on thirty-five different medications at one time or other. The Franciscos had taken their daughter to doctors and clinics around the country without finding any answers about their daughter's mysterious condition. Finally, in the winter of 1984, the Children's Epilepsy Center at Children's Hospital in Denver diagnosed her condition as Rasmussen's encephalitis, a rare inflammation of the brain.

Doctors in Denver sent the family to UCLA, where doctors who had experience treating the disease gave them this devastating prognosis:

"It's inoperable. There's nothing we can do." Maranda, the doctors explained, would slowly but surely get worse, eventually becoming permanently paralyzed on one side. Additional brain damage would cause progressive mental retardation. Then Maranda would die.

But the Franciscos refused to give up. They called every medical expert around the country who would talk to them, which is how they reached my colleague Dr. John Freeman at Johns Hopkins, our pediatric chief of neurology who has a well-earned reputation for seizure treatment. John listened to Mrs. Francisco's summary of her daughter's condition and asked her to send Maranda's medical records. He thought he might have an idea.

He carefully studied the records when they arrived; then he came to my office. "There's a procedure called a hemispherectomy, which you may not have heard of," he said after asking me to look at the charts.

"I've heard of it," I assured him, "but I've never done one." The surgery, I knew, involved the removal of one entire half, or hemisphere, of the brain. It had been attempted years earlier as a treatment for life-threatening seizures but had fallen out of favor because of serious side effects and a high mortality rate. John explained that he had been at Stanford when they performed several of them there. He knew of two successful hemispherectomies and believed it was a viable surgical option for someone like Miranda whose seizures were limited to one side of the brain. He was convinced this radical procedure was this girl's only hope.

"Think you could do a hemispherectomy on this girl, Ben?"

I told him I'd study the literature. I thought long and hard about how to avoid the complications other surgeons had faced in the past. I studied Maranda's scans and eventually asked Maranda's parents to bring her in for an evaluation. John Freeman and I talked and studied some more. Then I sat down with Mrs. Francisco. "I'm willing to attempt a hemispherectomy," I told her, "but you need to know I've never done one before."

"Dr. Carson," she said, "if you can do anything ... Everyone else has given up."

"It's a dangerous operation. Maranda could die in the operating room. She might have severe brain damage or other limitations." I hated to frighten this mother, but I couldn't give her false hope.

"And what happens if we don't agree to the surgery, Dr. Carson?" she wanted to know. "What happens to Maranda then?"

I replied as gently and matter-of-factly as I could. "She will get worse and die."

"Then it's not much of a choice, is it? If there's any hope ... please operate."

The night before the surgery, I sat down with both Mr. and Mrs. Francisco and reviewed a long list of possible complications. Again I told them that we couldn't predict the result of the surgery. The lesion affected her dominant (left) side of the brain. In most right-handed people, the left hemisphere dominates speech, language, and movement on the right side of the body. So a major long-term risk for this surgery, even if she survived it, could be loss of speech or complete paralysis of the right side of the body.

The Franciscos assured me they understood the risks. They realized this was their daughter's only chance.

I told them I had a homework assignment for them that night.

"Anything," they said, "whatever you want us to do."

"Say your prayers. And I'll say mine. Because I really think it helps."

Although I felt some anxiety that evening, I had been a surgeon long enough to know that if someone is going to die without an operation, then you have nothing to lose by trying. So I went to sleep at peace, knowing the risk we were taking and knowing we would give this pretty little girl a chance to live.

The complications started almost as soon as the surgery did. Maranda's brain was so inflamed that anywhere an instrument touched it, she began to bleed. We kept calling for more and more blood from the blood bank. Gradually I eased away the left hemisphere of her brain, cutting away tissue and cauterizing blood vessels as we went. Finally we were done. We sewed her skull back into place and sutured her scalp back over the wound. We'd successfully removed the entire left half of Miranda's brain.

Not only was it one of the most difficult operations of my career up to that point, it was also one of the longest. We had planned on five hours at the operating table. It took ten. By the time we finished, we had replaced almost twice Maranda's blood volume—nine pints in all.

Now all we could do was wait. Would she walk or talk again? I watched for the slightest sign of movement. The anesthesiologist unhooked the ventilator, so at least she was breathing on her own. A nurse called her name. Nothing. I felt confident she would wake up soon, but I couldn't be certain.

I followed the gurney as we wheeled her out of the OR. When her parents heard us coming down the hall, Mrs. Francisco called out, "Wait!" The two of them ran to meet us.

After Mrs. Francisco bent down and kissed her daughter, Maranda's eyes flickered open for just a second. "I love you, Mommy and Daddy," she said.

Her parents wept. A nurse shouted, "She talked!"

I stood in amazement. We had removed half of this little girl's brain, the dominant half that controlled her speech. Yet she talked. She could hear. She could think. She could respond. As she lay there on that gurney in the hallway, she even began to move her right arm and her right leg.

Unbelievable!

The media began clamoring for interviews and pictures. By the time Maranda went home, she had become something of a celebrity. So had I. That little girl went on to have a happy childhood with only a few minor limitations, and the last time I saw her, she was tap-dancing and talking about going to college.

Our success with Maranda prompted more hemispherectomies at Hopkins, but none of them garnered quite as much public attention as the first. So I figured I'd had my allotted fifteen minutes of fame, which was fine by me. I had no idea how many other unprecedented and potentially risky procedures lay ahead.

———

Because of the questions raised by the Bijani twins' case, and because of my willingness to accept the uncertainty of the most difficult of surgical cases like Maranda's, agreeing to write a book on the subject of risk was a relatively easy decision for me.

I knew what I hoped to accomplish in a book like this—to think big in terms of audience and subject matter. But I also wanted my advice to be fresh and practical, for the topic is broad and complex. Writing such a book has proven to be a more time-consuming and imposing challenge than I ever expected.

Our Schizophrenic Obsession with Risk

Risk has become an increasingly significant word in our American lexicon. If you Google this simple four-letter term, you'll receive more than a billion references in less than an eighth of a second. Indeed, it's safe to say that people are more sensitized to risk today than at any other time in history.

This may explain why so many people are not merely preoccupied with risk but often downright schizophrenic about the topic. Think about it. On one hand our pop culture idolizes the edgiest athletes—from the professional bull-riding circuit to the high-flying, mind-boggling, body-twisting, death-defying, made-for-entertainment extreme sports events featured on television's X Games. We glorify these "Do-the-Dew" heroes. We are drawn to those broadcasts like rubberneckers to the scene of a traffic accident. We stare in open-mouthed awe, anxious and ready to cringe at their bone-jarring failures and to cheer and marvel at their trophy-worthy successes.

And yet, at the same time, every public school in the country is required to have six to eight inches of rubber tire fragments, wood chips, or some other cushioning agent under every teeter-totter, swing set, and monkey bars set to cushion every little jump, drop, or fall so that no child will suffer an accidental injury.

We routinely celebrate risk in such mega-hit reality television shows as *Survivor* and *Fear Factor*, where we (and a nationwide audience of millions) cheer for, identify with, and laugh at other human beings as they publicly test the limits of their bodies, minds, and spirits in the most unfamiliar and threatening circumstances.

But no sooner do we hit the off button on our remotes than we join our fellow citizens in a public outcry to enforce more specific and rigid safety regulations. We demand far-reaching legislation and ground-breaking legal judgments to help eliminate every possible element of risk we might encounter in everyday life.

Could our culture be any more schizophrenic?

No Joke?

While we might simply laugh off such inconsistencies, a better response might be to examine what these risks really are. For instance, did you know that

- your risk of being injured by a malfunctioning television this year is 1 in 7,000?
- 28,000 people are treated at trauma centers every year for handling or swallowing cash?
- your chances of being seriously injured by Christmas decorations are 1 in 65,000?

It makes you wonder who compiles such statistics and why.

And don't tell me such "risks" as those don't project some bizarre images on the big screen of your imagination. For example, hearing that buckets and pails injure about 12,000 people every year conjures up visions of the slapstick comedy of Larry, Moe, and Curly. Yet the families of some 50 toddlers who die by drowning each year in five-gallon buckets would have a hard time finding any humor in this statistic.

Statistics show that women are generally safer drivers than men until about the age of thirty-five but that middle-aged men retake the safe-driving trophy and that, statistically, a forty-two-year-old man is the safest driver on the road—all of which makes great fodder for jokes about either gender. What's not so funny is the fact that a sixteen-year-old male driver is forty times more dangerous on the highways than a forty-year-old woman, and none of us can laugh about the fact that one out of every twenty-five drivers we encounter on the road at night is legally intoxicated.

Some risks will never be laughing matters.

This anxiety about risk permeates our society and impacts it in countless ways. Good. Bad. Ugly. And sometimes ridiculous. It's why we have a surgeon general's warning on every pack of cigarettes, but also why McDonald's now gives customers notice that their hot coffee is ... well, actually *hot,* and why those annoying and scratchy tags sewn into the seams on our mattresses and pillows threaten legal action if removed. It's why every medical patient now has the right of informed consent, and why so many of my doctor friends must pay hundreds of thousands of dollars a year for liability coverage. It's why sound-minded individuals seeking immediate medical care and their highly educated, experienced caregivers have to call an insurance company and wait for some nineteen-year-old clerk to give approval for a procedure or treatment he or she has never heard of and probably can't even spell. It's why we have seat belts and shatter-resistant windshields in our cars and metal detectors at the doors of schools, hospitals, and other public buildings. It's why we have childproof prescription bottles and tamperproof seals on milk jugs. It's why, for a time during the final stages of writing this book, the airline industry responded to a new round of terrorist threats with a total ban on liquids in carry-ons, which necessitated that passengers finish their coffee, chug that bottled water, and squeeze those tiny packets of dressing onto their salads before boarding. It is also why ladders are now sold with attached notices warning about the possibility of falls, why some Halloween superhero costumes include the disclaimer "Cape does not enable user to fly," and why one manufacturer attached to its product a detailed warning notice that read, "Do not use if this sticker has been removed!"

How did we become so intrigued by risk—and so worried about it at the same time?

My psychiatrist friends might offer some complex Freudian answers to this question, but my conclusion is more pragmatic—even simplistic. Like the adventurer who was asked why he climbed the mountain and answered, "Because it's there!" I think our culture has developed this intense love-hate relationship with risk, in part because it's always there. I think we've learned more about risk than any other generation in history because we can. Let me explain.

Risk Is Nothing New

Risk is hardly a modern development. Even the sketchiest overview of American history proves that point. The first European explorers to reach America (whether the Vikings, Columbus, or whoever) and those who followed after them faced incredible risks. Subsequent colonists lived here at great risk—as evidenced by the abandoned ruins of settlements scattered along coastal sites from the Caribbean to the maritime provinces of Canada. Those of my ancestors who arrived here in the holds of slave ships experienced a different dimension of risk. Of course, the Native Americans already living here had overcome their own risks to populate this land. While those Indians posed a certain risk to the newcomers, their tribes themselves were even more at risk—to the powerfully contagious diseases and ideas that arrived from the Old World.

The establishment of the United States was itself an extremely risky experiment, an audacious declaration of independence from the king of the most powerful nation on earth. The expansion and settlement of our young country were fraught with additional danger. By the time the North American continent was finally "civilized," we risked involvement in two armed conflicts so far-reaching and deadly that history designated them as "world wars."

Those echoes of gunfire and bombs had barely faded away in Europe and the Pacific before the nuclear Cold War and the first real threat of total annihilation of all humankind raised the concept of risk to an apocalyptic level. No sooner did the Cold War begin to thaw with the onset of détente and the melting away of the old Iron Curtain than we found ourselves in an unprecedented conflict marked by a perilous pattern of worldwide terrorism and violence that finally got our undivided attention on 9/11 and has been ratcheting up our awareness of risk ever since with no end in sight in the "War on Terror."

Of course, risk has been a fact of life not just throughout American history but since the beginning of time. Yet we are seeing a timely and unprecedented convergence of trends and historical developments that supports the contention that we are more focused on, and aware of, the risks we face today than any other society in history. Not just because the risks are there, but because the times we live in have uniquely equipped us to recognize, understand, catalog, measure, compare, and know more about the risks we face than any other society in history. Because we can.

At the Root of Risk

Most serious books on the subject of risk cite the great French mathematician-philosopher Blaise Pascal for laying the foundation of probability theory. Through correspondence with a couple of learned friends in the mid-seventeenth century, young Pascal used a complex combination of geometry and algebra to devise the first systematic mathematical method for calculating the probabilities of future events. One friend sought to apply the formula to eke out a living by means of a secret (albeit slight) winning advantage in games of chance. The true significance, however, of Pascal's pioneering work for business decisions, for fields such as risk management and insurance, and for the forecasting of economic trends and losses would be realized only gradually by others over the centuries following his death. As John Ross says in his book *The Polar Bear Strategy*:

> In essence, although on a limited scale at first, probability theory enabled its practitioners to quantify the odds of two different events occurring and then compare them. The effect of this simple but remarkable work was like letting a powerful genie out of its bottle. The insights gained by science and technology as a result, along with the new tools developed for analyzing risk decisions, radically changed the way humans thought about uncertainty and regarded the future. The theory bore directly on how people make

decisions and, consequently, how they live their lives, even among people who don't know the first thing about statistics.[1]

A long line of scientists and mathematicians expanded and expounded upon Pascal's foundation and began crunching data from the past to predict the future, to discover the phenomenon of the bell curve, to learn how a sample number of observations can be representative of a much larger population, to understand and draw distinctions between causation and correlation, and to develop the means of distinguishing between various risks and risk factors.

The revolution Pascal triggered in the 1650s eventually gave impetus to a mini-revolution that began in the 1950s when the concept of risk management was first introduced in an article in the *Harvard Business Review*. But not until the 1970s did everything come together to spawn the new science of risk analysis—a primarily academic, multidisciplinary field of scientific endeavor that arose, as Ross points out, "from the confluence of several factors: a critical accumulation of data in health and safety matters, the introduction of high speed computers that could contain and process this information, and the development of sophisticated analytical techniques to work with this information ... now risk numbers and comparisons are ubiquitous."

Probability theory provided the means to carefully examine the world through a more revealing lens. As economist Peter Bernstein noted, without such a systematic means of evaluating and then deciding whether or not to take a risk:

> We would have no way of estimating the probability that an event will occur—rain, the death of a man at 85, a 20% decline in the stock market, a Democratic Congress, the failure of seatbelts, or the discovery of an oil well by a wildcatting firm ... engineers could never have designed the great bridges that span our widest rivers, homes would still be heated by fireplaces or parlor stoves, electric power utilities would not exist, polio would still be maiming children, no airplanes would fly, and space travel would be just a dream.[2]

The by-product today from all this resulting risk analysis number crunching is a mind-boggling collection of sometimes fascinating, frequently helpful, often amusing, and occasionally shocking facts, figures, cautions, and comparisons, including the following examples:

- Alcohol is implicated in 44 percent of all accidental deaths.
- The risk that a bridge, during its lifetime, will collapse is one in a million. The lifetime risk that you will be on a collapsing bridge is one in four million.
- You are 400 percent more likely to die from falling than from something falling on you.
- Children are 600 percent more likely to be killed by a school bus hitting them than they are to be killed while traveling on a school bus.
- The risk that an obstetrician will be sued for malpractice is 70 percent.

We are bombarded by new data and warnings about risk every day. From the media ("Film at eleven about the unsuspected danger of . . ."); from science and medical experts ("The CDC issued a new report this week advising pregnant women to avoid . . ."); from friends and family ("I just called to make sure you knew about the horrible new E. coli outbreak. It's in eleven states already and three people have died. They still haven't pinpointed exactly how it got into the food chain, but if you have any fresh spinach in the house, don't eat it!").

The truth is that life *itself* is risky.

The question is, how do we respond to such an ominous onslaught of intimidating and alarming information?

The Truth about Risk

No one thinks of ice cream as a major childhood risk, but the ice cream wagon that hit four-year-old Bo-Bo Valentine when she ran into the street put her young life at risk. When I first saw her early one Monday morning, she had been in intensive care all weekend, comatose, with an intracranial pressure monitor in her skull. A resident summarized her case this way: "Isn't it about time to give up on this little girl? Just about the only thing she has left is pupilary response," which meant her pupils still responded to light. Otherwise, she had lost what little function, purposeful movement, or response to stimuli she had when she'd been rushed into the emergency room.

Before responding to the resident, however, I bent over Bo-Bo and gently lifted her eyelids. Her pupils were fixed and dilated. "I thought you said the pupils were still working."

"They were just a minute ago," he insisted.

"Then you're telling me her pupils just now dilated?"

"They must have!"

If that was the case, it meant something serious was currently happening and we had to do something right away if there was any hope of preventing further damage. "Call the operating room," I told the nurse. "Tell them we're on the way! Four plus emergency!"

Everything shifted into high gear. Two residents grabbed Bo-Bo's bed and rolled it down the hall on the run. En route to the OR, I bumped into another neurosurgeon in the hallway. He was one of the senior docs I respected greatly for his work with trauma victims.

While the staff set up the OR, I explained what had happened and what I was planning.

"Don't do it!" he said as he turned and walked away from me. "You're wasting your time."

His response startled me, but I didn't let it deter me. There wasn't time. Bo-Bo was still alive, and we had a chance, slight as it might be, to save her life. I didn't rethink my decision. I was going to do the surgery anyway.

Within minutes everything was ready to begin a craniectomy. First I opened her head and took out the front of her skull. Then I opened up the dura, the leatherlike covering that protects the brain tissue. Located between the two halves of the brain is the falx. By splitting the falx, the two hemispheres of Bo-Bo's brain could communicate together and equalize the pressure between her hemispheres. Removing some of the skull further reduced the pressure caused by the swelling. The entire procedure gave her brain room to swell until it began to heal.

Before I closed her up, I covered the opening temporarily with a piece of dura from a cadaver to hold everything in place. Then I closed the scalp over everything. The entire operation took about two hours.

Bo-Bo remained comatose for several days as we watched for some response, any response that would offer hope. Nothing. Then one morning her pupils responded just a little to light. *Maybe something is happening,* I dared to hope.

A couple of days later she started moving a little — stretching her legs and shifting her body as if trying to find a comfortable position. A week after that she was alert and responsive again. Once I was confident she would recover, we took her back to surgery and repositioned the portion of her skull we had removed. Within six weeks she was a happy, normal, charming four-year-old girl again.

I saw Bo-Bo recently, and she introduced me to her own little girl. That brief encounter was a wonderful reminder to me that experts don't always have the last word on risk. Sometimes they only add to our doubt and confusion about the uncertainties and risks we face in life.

So what risks do we really need to worry about? How in the world are we supposed to make reasonable and wise decisions about the risks we face when our perspective on the subject is so often distorted? How do we decide what risks are acceptable?

Answering those questions will take the rest of this book—and a lot of deliberate thought. As we begin to wrestle with them, I'd like to counter the distorted perceptions about risk we raised in the last chapter with a few truisms that will, I hope, help you better understand where I'm coming from and where we'll be going in the following chapters.

Truth #1: Everything Is Risky

The wide variety of risks already enumerated in the last chapter is evidence of the fact that *everything* in life is risky. A recent study of news coverage found that 35 percent of all stories in U.S. daily newspapers—and about 47 percent of front-page articles—deal with various risks of contemporary life. A computer search of one day's newspaper headlines came up with 634 "most relevant" results and omitted countless duplicate stories and other similar articles. A brief sampling of topics included the following:

- "Common Painkillers May Raise Risk of Heart Failure"
- "Risk Management Solutions Updates Hurricane Model"
- "Do Pets Increase Infants' Eczema Risk?"
- "Carp in Utah Lake Pose Health Risk for Humans"
- "Veterans at Risk of Identity Theft"

All these and more than six hundred other risks were highlighted in just one ordinary day's headlines. Not surprisingly, confusion is a common reaction to the onslaught of information we receive about risk—including information from the so-called experts.

Truth #2: The More We Know, the More We Worry

A couple of centuries ago doctors didn't understand the relationship between germs and disease; most of the populace throughout Western civilization believed more than one or two baths a year was excessive and might actually contribute to several dreaded illnesses. Today we know that the human body contains more bacteria than it does cells, and most of us are well aware that the state of our overall health is often determined at the invisible, cellular level where even the simplest jumbling of our DNA (the essential building blocks of life) can trigger the dreaded onset of cancer and thus cause our death.

Distorted Views

Those who are quick to declare that we're living today at a time of unique and unprecedented risk may need a little jogging of their memories, because our perspective has been and is greatly distorted by what I would have to diagnose as a serious case of societal amnesia. Consider how we hear so much speculation and read so many sobering statistics about the risks posed by modern technologies. For example, the odds of a core damage meltdown at a nuclear power plant releasing radiation into the atmosphere are five per million per year according to the Nuclear Regulatory Commission. Recent reports by the CDC suggest two million Americans a year will develop such serious staph and strep infections *after* they are admitted to a hospital that approximately 90,000 of those will die from their infections. Add to these kinds of alarming statistics the long list of common additives in our food supply that have been shown to cause cancer. Note that more than $30 billion is spent each year cleaning up hazardous waste. And don't forget that every year between 40,000 and 50,000 Americans die in motor vehicle crashes in which another 3 million are injured. Consider the countless other risks we know about (never mind the ones we'll be learning about in the years ahead), and it's no wonder 90 percent of Americans say they feel less safe today than they did growing up.

Yet the facts belie this sense of insecurity.

Consider that life expectancy in this country for those born in 1900 was under fifty years. Boys born in 2000 could be expected to live to seventy-two, girls to eighty. Doesn't that tell us something about the comparative risk of life today?

Let's recall for a moment the "safer" world of our own youth, a world before air bags and mandatory seat belts, before 911 phone systems showed the location of distressed callers, before cell phones allowed parents to check on their children anytime, anyplace. Remember the "carefree and peaceful" 1950s before CAT scans, before Doppler radar to provide weather warnings, before ultrasounds, organ transplants, and even coronary bypass surgery? We didn't have AIDS, but we all knew people with polio.

What about the oh-so-much-safer, idealistic, and revolutionary 1960s? Have we so quickly forgotten those who faced down the power of an establishment, the teeth of its police dogs, and the billy clubs of authority to take a risky and historic walk for freedom and justice? Have we blocked out the awful memories of the days when a series of assassinations claimed the most popular leaders of our nation? What about the violent protests that swept through the idyllic campuses and ivy-covered halls of our nation's colleges? I lived in Detroit through the race riots that threatened it and so many other great American cities in those years. Like millions of other American schoolchildren, I crouched under my classroom desk during air raid drills that were some impotent educational bureaucrat's feeble reaction to the terrifying reality of a world whose greatest superpowers spent much of that decade rattling nuclear sabers and threatening each other with the prospect of mutually assured destruction.

Through a (Looking) Glass Darkly

We can debate the relative seriousness of the threats we face versus those our parents and grandparents faced, but the reality of risk isn't new. Our perspective, however, is undeniably distorted not just by our limited historical recall, but by the way we *see* everything today.

The violence we see today seems more gruesome. The suffering we see seems more heart-wrenching. The dangers we see all around us seem more immediate, more ominously threatening to us and our families. The key word in our media age is *see*, for the greatest difference between our day and any other time in history is what and how we *see* today. As Gavin de Becker says in his book *The Gift of Fear*,

"Years ago we had a smaller catalog of fears to draw upon. That's because in our satellite age we don't experience just the calamities of our lives; we experience the calamities of *everyone's* lives. It is no wonder so many people are afraid of so many things."[3]

The ratings-driven nature of the media today only further distorts our perspective on the risks we face. Newspaper headlines and late-night news shows have to grab our attention, so they do it with the sensational and the graphic—and we react accordingly.

Remember back in the early 1990s when one of the biggest stories in the news for several weeks was a rash of tourist murders in Florida? Several million potential visitors changed their vacation plans and went elsewhere. They did so without ever doing the math to make an informed decision because the media focused only on the twenty-two murders. The reports didn't point out that Florida had forty million tourists that year, and if you figure they each stayed an average of one week, the murder rate was only one-third that of the average American city. So in truth, being a tourist in Florida during that time would have posed less chance of being murdered for most Americans than staying home. I guess it's hard to hook viewers and readers with such facts.

The unusual also draws a lot more attention than the ordinary, which is one reason we see so much coverage of every rare, horrific-sounding condition such as "flesh-eating bacteria" that affects one person in millions. Yet we never read stories about the one in seven thousand (adding up to tens of thousands of victims) who seek medical attention every year because of shaving accidents.

Since any commercial plane crash anywhere in the world makes CNN, the Fox News Channel, the network evening news, plus all the local evening news roundups, we forget that the chance of being killed driving to the airport is far greater than the odds you will die in a lifetime of flying. As a result of our common misperceptions, we overrate and worry more than we should about the danger of uncommon and exotic risks while dismissing many everyday dangers we're more apt to encounter and can actually do something about.

The degree to which we fear an actual risk is also influenced by media exposure. Studies have shown that the word *shark* prompts a greater fear response from people than *spider, snake, death, rape,* or even *murder*. So how many Americans go to the beach every year more concerned about and alert to the threat of a deadly shark attack (which may occur only a time or two or three—if at all—this year on U.S. beaches) than the likelihood of someone in their party drowning (which happens thousands of times every year, year after year)? Could that be in part because stories of any shark attack, from New Zealand to Zanzibar, make the news even in Kansas? Drowning stories, which may get local media coverage, simply don't provoke the same level of dread (perhaps because they don't inspire the same sort of breathless reporting—pun intended) as do tales of fins and jaws and killer whites.

Despite, and sometimes because of, the mind-boggling amount of information available today, there's clearly a huge gap between our perception of some risks and their actual magnitude. For instance, the average American estimates the odds of dying in an automobile accident this year to be about 1 in 70,000; instead, the actual risk is 1 in 7,000. Most people reckon the prospect of a fatal heart attack at about 1 chance in 20; the real risk is close to 1 in 3.

Rather than reacting to every risk we hear and see, we should make an effort to discern which ones we can do something about.

Truth #3: A Lot of Risks Aren't Worth the Worry

Processing the sheer volume of risk data that bombards us every day is clearly impossible. The information we do understand can seem frightening, overwhelming, and confusing. We can't hide from it. Nor can we laugh it all off. Worrying accomplishes nothing. We don't know where to turn, who to believe, what dangers are real, or which risk poses the greatest threat to our family's future and the world's survival. The more we think about risk, the more risks there seem to be. Which may be why it's tempting to shrug off the warnings, ignore all the disturbing talk about risks, and refuse to be troubled by the myriad threats life throws at us. Sometimes that's a reasonable strategy.

Most of us don't lie awake at night worrying that we might be one of 3,300 Americans who are injured by room deodorizers every year. I know that while I'm relaxing with my sons and sharpening my eye-hand coordination around the pool table in my basement, I never give a thought to the chance that I could be one of the 5,000 people a year who sustain injuries while playing billiards. Listening with pleasure while my wife and sons practice for a performance of the Carson family's string quartet, I've never worried about the fact that every year 8,000 Americans are injured by musical instruments. And all three of these risks are thousands of times more likely than my catching the plague this year—chances of that being 1 in 25 million.

Here are some other risks that aren't worth worrying about:

• The most likely month to die in is January. The least likely is September. (Is this a good argument for not making a New Year's resolution to take up skydiving?)

• An infant is three times more likely to be injured in a high chair than in a playpen. (Should we cut the legs off Junior's high chair or get down on the floor ourselves to feed baby Ruth her strained carrots through the mesh of her playpen?)

Such risks are easy to shrug off.

But then, there are many personally pertinent risks, such as the 3 in 10 chance that any American will eventually have some form of cancer. The most common cancer for a man is cancer of the prostate; one man in every 1,000 is diagnosed each year. Black men have almost double the risk of white men for the disease, and that risk increases dramatically with a man's age: at forty-five it's 5 percent, at fifty-five it's 9 percent, at sixty-five it's 15 percent, and at seventy-five it's 20 percent.

Knowing those risk statistics is one reason I have been diligent in recent years about getting annual physicals and regular PSA (prostate-specific antigen) tests. Indeed, being aware of the dangers, understanding the risk factors, and recognizing the warning signs of prostate problems actually saved my life a few years ago. (More details and the risk lessons I learned from that experience a little later.) So I know from personal experience that simply shrugging off and ignoring risks could be a senseless and tragic mistake.

But it can be very confusing when some studies highlight a risk only to have other researchers contradict or downplay those findings. Consider the ongoing debate about secondhand smoke or the effectiveness of air bags in cars where this now-required safety feature (which un-deniably saves lives in thousands of accidents each year) can actually inflict serious injury and even death in some crash scenarios, which leads us to yet another troubling point of confusion.

Sometimes the very same experts who can't agree (and thus give us conflicting signals about the seriousness of a particular risk) are even less certain about the consequences of many proposed *solutions*. So how do we know when "erring on the side of caution" is going to be a more serious problem than the risk we want to avoid? Sometimes we don't.

Two quick cases in point. DDT was banned for use as an insecticide in 1972 because some experts thought it *might* pose a carcinogenic risk. There was no clear evidence that it actually caused cancer in hu-mans, though there was some basis for thinking it *might*. For caution's sake, farmers and others needing to control insect populations were forced to switch to organophosphate insecticides (such as parathions), some of which were eventually proven to be hundreds, even thousands of times *more toxic* than the DDT they replaced.

The second example is saccharin. Several 1970s rodent studies indi-cated that mega-massive doses of the then-popular artificial sweetener *might* increase the chance of bladder cancer in humans. Though the cautious plan to ban it stalled in Congress over the next few years, millions of consumers shied away from saccharin for fear that it might harm them. The irony was that while saccharin *might* harm people, there is no doubt that the same amount of sweetening in the form of sugar is much more harmful. Obesity—and its associated ills of high blood pressure, diabetes, heart trouble, and so on—kills far more Americans today than bladder cancer ever did.

So what are the genuine threats you face, and what are you going to do about them? It's all so confusing!

Worry Not

Most of us refuse to be traumatized by the risks we know we face. But we all probably do know someone (or many someones) who seizes on every imaginable worry, whose favorite prayer seems to be "Give us this day our daily dread." Folks who seem to endure and even enjoy a constant state of worry about anything and everything. Have you noticed they are never happy unless they are trying to convince us to worry with them?

But as I regularly tell the anxious parents of my young patients, "I've never had a case where worry did anyone any good." Neither is worry a productive response to the seemingly endless and overwhelming risks we encounter in our world today.

So how in the world can we possibly cope with all this risk?

Truth #4: We Can't Eliminate All Risk

In an age that views information as power and places its highest trust in education, science, and technology, many people mistakenly believe that any threat we can identify, observe, or measure can and should be completely nullified.

Some years ago, in a major American newspaper article on childhood injuries, an official for the Centers for Disease Control made the absurd claim that "there is no such thing as an accident, only lack of parental forethought." The same sort of disconnect from reality is behind the misguided hunt for *zero risk*, a standard raised fifty years ago when Congress mandated that no degree of cancer-causing risk would be tolerated in food additives. That seemed a stringent enough standard at a time when scientists measured the presence of a substance in parts per million (meaning in a million molecules, scientists could detect a single foreign molecule). But scientists today can detect substances down to parts per quintillion (that's a one followed by eighteen zeros). In layman's terms that's the ability to find and measure a tablespoon and a half of some substance, let's say dioxin, thoroughly stirred and spread evenly throughout the Great Lakes. Does anyone think *that* standard of "purity" is practical or economically affordable?

Paralyzed by Peril

On the other hand, if we seriously attempt to inform ourselves of every possible danger and take every risk factor and warning to heart, we might soon feel so overwhelmed that we don't want to get out of bed in the morning to face all the threats we can expect to encounter on any given day.

Before getting up and heading for the shower, you might just lie there a little longer and consider this: Hundreds of people die in their bathtubs every year. If you're one of the 53 percent of Americans who get their tap water from underground aquifers, before you brush your teeth, you don't want to hear the EPA's estimate that of the 100,000 leaking underground fuel storage tanks in the United States, 18,000 are known to have contaminated nearby groundwater. Once you've finished up at the bathroom sink, you should be warned that just getting dressed is more dangerous than most people ever suspect; 150,000 Americans are seriously injured by their clothing every year. And more than 100,000 of us get rushed to the emergency room when our shoes or shoelaces don't perform as designed.

If you feel the need for a little extra fortification to jump-start your day, you might not want to know that there are more than 1,000 different chemicals in roast coffee—only 26 of which have been tested for carcinogenicity and 19 of those caused cancer in rodents. In fact, some experts calculate that there are more carcinogens in one cup of coffee than in the total amount of pesticide residues ingested by the average person in a year. And before deciding what to eat with your breakfast coffee, you probably shouldn't think too much about a recent report from the National Academy of Sciences that concluded, "It is plausible that naturally occurring chemicals present in food pose a greater cancer risk than synthetic chemicals."

You probably don't need a reminder of all the potential risks faced while commuting to work, and I won't bother to list any of a multitude of common on-the-job dangers.

Let's consider instead your plans for coming home at the end of the day to spend a relaxing evening entertaining friends. Before you do any last-minute straightening up, you might want to note that the odds of being injured by your toilet bowl cleanser are one in 10,000—only slightly more likely than the odds you will be murdered this year, which is one in 11,000. Oh yes, be careful around your windows, because twenty people a year are accidentally strangled to death on drapery cords.

Then, before you finalize plans for serving a picnic out on your patio, you might need to consider the fact that every year more Americans are injured by their barbecue grills than by the use of fireworks. And those charbroiled steaks you were going to serve? They contain billions of atoms worth of benzopyrene, which ranked number eight in the top twenty hazardous substances listed by the federal government's Agency for Toxic Substances and Disease Registry at the outset of the twenty-first century. It might also interest you to know that three carcinogenic nitropyrenes found in diesel fuel are also present in grilled chicken. In fact, the browned and blackened food you eat over the course of an average day is several hundred times more carcinogenic than what you inhale if you live in a metropolitan area with severe air pollution.

So who could blame you for pulling the covers over your head tomorrow morning and refusing to face another day full of so many risks? But if you do stay in bed, you will need to be warned: you could find yourself among the 400,000 or so Americans each year who are injured by their beds, mattresses, and pillows. Even if you dodge those dangers, staying in bed could eventually result in muscular atrophy, elevate your risk of high blood pressure, or even bring on a life-threatening pulmonary embolism. Not to mention your almost certain risk of unemployment should you pursue this strategy for long.

Surrendering to fear and allowing ourselves to be paralyzed by peril isn't something most of us can afford to do. But if we're all much more aware today of the risks we live with in our society, and yet we're still never able to fully eliminate them, how can we think about the risks still before us?

Truth #5: Minimizing Risk Is Often the Best We Can Do

The scientist who developed the Saturn 5 rocket, which launched the first Apollo mission to the moon, once said, "You want a valve that doesn't leak, and you try everything possible to develop one. But the real world provides you with a leaky valve. You have to determine how much leaking you can tolerate."

Which brings us to the next point . . .

Truth #6: Each of Us Has to Decide
What the Acceptable Risks Are

When it comes to determining how you will react to any particular risk, you ought to think for yourself. We've already noted some of the dangers in trusting the media presentation of risk. Yet sadly, the Harvard School of Public Health says people get more information about risk and hazard from the media than they do from their physicians or anyone else. While some experts may be more reliable than others, we often get conflicting messages from them. We are warned to "avoid aspirin because it causes stomach ulcers" at the same time we are advised to "take aspirin to avoid the risk of stroke."

A little later I'll give you a simple, practical framework for thinking about risks and deciding for yourself a reasonable course of action.

Know Risk?

You and I are forced to consider and cope with countless potential dangers we encounter all around us every day. Which threats truly deserve our concern? We've looked at all-too-common reactions that don't help. What might be a reasonable, practical, productive response to the serious hazards our world holds for us? In the constant and confusing cacophony of warnings we hear, to whom should we listen? Why do we deem some risks acceptable? When do we wisely walk away from other dangers? How do we decide the difference?

If you've read any of my previous books—*Gifted Hands, Think Big,* or *The Big Picture*—you probably won't be surprised if I revisit one of my favorite themes and remind you that the greatest and most valuable resources we have for making crucial decisions are *knowledge* and the amazing brainpower God gave human beings when he created us. That's certainly true for deciding our best response to any risk we ever face.

I would reemphasize, however, another favorite point: that *wisdom* is different from, and often more critical than, *knowledge.* In fact, too often all the information we've been given, all the risks we've encountered, all the warnings we've received from so many different sources actually combine to skew our perspective so that effective risk analysis and decision-making becomes *more* difficult rather than less.

Instead of losing ourselves in all the knowledge before us and sliding into worry, we can exercise a little wisdom to help us recognize the other side of the equation ...

Truth #7: Not All Risks Are Bad

We'll spend considerable time in the chapters to come looking at the upside of risk. After all, when you think about it, life without any risk would be dull indeed—which brings us to the final truth I'd like to point out regarding one of the most significant risks of all.

Truth #8: We Are All Going to Die of Something Eventually

Consider your chances of dying from the following causes this year:

- Cancer: 1 in 500.
- Drowning: 1 in 50,000.
- Riding your bicycle: 1 in 130,000.
- An airplane crash: 1 in 250,000.
- In your bathtub: 1 in 1,000,000.
- Falling out of bed: 1 in 2,000,000
- Freezing to death: 1 in 3,000,000.
- Struck by lightning (if you are a man): 1 in 2,000,000.
- Struck by lightning (if you are a woman): 1 in 10,000,000
- Rabies (in the U.S.): 1 in 100,000,000.
- A foreign object inadvertently left in your body during surgery: 1 in 80,000,000.
- A falling meteor: roughly 1 in 5,000,000,000.

Odds that you will die at some point in your life: 1 in 1.

Thus, you might say the greatest, most significant, and universal risk factor in death is being born. This implies that it really isn't very helpful to approach the subject of risk by focusing on how we might die; rather, it's far wiser to consider how we should live and what risks we will live with.

I agree with Teddy Roosevelt, who once declared, "Far better is it to dare mighty things than to rank with those poor spirits who neither enjoy much nor suffer much." His words resonate with me because all my life I've observed two groups of people who have made serious life-impacting mistakes in their approaches to risk.

First are those people who sadly are so afraid to take any risk that they never actually manage to do anything of true significance in their lives. Second are those individuals who take all the wrong risks and tragically end up hurting or destroying themselves or others in the process. Lives are ruined either way, and both groups fail to reach their potential. They never discover or enjoy the true purpose for which God placed them on earth.

Over the years I've discovered a simple prescription to use when confronting risk, a remedy that will help people in either fraternity—the fearful and the foolish—plus all of us who live somewhere between the two.

Indeed, I'm convinced most of the success I've experienced and the majority of my personal and professional accomplishments over the years can be traced back to my application of this practical little formula in any number of significant life risks—starting with what most people today would consider an *at-risk childhood.*

Growing Up "At Risk"

IF SOCIOLOGISTS HAD COINED THE "AT-RISK KIDS" DESIGNATION BACK in the 1950s, I could have been its poster child. Since I never thought of my life as being any riskier than anyone else's, I might well have taken offense at the label. But I certainly met the criteria: A (1) black (2) male, raised in (3) poverty in a (4) ghetto culture on the (5) streets of urban Detroit and Boston, the product of a (6) broken home headed by a (7) poorly educated and (8) very young (9) single mother (married at thirteen, divorced by her midtwenties when I was eight) who had (10) no professional training or job skills.

I've recounted much about my upbringing in my previous books. It's even been the subject of a children's book,[4] and I retell the basic facts virtually every time I'm asked to speak. A theatrical portrayal of my life has been performed for years on stage before hundreds of thousands of schoolchildren, and plans for a movie have been in the works for some time now.

So, as strange and unlikely as it still seems to me, millions of people know the general outline of my life story. If you're one of them, I beg your indulgence for the following quick recap. I promise there will be a few new details—and I hope a fresh perspective—as we reexamine the highlights of my early life, looking back through the revealing lens of risk.

At the time, my own young life seemed exceedingly ordinary to me—certainly more dull than dangerous. Only recently have I begun to appreciate the role risk played in making me the person I am today—and not just one risk, but many different ones that recurred even before I was born. Risks suffered. Risks endured. Risks ignored. Risks realized. Risks encountered. Risks refused. Risks taken. Risks regretted. Risks survived. Risks faced. Risks accepted. Risks weighed. Risks chosen. Risks embraced. Risks overcome.

My life is not so different from most people's on this score. Every human being experiences risks; some of the risks are common to all humans, and some are unique to the life each of us has been given to live. But I know for certain that risk—both its shadow and its reality—has shaped my life inside and out.

My mother took a huge risk in marrying an older "Prince Charming" who courted and wooed her by promising to whisk her away from the grueling hardship she lived with growing up as one of twenty-four children in a family that eked out a bleak subsistence on a little, hardscrabble farm in rural Tennessee. Her risk paid off big-time—at least in the short run—as Sonya Carson moved overnight from the post-Depression adversity of Appalachia to the promising bright lights and big-city excitement of Detroit. All seemed grand for a time. Mother gave birth to my brother, Curtis, and a couple of years later I followed.

As a young child I remember understanding that my father's job kept him away a good part of the time. Yet whenever he was home, he was affectionate and played with me. So I loved my daddy and thought we had a happy family.

Daddy was gone a lot more as I got older, and I never knew why. There seemed to be a tension between him and Mother, but I didn't grasp the reason. Then one day when I was in third grade, Mother explained to my brother and me that our father was moving out and would not be living with us ever again.

In tears I pleaded with Mother to explain why. She tried to tell me it just had to be that way. I begged her to make Daddy come back. She said she couldn't—she just couldn't. I kept pressing because nothing made any sense. She finally went so far as to tell me, "Your father has done some really bad things." I told her I knew she could forgive him. She said it wasn't that easy.

Not until years later did I learn it wasn't his job that had kept my father away from our family. He had been living a double life for years—complete with a second wife and another set of children.

The risk Mother had taken in getting married and leaving her family back in Tennessee could not have looked good to her at the time my father moved out. Yet I'm well aware that I owe my very existence to that foolish risk made by a poor, innocent, and naive thirteen-year-old girl so many years ago.

We faced an even bigger risk after my father left. He soon quit paying the required child support, so Mother determined she and her two sons would "make it on our own." She found the only jobs she knew how to do—cleaning houses, taking care of children, and sometimes cooking for two, three, or more well-to-do families at a time. Many mornings she left before dawn and didn't return from her second or third job until sometime after Curtis and I were in bed for the night. Two or three days at a time would go by without our ever seeing her.

The long hours of tedious work and the risk of raising two boys by herself under those circumstances weighed heavily on my mother. But she never let on. Only after we became adults did my brother and I learn the truth about those occasional "special" times when we would get to stay with friends while Mother "went away." Mother simply told us she had to "visit" or "care" for some "loved one"; she'd be gone anywhere from a few days to three or four weeks. We never suspected those were occasions when she would feel so threatened and overwhelmed by life that she would temporarily check herself into a mental facility to get treatment for depression and emotional distress. Then when she felt capable of coping with life again, she'd check herself out, we'd welcome her home from her "trip," and life would go on.

Looking back now, knowing what my mother was actually going through, I have more respect for her than ever. Throughout that immensely painful and difficult period of her life—when she suddenly found herself all alone in the world, devastated and disillusioned by the end of her marriage, and completely and solely responsible for the raising of two young boys—she summoned the necessary strength and reserve of character to risk facing her own weakness *and* to find the help she needed to deal with it.

The constant financial strain soon took a toll of its own. Rather than falling behind on the monthly payments and losing our little house, Mother made another difficult and somewhat risky decision. We rented our home out to another family for enough money to cover the mortgage, and we moved halfway across the country to Boston, where we lived for a time with my mother's older sister Jean Avery and her husband, William — a warm and wonderful couple whose own children were already grown.

While we were there, Mother made two or three more "visits to relatives," but Curtis and I didn't mind, because Aunt Jean and Uncle William took such great care of us that we were a bit spoiled by the time Mother returned. Not only did the sojourn in Boston give our family a chance to regain our financial footing, but Mother seemed to recover a lot of emotional and spiritual strength while we lived with the Averys.

Ironically, the gains in family stability we experienced during our time in Boston were accompanied by a level of risk we hadn't felt so much before. I really do think it was more than just the difference in familiarity that made life in the Boston tenements feel a lot more dangerous than the streets back home in Detroit. The Beantown rats that seemed big as cats, the winos sprawling on the sidewalks around the neighborhood, and the squad cars constantly racing up and down the streets with their lights flashing and sirens screaming all contributed to the atmosphere.

That sense of danger wasn't just the result of a young boy's fertile and overactive imagination. One of Aunt Jean and Uncle William's sons was tragically shot to death on those streets one night. I had liked and looked up to my young adult cousin, but in addition to the terrible personal grief I felt at his senseless passing, I realized that by associating with drug dealers, he had been doing something he shouldn't have been doing when he was killed. I remember concluding, "There are things out there that just aren't worth the risk!"

By the time two years had passed, Mother decided she had the emotional and financial wherewithal for us to move back to Detroit and live on our own again. She wasn't confident we could yet afford the mortgage on our own house, so we moved into a top-floor apartment of an old building in a smoggy industrial neighborhood crisscrossed with train tracks.

We were all glad to be "home" again, but when time came to enroll in fifth grade at Higgins Elementary School, I was in for a rude awakening. I thought I'd gotten a good foundation my first three years in the Detroit public schools. Then in Boston we'd attended a small private church school because Mother believed we'd get a better education there. Unfortunately, it wasn't good enough.

Classes at predominantly white Higgins Elementary were tough. The other fifth graders were not just ahead of me; I felt lost in every subject. Instead of being one of the better students in my class as I'd been in Boston, I found myself at the bottom, with no real competition for the "honor." Perhaps the worst part was that I began to believe the assessment of some of the kids who teased and taunted me by labeling me the class "dummy."

My most vivid fifth-grade memory is of the day we had a math test and our teacher had us hand our papers to the person behind us for grading while she read the answers to the class. Once the tests were graded, they were handed back to their owners, who then listened for the teacher to call out our names so we could report our scores out loud.

Waiting in dread, I finally heard my name. "Benjamin?"

I mumbled my reply, and the teacher enthusiastically exclaimed, "*Nine!* Why, Benjamin, that's wonderful." (There were thirty questions on the test, but nine out of thirty would have been incredible for me.)

The girl behind me snickered loudly and announced in an even louder voice, "Not *nine*! He got *none*!"

The entire classroom erupted with laughter. I wanted to sink through the cracks in the floor. I was close to tears but refused to let anyone see how much the laughter hurt. So I slapped a big smile on my face and pretended not to care.

But make no mistake; I did care. Not just because it hurt my feelings, but because I knew my recent performance in the classroom was putting my dreams at risk.

More than two years before, I'd made a heartfelt commitment one day in church when I had heard a memorable sermon about "always being safe in Jesus Christ if we place our faith in the Lord." At the close of the service, I walked to the front of the church to signify my decision and my determination to be a follower of Jesus.

About that same time I also decided that I would someday serve God as a doctor—a missionary doctor. The Bible-lesson papers we received at church often featured stories about medical missionaries, and their settings in fascinating far-off lands in Africa and India intrigued me. The stories of dedicated physicians relieving suffering and helping thousands of people live healthier, happier lives inspired me.

"That's what I want to do," I announced as we walked home from church one day. "Can I be a doctor, Mother?"

She stopped right there, placed her hands on my thin shoulders, and looked me right in the eyes. "Listen to me, Benny. If you ask the Lord for something and believe he will do it, then it'll happen!"

"I believe I can be a doctor," I told her.

"Then, Benny, you will be a doctor," she assured me, and we resumed our walk home. From that time on I knew what I wanted to do with my life.

Of course, like most kids, I didn't have a clue what was required to become a doctor. But I was pretty sure being the class dummy was not the surest, quickest, or most recommended path to my chosen profession.

I don't think Mother worried much about my prospects for a medical career at that point. Her immediate concern was whether or not I'd ever get out of elementary school. Curtis wasn't doing much better in his first year of junior high, so she sat us down one afternoon and told us she was so disappointed in our recent schoolwork that she didn't know what she was going to do. We loved our mother and hated to disappoint her. But we'd come back to Detroit to find ourselves so far behind our peers that we didn't know what to do either.

Mother finally sent us to bed saying she was going to stay up and pray about the sorry situation we were in at school. She was going to ask God what he would have her do, because after all, there are a lot of verses in the Bible about God's having a special concern for the poor, the widows, and their children.

I don't know about Curtis, but I had a hard time falling asleep that night. I'm not sure whether it was curiosity or worry that kept me up listening, thinking, and wondering what God was going to tell our mother.

Sure enough, when she told us the next morning, my brother and I didn't like it at all. Mother insisted God had impressed upon her that we were spending too much time watching television and not enough studying. "We're going to turn off the TV, and from now on you can choose only three television shows to watch each week ..."

Three? We were already protesting. But she went on.

"... and every week you are going to read two books—you get to choose which books—and write me a report on each one."

Again we argued. Two books a week was even more unreasonable than three television shows. But she held her ground.

Curtis and I weren't the only ones to question whether she heard the Lord right. Even some of her friends, other mothers, told her she was being too hard on us, that boys needed time outside to play. Some people actually warned Mother she would risk making us hate her for demanding we turn off the TV to read books and write reports.

But those folks were all wrong. We didn't hate Mother for instituting the new plan. Oh, sure, for a time we regularly complained that she was being too hard on us and begged her to relax the new policy. But deep down we never doubted that she loved us and only wanted what was best for us. So we abided by her restriction on TV—even when she was at work and we were home alone, because we respected her too much to disobey.

We complained about the reading assignment as well. I had never read a whole book in my life, except what they made us read in school. I couldn't imagine finishing one book a week, let alone two.

But Mother insisted, "Benny, honey, if you can read, you can learn just about anything you want to know. The doors of the world are open to people who can read."

So Curtis and I went to our local public library. Mother had said we could read any book we wanted. Since I'd always loved animals, I started reading animal books. Two a week. Then I'd write reports on the books for Mother, who would ask us to read our reports aloud to her. (We didn't know until later that she couldn't read them herself.) When we were done, she'd take the paper from us and look through it carefully as if she were really reading. Then she'd smile, put a big checkmark on the report, and hand it back to us.

When I'd read the most interesting animal books in our neighborhood branch of the Detroit Public Library, I began checking out books on plants. Then I went on to rocks. After all, we lived in a dilapidated section of the city near a lot of railroad tracks. What is there along railroad tracks? Rocks. So I would collect boxes of rocks, take them home, and compare them to the pictures in my geology books. Before long I could name virtually every rock, tell how it was formed, and identify where it came from.

I was still in fifth grade, gradually improving in some of my subjects, but still considered the dummy in the class. No one at school knew about my new reading program.

Then one day our fifth-grade science teacher walked into the classroom and held up a big, black, shiny rock. "Can anyone tell me what this is?" he asked.

I had never raised my hand in class. I had never volunteered an answer. So I waited for the smart kids to respond. None of them did. I waited for the slow kids to raise their hands. None of them did, so I figured this was my chance.

When I raised my hand, I think I shocked my teacher. Everyone in the room turned and looked at me. Classmates were poking each other and whispering, "Look, Carson's got his hand up. This is gonna be good."

The teacher finally overcame his surprise to say, "Benjamin?"

I said, "Mr. Jaeck ... that's obsidian."

The entire classroom fell silent. My answer sounded good, but no one knew whether I was right or wrong. So they just waited.

Finally the teacher broke the silence and said, "That's right! This is obsidian."

I went on to explain, "Obsidian is formed after a volcanic eruption. Lava flows down, and when it hits water, there is a super-cooling process. The elements coalesce, air is forced out, the surface glazes over, and ..." I suddenly realized my classmates were all staring at me, absolutely amazed at the words coming out of the mouth of the class "dummy."

But do you know who was the most amazed of anyone? I was. For at that moment it dawned on me that I was not a dummy after all. The reason I could answer a question no one else could answer was because I had been reading science books about animals, plants, and minerals. *What if I read books about all my subjects?* I thought. *Then I'd know more than all these students who have laughed at me and called me "dummy."*

So, beginning that very day, that's just what I did. By the time I reached seventh grade, the same students who used to tease me about being the dumbest person in class were coming to me and asking, "Benny, how do you do this problem?"

I would say, "Sit at my feet, youngster, while I instruct you." I was perhaps a little obnoxious. But after the teasing they gave me, it felt good to dish a little of it back on them.

In two years of disciplined, weekly reading, I went from the absolute bottom of my class to the top—in almost every subject. Mother was thrilled. No longer was I at risk of failing out of school, and I was more convinced than ever that I was going to be a doctor. Both my mother and I were grateful to God for the guidance he had given her when she'd prayed and asked him what she needed to do with her two sons. Curtis and I were thankful that Mother had risked our resentment to stick to her guns and follow through on her decision to pull the plug on TV and turn us on to reading instead.

Getting my act together in the classroom, however, didn't shield me from all of the other risks life presented for my brother and me as we grew up in a less-than-desirable neighborhood. We didn't think twice about it at the time, and Mother certainly didn't know about the risks we took, but just getting to and from school in our new neighborhood was a dangerous proposition. The fastest and most exciting way to commute was to hop one of the freight trains rolling on the tracks that ran alongside the route Curtis and I took to Wilson Junior High School. Curtis liked the challenge of fast-moving trains, tossing his clarinet onto one flatcar and then jumping to catch the railing on the very last car of the train. He knew if he missed his chance, he risked never seeing his band instrument again. But he never lost that clarinet.

Since I was smaller, I usually waited for slower trains. But we both placed ourselves in great danger we didn't ever seriously stop to consider. Not only did we have to run, jump, catch the railing, and hold on for dear life to a moving freight train, but we had to avoid the railroad security who were always on the lookout for people hopping their trains.

They never caught us. And we never got seriously injured like one boy we heard of who was maimed for life after falling onto the tracks under a moving train.

Hearing that story wasn't what ended our risky commutes. We stopped after an encounter I had with a different threat as I trotted along the railroad tracks on my way to school alone one morning. Near one of the crossings, a gang of bigger boys, all of them white, approached me. One boy, carrying a big stick, yelled, "Hey, you! Nigger boy!"

I froze and stood staring at the ground. He whacked me across the shoulders with the stick as his buddies crowded around. They called me every dirty name they could think of and told me "nigger kids" weren't supposed to be going to Wilson Junior High. I was too small to fight them and too scared to run. But when they tired of dishing out the verbal abuse, they told me, "Get out of here as fast as you can run. And don't let us catch you around here again, because next time we'll kill you."

I took off running and didn't slow down until I reached the school yard.

I told Curtis what had happened, and from then on we took a different route to school. I never hopped another train and never saw that gang again.

The only other time I encountered such a direct threat was during junior high when Curtis and I decided to try out for our neighborhood football team. Football was big in Detroit in those days—but unfortunately, my brother and I weren't. Compared to everyone else on the team, we were quite small. We were so fast, however, that at practice we could outrun everyone else on the field—which evidently upset a few of our teammates, or at least some of their family and friends.

One afternoon, as Curtis and I left the field after practice, a group of white men surrounded us. We could sense their anger before they even said a word. One guy stepped forward and said, "If you guys ever come back, we're going to throw you in the river!" That said, the whole bunch of them turned and walked away.

As we hurried toward home, I said to my brother, "Who wants to play football if your own supporters are against you?"

"I think we can find better things to do with our time," Curtis agreed.

And that was pretty much how we explained our decision to Mother. We told her that we were planning to study more than ever. Not wanting to upset her, though, we decided not to tell her about the threat, nor did we say anything to anyone else. We simply never went back to practice. No one ever asked why.

But despite all the risks that surrounded us in those days, the greatest risk I faced during my teenage years was the threat I posed to myself.

My Risky Behavior
Nearly Got the Best of Me

I STILL WANTED TO BE A DOCTOR. I HAD ALSO DECIDED I WANTED TO be rich. That meant that I adjusted my sights from being a missionary doctor to becoming a psychiatrist. I had never met a psychiatrist, but on television they always seemed to live in fancy mansions, drive Jaguars, and work in big, plush offices where all they did was talk to crazy people all day long. I thought, *Since I seem to be talking to crazy people all day long already, this could work out pretty well.*

My brother gave me a gift subscription to *Psychology Today*. Though I didn't yet understand everything I read, I gradually got comfortable with the language and terminology. I began thinking very seriously about my new career goal.

There was one major obstacle, however, to my becoming a doctor of any kind.

From the time I made that first personal Christian commitment when I was eight, I had tried to live my life by the biblical teachings I learned at church. But my biggest stumbling block during the early years of my adolescence was anger. I struggled with an often intense and sometimes unmanageable temper. It erupted out of nowhere and became so all-consuming that it posed a threat not only to me, but to those around me.

One day I got into a shouting match with my mother over a pair of pants she'd bought me that I refused to wear and insisted she take back. She informed me she couldn't return them because she'd bought them on sale. I screamed that I would not wear them because they weren't what I wanted.

"Benny," she told me, "you don't always get what you want."

"But I will!" I yelled as I instinctively raised my right arm and without a conscious thought launched my hand at my mother. Fortunately, Curtis was standing nearby. He grabbed me from behind and wrestled me away before I could do our mother any physical harm.

I knew in my heart I had never really wanted to hit my mother. After all, I told myself, I was a good kid who seldom got into trouble. But the truth was, I was having more and more temper issues. I had never been the kind of child who angered easily, but now as a teenager, when I did get upset, I seemed to lose control—quickly and completely. Yet even now, after almost striking my own mother, I didn't want to admit that my anger problem was serious.

Then one day I hit a boy in the hallway at school. Because I had my locker padlock in my hand at the time, the blow opened a three-inch gash in the other kid's forehead. Naturally, and rightfully so, I ended up in the principal's office. But I was so obviously horrified and regretful of my behavior that the boy I hit forgave me, and the principal didn't expel me from school as he could have.

Again I brushed the incident off, telling myself, *I didn't mean to hurt anyone. I simply forgot what was in my hand. My temper isn't really that big a problem. I'm a good kid. I can handle it.*

Finally something happened I couldn't ignore, something that could have *ruined* my life.

Instead, it *changed* my life. Forever. And I'm thankful.

One day, as a fourteen-year-old in ninth grade, I was hanging out at the house of my friend Bob, listening to his radio, when he suddenly leaned over and dialed the tuner to another station. I'd been enjoying the song playing on the first station, so I reached over and flipped it back. Bob switched stations again. Then something snapped inside of me. A wave of rage welled up, and almost without thinking, I pulled out the pocketknife I always carried. In what seemed like one continuous, involuntary motion, I flicked open the blade and lunged viciously, right at my friend's stomach. Incredibly, the point of the knife struck Bob's large metal belt buckle and the blade snapped off in my hands.

Bob raised his eyes from the broken piece of metal in my hand to my face. He was too surprised to say anything. But I could read the terror in his eyes.

"I ... I ... I'm sorry!" I sputtered, then dropped the knife handle and ran for home, horrified by the realization of what I'd just done. I burst into our empty house, rushed straight for the bathroom, locked myself in, sank to the floor, and tried in vain to erase the memory of the past few minutes. I squeezed my eyes shut, but I couldn't stop the visual horror of the replay—my lunging hand ... the slashing knife ... the belt buckle ... the broken blade ... Bob's shocked face. I couldn't get rid of the images.

There was no explaining it away. *I tried to kill my friend!* I thought. *I must be crazy. Only a crazy person would try to kill a friend!*

For hours I sat on the floor of that locked bathroom. Thinking. Remembering. And feeling more sick, more miserable, and more frightened than I had ever been in my life.

Finally I admitted to myself what I could no longer deny—I had a severe problem with anger. Even harder to acknowledge was the fact that there was no way I could control my temper by myself.

That's when I prayed: *Lord, please, you've got to help me. Please take this temper away!*

I had been reading *Psychology Today* long enough by that point to know that a person's temper is considered a personality trait and that much expert opinion held that people have to accept and compensate for their personality traits—that people can't usually change them.

But I also realized I would never achieve my dream of being a doctor with an uncontrollable temper. *Lord*, I persisted, *please change me! You promised in the Bible that if I ask anything in faith, you will do it. And I believe you can change me!*

I slipped out of that bathroom and got a Bible. Back on the bathroom floor, I opened the pages to the book of Proverbs, and the first verses I saw there were about anger and how angry people have nothing but trouble. Those words from God seemed to be written just for me. One verse I read and reread was Proverbs 16:32: "He who is slow to anger is better than the mighty, and he who rules his spirit than he who takes a city" (NKJV). Those words convicted me, but they also gave me hope.

Truly it was as if God was speaking directly to me. Assuring me that he saw and knew everything about me, uncontrollable temper and all. That he still loved me. And that because he was the one who made me, he was the only one who could help change me. And he would.

I read and prayed and wept for a long time in the bathroom that afternoon. Gradually I was filled with a genuine, unexplainable sense of peace. I stopped crying. My hands quit shaking. The horrible image of what I had done slowly faded from my mind. I knew God had answered my prayer.

I had locked myself in that bathroom alone with God for four hours. But when I walked out, I knew he had done something very significant in my heart. He had changed me in an undeniable and palpable way.

I don't just *believe* that, I *know* it.

I know it because the problem of uncontrolled anger was never again a threat to those around me, to me, or to my dreams. I can't put into words how empowering it was for me to realize that other people could no longer control me by getting me mad. It's still an extremely empowering thing today to realize that no one else can trigger an eruption of unmanageable anger in me, that God has provided and will provide whatever strength I need to control my temper and handle all of my other emotions.

I learned an even more important lesson from coming within a fraction of an inch of killing my friend and nearly dooming myself to spend years locked behind bars. It was a new conviction and understanding that the Lord really had provided in the Bible a seemingly inexhaustible source of practical wisdom that could serve as a valuable resource for everyday living.

It took me awhile to begin applying some of that wisdom, but eventually much of what I found in my daily habit of Bible reading slowly sank in. For example, Proverbs not only contains helpful advice on anger, but also includes so many warnings about fools and foolishness that I began to realize how susceptible I was to yet another risk that threatened to derail my dreams. A subtler danger perhaps than my anger had been, but a serious problem nonetheless.

When I was partway through eighth grade, Mother managed to make good on her goal of moving us back into our own house. After five long years of renting since my father left, after more than two years back in Detroit since our return from New England, the move back to Deacon Street felt to all of us like we had finally come all the way home.

The midyear transfer from Wilson Junior High to Hunter Junior High, however, was not a smooth or welcome transition. At Wilson I had earned the respect of my old classmates who'd watched me progress from class dummy to the top of the academic pack. But my new classmates at Hunter (which was 75 percent African-American) didn't seem nearly as impressed by what you *knew* as by what you *wore*.

Though I longed to be accepted, our family just didn't have the money to buy the clothes I needed to fit in with the cool crowd. That peer pressure I felt became a point of contention between Mother and me for a couple of years. I would beg her to buy me some of the hot new fashions popular with my friends. She'd sadly explain once more that she couldn't afford such clothes. Then I would complain that she didn't care if I became a friendless outcast, and she would tell me that anyone who judged me on the basis of clothes wasn't going to be a worthy friend anyway. And so it went.

Curtis usually sided with Mother. As much as I resented her position at first, in my heart I realized that what she said was true. Then as I read Proverbs in the Bible, I realized that all those verses about fools and their foolishness were actually describing me and my friends.

I was a fool following fools, and the peer pressure I felt inspired even more foolishness. Not only did my new pals overemphasize clothes, but they placed a low priority on studying. Although I couldn't afford to dress cool, at least I was always ready to hang out after school to play basketball in the park until bedtime. As a result, the grades I'd worked so hard to bring up began to slide. The straight A's I'd earned in eighth and ninth grade went back down to the C–range, which seemed to satisfy most of the in-crowd during tenth grade at Detroit's Southwestern High School the following year.

But about that time, an opportunity popped up that provided a welcome escape from the peer pressure that threatened my dreams, an opportunity that required a risk on my part.

ROTC units played an active role in many of Detroit's public high schools during the 1960s. At the beginning of his tenth-grade year, my brother, Curtis, had joined the program. By his senior year, he had risen to the rank of captain and served as our school's company commander. But as much as I looked up to and admired my brother, I was not inclined to follow in his footsteps. The discipline and demands of ROTC held little appeal for the guys I hung out with, so the program didn't interest me either.

Then one day I saw Colonel Sharper striding down the halls of school.

Like Curtis, Sharper was a senior. He had achieved a much higher rank than Curtis, however, and he became one of only three colonels in all the ROTC programs at all the high schools in Detroit. But the authority he commanded and his many achievements did not impress me nearly as much as his colonel's uniform. He had a three-diamond cluster on each shoulder, row after row of medals, plus a host of ribbons and even some fancy ropes. It struck me that if I could show up at school every day in a snazzy uniform like that, I would no longer have to endure the humiliation of wearing the outdated clothing my mother said was all she could afford. Suspect though my motives might have been, I was suddenly enthralled by the prospect of a uniform like Colonel Sharper's.

I must have surprised Curtis when I asked him how and where I could sign up for ROTC. That's when I learned about one serious and unexpected obstacle to my ever achieving the rank of colonel.

Not until their first semester of tenth grade were students given a chance to join ROTC. That means they had six whole semesters of high school to earn the promotions needed to rise up through the ranks. Like all good military organizations, ROTC had rigidly prescribed formulas and timetables for each and every promotion.

Since I was enrolling a whole semester behind my sophomore classmates, that meant I would always be a half year behind them. Although achieving the rank of colonel in just five semesters was not impossible, it was a long shot at best. So I asked myself, *Is it worth the risk? Do I really want to accept the rigors of ROTC if there's only a distant chance of achieving the top rank?*

So even though the odds of my ever wearing a fancy colonel's uniform were slim, I was smart enough to realize that whatever rank I achieved, I would still be able to wear my ROTC uniform most days of the week for the remainder of my high school career. No more uncool clothing.

I signed up.

As it turned out, I enjoyed everything about ROTC—military science and strategy, disassembling and assembling rifles, target practice, drill instruction, the whole nine yards. I did so well that by the end of my first semester, I was promoted, not to private first class or to corporal, but straight to staff sergeant. By early the next year, I had been promoted to sergeant first class, then master sergeant. That was when Sergeant Hunt, a real sergeant in the real Army, challenged me to take over the fifth-period ROTC class, an unruly band of brothers who were notoriously disruptive, uncooperative, and exasperating.

Sergeant Hunt promised me that if I could shape up that bunch, he would promote me to second lieutenant at the beginning of my third semester in ROTC. If I could manage that, not only would I have caught up with and passed most of the cadets who had started a semester ahead of me, but it would give me an opportunity to sit for the field-grade examination. Only those who achieved the rank of second lieutenant or above qualified for this exam, which, in turn, determined what level of promotion they were eligible for next. Beyond that, all promotions were made strictly on merit.

Of course, accepting Sergeant Hunt's fifth-period challenge could mean possible failure, and knowing the hooligans in that group as I did, I knew there was a real risk of being beaten up or humiliated. But success looked like my best chance to leapfrog over a lot of other people and position myself to move up the ranks. It was that "bigger picture" consideration that gave me the courage to take on the challenge and accept the risks.

As it turned out, that fifth-period class only seemed incorrigible. I soon discovered that they actually had a lot of pride, so I worked them hard on their drilling and their knowledge of rifles. Then I appealed to their pride and challenged them not just to do better, but to become the top ROTC class in the school by semester's end. And they did.

I received my promotion. I took the exam and posted the highest score in the city, beating out not just other second lieutenants, but all of the first lieutenants, captains, majors, and lieutenant colonels — everyone. The ROTC board called me in for an interview, after which they promoted me to the rank of lieutenant colonel, an unprecedented jump from second lieutenant.

That new role not only gave me more responsibility, but also qualified me to sit again for the field-grade exam during my next semester. Not only did my performance on the second test earn me my coveted promotion to colonel, but I was given the title of city executive officer over all of the high school ROTC programs in the Detroit public school system.

I learned that with great responsibility often come great honor and opportunity. As the ROTC's city executive officer, I had the chance to meet General William Westmoreland, have dinner with Congressional Medal of Honor award winners, march at the head of a Memorial Day parade, and be offered a full scholarship to West Point.

I was thrilled by the whole ROTC experience. Not only did it serve as an impressive entry on college applications, but it taught me a wide variety of skills. It also bolstered my confidence to believe I might find a military career quite satisfying if I accepted that scholarship to West Point.

But when I sat down to think through my longtime dream of becoming a physician, I decided I couldn't risk interfering with that. So even though ROTC was a wonderful time in my life that taught me a lot about how great risks pay off with great rewards, I decided to move on. I was able to do that in part because my ROTC lessons helped in so many ways to prepare me and pave the way for the next big life risk I would soon have to take — choosing a college.

I've told this story many times, but it was a television show (one of the three I chose to watch every week) that played a pivotal role in my college selection. I dreamed of being selected as a competitor on the *General Electric College Bowl*, which aired on network television every Sunday afternoon. Teams of undergraduates from various colleges competed each week to answer questions on subject matter ranging from science and math to language and history to art and music. It was my desire to one day appear on that show that spurred me to learn about the great classical composers and to recognize and appreciate their music—knowledge that did nothing to further my high school popularity during a time when my peers were more in tune with rock groups like the Beatles, the Rolling Stones, and Three Dog Night, and the popular new Motown sound of the Supremes, Smokey Robinson, Dionne Warwick, and Marvin Gaye.

The GE College Bowl broadcast that made the most impact on me took place the summer before my senior year in high school. On that program a team of scholars from Harvard battled a group from Yale. I hadn't yet decided on a college, but both of those Ivy League institutions were on my dream list. The trouble was, I only had enough money to pay one ten-dollar college application fee. So that one television show, when the Yale squad trounced Harvard by a score of something like 510 to 35, sealed the decision for me. I would apply to Yale!

If I knew then what I know now, I never would have risked the only college application money I had to apply at Yale. Considering the caliber of the thousands of students from around the world who apply there every year, how realistic were my chances? And yet ...

Once in a while, when it comes to taking risks, youthful naiveté pays better dividends than do knowledge and experience, because I never once considered sending an application to a less exclusive school, even though I would have been guaranteed entrance.

When I came down to the deadline, it wasn't that difficult a risk to take. Not only did I remain convinced that God wanted me to become a doctor, but I had read many Bible verses telling me God would answer my fervent prayers and grant the desires of my heart. My desire was to go to Yale, and I prayed for that fervently. I remember reading Proverbs 10:24, which says, "The expectations of the righteous shall come to pass." So I kept looking for my acceptance in the mail every day because that was my expectation. When it finally came, I wasn't at all surprised.

I was, however, very excited.

I had many reasons to celebrate. My dreams were one step closer to fruition. Though I didn't yet think of it in these terms, I had survived an *at-risk* upbringing. I had achieved at a level beyond all expectations — except those of my mother and myself. I felt well prepared for whatever the next stage of life would bring.

But I had no idea I'd only begun to learn the risk lessons I would need to survive and succeed personally and professionally in the years to come.

Risks I Took That Changed
My Life Forever

SINCE I ONLY HAD ENOUGH MONEY TO APPLY TO ONE COLLEGE, JUST *getting into* Yale had been a real risk. I soon discovered, however, that *staying in* school at Yale posed an even greater challenge—the risk of failure.

I arrived on campus feeling confident, maybe even a little cocky. I'd won all sorts of honors during high school, received the highest SAT scores in the Detroit Public Schools the previous year, and talked to a number of college recruiters who told me how much their schools wanted me. I figured Yale was fortunate to have me.

Then during supper one evening the first week of my freshman year, the students sitting with me around a cafeteria table somehow began comparing SAT scores. I just listened. Curious. Then shocked. Every single one of them had outscored me. I think that little reality check was my first real clue that the Ivy League was a huge step up from my high school back home.

Still, the real risk of failure didn't sink in until almost the end of my first semester. My old high school study routine—read the assigned material in the text, show up for class, cram for a day or so before any tests, and collect my A—didn't work well at Yale. Each day, each week I felt myself slipping further and further behind, particularly in chemistry (a required course for pre-med majors), in which I earned the lowest grade in a class of six hundred students.

I had done so poorly that by the end of the semester I knew I had only one faint hope of avoiding failure altogether. The chemistry prof had a rule that no matter what grade a student got during the semester, if he or she did well enough on the final exam to demonstrate mastery of the material, he would toss out all of the earlier grades and count only the final.

I wasn't at all sure I could learn what I needed to know for the final, but I determined to try. As I opened my chemistry book to study, I prayed, "Lord, I need your help! I've always thought you wanted me to be a doctor. But I can't stay in pre-med if I fail this class. Please, either let me know what else I ought to do, or perform a miracle and help me pass this exam."

I spent hours memorizing formulas and equations and reading through the text, trying to understand what I'd not been able to grasp all semester. Finally, at midnight the words on the page began to blur. I turned off the light, and before I went to sleep, I whispered into the darkness, "God, please forgive me for failing you."

During that night I dreamed I was sitting in my chemistry class all alone. A shadowy figure walked into the dream and began writing chemistry problems on the board. Then the figure began working the problems as I watched.

When I woke the next morning, I remembered enough of the dream to get up and start writing down the problems. A few answers were fuzzy, but I recalled most of the problems with surprising clarity.

Then I showered, dressed, and headed for my chemistry class, numb from exhaustion and the sure knowledge that I was woefully unprepared for the exam. But when the professor passed out the exam, I was shocked to look at the first page and see that question number one was the first problem written on the board in my dream. I quickly scanned through the rest of the test to discover all of the problems were identical to the ones worked out on the board in my dream.

My pencil flew across the pages. I knew the answer to question after question. Toward the end, as my recall of the dream began to fade, I missed a few. But when I turned in the test at the end of period, I knew I had passed.

After leaving the room, I strolled around the Yale campus for an hour thinking about what had happened and what it all meant. In my mind, God had confirmed once again that he wanted me to become a doctor.

"Thank you, Lord," I prayed. "You gave me a miracle today!" But I also promised God this would be the last time I would ask him to rescue me from poor grades. I would learn how to study throughout a course and wouldn't risk my grades by depending on last-minute cramming again. And that's what I did.

———

At college, I also decided to face another kind of serious risk—although it took me awhile to take the plunge. I met Candy Rustin just before my third year at Yale, though I almost missed out on romance because I was so focused on my studies and other responsibilities.

I'd had a few dates in college and had gone out occasionally with groups of friends. But working hard to pay my expenses and make the best possible grades, I found little time for dating or even thinking about women—until I represented Yale at a special reception for incoming freshmen from Michigan.

I couldn't help noticing a pretty young woman with a bubbly laugh who seemed to be talking to everyone. *That's one good-looking girl!* I thought. I made a point of introducing myself, and a few weeks later I spotted her walking across campus. I smiled and asked how her classes were going.

"I think I'm making all A's," she told me.

Wow! I remember thinking. *She must be really smart!*

After that, I made a point to stop and talk to Candy whenever I saw her. Not only was she in pre-med, but I learned she played violin in the Yale Symphony and the Bach Society. *This is also one talented girl!* I concluded.

From my first year at Yale, I had regularly attended worship and sung in the choir at a nearby Adventist church. We needed an organist. So one day as Candy and I talked, I suggested she come with me to church and audition for the position. Someone else got the organist job, but Candy came to church with me anyway and joined the choir. Not only would I now be seeing her regularly on campus, but I'd be seeing her at church every weekend as well. Before long we began attending a church-sponsored Bible study and meeting after those classes to talk. Still, we were just friends. I was too busy with school to think about anything more.

During the Thanksgiving holiday my senior year, Candy and I were both hired by the university to interview prospective students from Michigan with high SAT scores. Yale even provided a rental car, which we drove from town to town for the interviews, and, of course, we also spent time visiting our own friends and families.

On the last day of our trip, we left Detroit later than we had planned. Since I had to return the rental car in Connecticut by eight the next morning, we decided to drive all night. Since the route was mostly interstate, I didn't worry much about the risk of an all-night drive. But I was exhausted. "I don't know if I can stay awake," I told Candy.

Shortly after crossing into Ohio, Candy dropped off to sleep. I figured I'd give her a chance to get some rest before asking her to drive a little later. About one in the morning, I noticed a sign reading "Youngstown, Ohio." The speed limit was seventy, but we hadn't seen another car in almost half an hour. So I cruised along at about ninety miles per hour, confident we would make it back in time after all.

The car was warm, Candy dozed quietly beside me, my eyelids began to feel like lead, and the dotted line in the middle of the interstate slowly blurred as I drifted off to sleep at the wheel.

The vibration of the tires as they hit the metal illuminators between the lanes awakened me with a start. All I saw in the headlights was the blackness of a ravine ahead, dropping steeply off the side of the road, and the car was heading straight for it. I instinctively jerked the wheel as hard as I could to muscle the car back onto the roadway. We could have flipped. Instead, we went into a wild spin — around and around and around, I don't know how many times — in the eastbound lanes of that interstate. Scenes from my childhood flashed through my mind with the thought, *So this is what it's like to die.*

When we finally stopped spinning, we were in the far right lane, the motor still running and pointed in the right direction.

Shaking, I eased the car off onto the shoulder of the roadway and turned off the engine — just seconds before a speeding eighteen-wheeler barreled by. "We're alive. God saved our lives. Thank you, God," I said aloud.

The sound of my voice awakened Candy. "What's wrong?" she asked. "Why are we stopped?" She thought maybe something was wrong with the car.

"Nothing's wrong!" I told her. "Go back to sleep!"

But she sensed the tension in my voice. "Ben, don't be like that. Everything can't be fine if we're not moving. Why are we stopped?"

I twisted the key in the ignition and tried to sound casual as I accelerated back onto the highway. "Oh, just a quick rest ..."

"Ben! Please ..."

I coasted back onto the shoulder, put the car in park, and turned off the engine. "Okay," I sighed, "I fell asleep back there ... and ... I thought we were going to die." I could hardly get those last words out.

Candy reached across and put her hand in mine. "The Lord spared our lives, Ben," she said with certainty. "He's got plans for us."

"I know," I replied, feeling just as certain as she was.

Neither of us slept another wink that night. We talked easily and freely all the way back to campus. At some point in Pennsylvania or New York, Candy turned to look at me and asked, "Ben, why are you so nice to me? Like tonight, I should have stayed awake to help keep you alert, but you let me sleep."

"I guess I'm just a nice guy."

"It's more than that, isn't it?" she pressed.

"I'm always nice to second-year Yale students," I teased.

"Ben. Be serious."

I guess that was the issue—whether or not I should risk being serious. It was hard not to joke. Hard to risk what I then said to her: "I guess it's because I like you. I guess I like you a lot."

"I like you a lot too, Ben. More than anyone else I've ever met."

An unfamiliar sensation filled my chest when she said that. I didn't answer—at least not with words. I sensed I was about to take one of the most important risks of my life. But it felt so right that I didn't hesitate. I took my foot off the gas and once again eased the car to a stop on the shoulder. I put my arms around Candy and kissed her. She kissed me back. Our first kiss. So the risk was definitely worth it.

Neither of us really understood what we were getting into, yet we knew we were in love. From then on we were inseparable. Strange as it may seem, our relationship never put our studies at risk. We spent a lot of our time together doing homework. We encouraged one another. And with Candy by my side, I was more determined than ever to work hard and make my dreams come true.

I didn't realize it at the time, but the nature of the risks I faced had begun to change. Many of the risks I faced as I grew up had been just a natural part of the fabric of my life—risks I had no real control over. But as a young adult in school and then as a young professional after that, more and more of the life risks I encountered involved uncertain choices that I could, or in some cases had to, make.

Some risks I avoided. Others I embraced. But always I tried to make wise and good decisions about what risks to take. I didn't always make the best choices, in part because I hadn't yet hit upon the simple risk-analysis formula that I have since made a crucial part of my regular decision-making process, both personally and professionally.

Yet I think a few examples of my early encounters with risk would be instructive here, if only to show how those experiences with personal risk analysis (an evolving, trial-and-error proposition for a while) eventually led me to the simple and effective prescription I want to offer as the crux of this book. Before we get to that prescription, I want you to gain a sense of how I came to develop it, understand it, and apply it to making decisions about my own life risks.

One of the biggest, most crucial risks I ever took was in my first year of med school. Indeed, it's not just possible but probable that if I hadn't taken that risk or if my decision to take that risk had not worked out the way it did, I would not be writing this book. I would not even be a doctor today. I'll explain.

After a successful undergraduate career at Yale and more convinced than ever that God intended me to be a doctor, I was not intimidated in the least by what I'd heard about the academic rigors of medical school. I believed I was ready.

But during that first semester at the University of Michigan School of Medicine, I found myself stuck in the lecture hall for six to eight hours every day, exposed to such a flood of facts and information that I understood why the first-year learning process has been likened to the challenge of having someone open a fire hydrant and expect you to swallow it all. To describe the amount of material we were required to learn as "overwhelming" would be a grave understatement. I did so poorly on the first set of comprehensive exams, which were given just six weeks into the school year, that I was sent to my faculty advisor for help and advice.

After spending a few minutes looking at my records, he said, "Mr. Carson, you seem like a very intelligent young man.... I bet there are many things you could do outside of medicine."

So his recommended Plan A for me was to drop out of med school. He felt I didn't have what it took to cut it as a physician. He thought I would save myself—and a lot of other people—considerable grief if only I would quit now, before investing more time and effort in a pointless endeavor.

What a devastating assessment for someone who had planned to be a doctor since he was eight years old! I'd never seriously considered anything else. I guess my advisor picked up on my reluctance to heed that advice. So he proposed Plan B: perhaps I should consider taking a reduced load. Study one or two courses at a time rather than multiple courses. Though it would take longer to graduate, I might eventually be able to finish.

I thanked him for his advice and went home, my head spinning. I could feel my dreams beginning to crumble. I just didn't know what to do. So I prayed. I asked God to give me wisdom, and at a calm moment, I began contemplating my situation in terms of risk. *What if I drop out?* I thought. I was genuinely afraid my self-esteem would plummet so low I might never recover and would go on to have an absolutely dismal life.

Those prospects were so disturbing and unacceptable to me that there really wasn't any more analysis to do at that point.

So I moved on to asking myself, *How can I turn this situation around?* I thought about courses in which I had always done well and courses in which I had struggled. An obvious pattern emerged: I usually struggled in courses that revolved around a lot of boring lectures, because I'm not an auditory learner. In contrast, the courses I did well in were those that relied on a lot of reading to convey the basic information. I also got a great deal out of repetition.

So what did I do with this self-assessment?

I made the decision not to pursue either course of action suggested by my advisor. Then I took what sounds like (and probably was) an even more drastic risk. Since I wasn't learning the necessary material from listening to lectures, I quit going to class altogether and spent all of those hours using the most effective learning techniques for me — first reading, then repetition in the form of flash cards I created for every one of my classes.

I didn't completely ignore the lectures. We had "scribes" at the med school, people who earned money by taking and typing up detailed notes of every lecture in every class. You could subscribe to their notes for a reasonable price, so that's what I did. I quickly discovered that by reading the lecture notes, I absorbed much more information much faster than I had when I attended class.

Again, with the understanding that reading was my optimum learning method, I made great use of the abundance of old exams available in the library. By reading through the exams for last year and the year before and the year before that, I was able to get a good idea of what might be on this year's exam. While the questions might change, the body of information (or in this case the information of the body) addressed in last year's questions was going to be important again this year, unless some dramatic change had occurred in scientific knowledge.

For example, I saw that to answer a question, I needed to understand the first three parts of the Krebs Cycle, which pertains to certain types of metabolism and energy production. Rather than trying to memorize the answers to that specific question, I realized it was much smarter to go to the text thinking, *I need to understand the first three parts of the Krebs Cycle*, because that was almost certainly going to show up again in the examination.

Once I learned to study like that, to create appropriate flash cards, and to read the scribes' notes along with my textbook, there was virtually no risk of me ever getting a bad mark again on any exam for the rest of medical school. More important, studying that way allowed me to become a first-class physician because I understood the materials in a way that would stick with me.

Candy and I were married the summer between my second and third year of medical school, about a month after she graduated from Yale with a double major in music and psychology. We began our lifetime adventure of marriage by accepting the fact that years of professional training lay ahead for me. In those years we encountered, analyzed, and acted upon some additional meaningful risks. We'll quickly look at three here.

Risk Number One — Thinking in New Ways

One day while in my clinical years of medical school, during a month-long neurosurgical rotation, I watched as one of my instructors performed a delicate surgical procedure on a patient.

"The hardest part," explained my instructor, "is locating the foramen ovale," and he probed with a long needle in search of this tiny hole every person has at the base of the skull.

As I watched the tedious, trial-and-error approach to locate this minuscule access point through the bone and into the brain itself, I kept thinking, *There must be a better way, a less invasive means, of pinpointing the spot than poking around the base of a patient's skull with a needle.*

After rounds that day, I went to the radiology lab where I'd worked one summer and asked permission to use their equipment. It took me several days to refine the idea. I started with a simple truth: that two points determine a straight line. I postulated that I should be able to place one very small metal ring at the front of the skull and another ring at the back of the head. Then by passing an X-ray beam through the head and turning the head until the rings lined up, I would know the foramen ovale would lie on that line.

The basic procedure seemed simple enough once I reasoned it out, but I couldn't help wondering why no one had thought of it before. I didn't risk saying anything about my discovery to my teachers for several days. I thought, *If I'm wrong, I'll embarrass myself. If I'm right, these experienced surgeons might be offended that a mere medical student would propose a new procedure.*

Then I used the technique in a couple of tests on cadaver skulls and discovered that it really did work. So I explained to my neurosurgical professors what I was doing and then demonstrated the technique for them. The neurosurgical chief watched, shook his head slowly, and smiled. "That's fabulous, Carson," he told me.

I encountered no resentment from the surgeons, some of whom even started using my technique. The willingness to think differently about a problem and then risk sharing the idea with others certainly paid off.

Risk Number Two—Weighing the Alternatives

Once I'd made the decision early in med school to specialize in neurosurgery, choosing a residency program wasn't difficult. I'd wanted to come to Johns Hopkins, which is considered by many people the top medical teaching and training hospital of its kind in the world. The experience proved everything I had hoped for and more. It gave me, among so many other things, an initial introduction to the type of risks common to the career of a brain surgeon.

During my fourth year in Baltimore, I served as chief resident of neurosurgery at Francis Scott Key Medical Center, which was owned by Johns Hopkins. One night I received a call from the emergency room about a teenager who'd just arrived, beaten severely on the head with a baseball bat. Unfortunately, this beating took place on a weekend during the meeting of the American Association of Neurological Surgeons being held in Boston that year. My attending surgeon, whom

I was to consult and get approval from on any case, was at that meeting. My other option was to call the faculty member at Johns Hopkins who was on call that night, who was to cover for all neurosurgical consults at all of the hospitals.

I tried again and again to reach the on-call doctor, but I couldn't get through. Each attempt became more and more desperate because my patient was comatose and deteriorating quickly. He had sustained so much brain damage that I was convinced he would die soon unless I performed a lobectomy and removed the damaged tissue to give the man space and time for the swelling of his brain to go down. But I'd never performed the procedure. And hospital regulations forbade me, even as a chief resident, to perform surgery such as this without an attending surgeon present.

As I watched my patient, I realized, *He needs the surgery now!* And yet I thought, *What happens if I get in there and run into bleeding I can't control? What if there is some other problem I've never encountered before? If anything goes wrong, people are going to second-guess the decision and demand to know why I broke the rules to operate.*

But then I had to ask myself, *What is going to happen here if I don't operate* now? The answer was clear as the proverbial bell: this young man would die.

The physician's assistant on duty with me that night saw the decision I faced. He said three words to me: "Go for it!"

By the time we opened up the skull, I was calm and remembered exactly what steps I needed to take in order to remove the frontal and temporal lobes (which are surprisingly expendable) from the right side of this young man's brain. There were no complications during surgery.

As relieved as I felt when the young man woke up a few hours later, neurologically normal, I worried for several days about the consequences I would face for taking such a risk. Fortunately, there were none. All of the medical staff present that night realized the patient would have died if I hadn't rushed him into surgery.

I encountered that patient not long ago. He came up after I spoke somewhere and introduced himself. Today he's living a normal life, married with a family, and working as a psychologist/counselor with the Baltimore City Public Schools.

Risk Number Three—Making Your Own Decision

As the end of my chief residency approached, I met a visiting neurosurgeon from Australia, Dr. Bryant Stokes, who invited me to extend my training yet another year by coming to work with him down under as senior registrar (a position similar to chief resident in our American system) at a major teaching hospital in western Australia.

Naturally Candy and I spent much time seriously considering the pros and cons. Bryant was an excellent surgeon and a great guy, and he assured me I'd have a steady supply of interesting and challenging cases. But a number of friends and colleagues cautioned me about the role of racism in Australia's colorful history. They warned me that Candy and I might not be welcome there, that working there might be a huge mistake, and that if I went, I'd regret the decision and probably be home within weeks.

With that kind of advice, it didn't take long to decide against Australia, especially since Candy was pregnant with our first child. But in the following days and weeks, we both began to feel uneasy about our hasty decision. We kept running into Australians everywhere we went, and they seemed warm, friendly, and accepting. Every time we turned on the television, there would be a special program featuring the world's smallest continent; it seemed a wonderfully appealing place. Was all this Australia stuff just a coincidence, or was God trying to tell us something? Had we perhaps been too hasty in rejecting our Australian invitation?

So Candy and I decided to do more research. We reconsidered some of the pros and cons. Going to Australia would mean another year of training—but one that promised to provide me with a lot of valuable experience operating under the best neurosurgeons in Australia and getting a chance to work on the most complicated cases. We might make new friends in a different and interesting part of the world. Not going would mean I could start my neurosurgical career as soon as my residency ended. I'd spent a lot of years in preparation already, so the thought of wrapping up that training and finally getting started on my own professional career held enormous appeal. Then there was the racism issue, on which we were now getting divided opinions.

Ultimately we decided to go. Our year in Australia turned out to be a fabulous experience. I was given the opportunity to perform the largest number of operations I've ever done in one year's time, many of them highly complex. In twelve months down under, I became proficient in many new techniques and gained a level of skill and experience that would have taken me years to acquire if I had stayed in the States and faced the challenge every new attending physician faces his or her first year—finding a position, trying to establish a practice, getting an initial feel for the profession, and so on. The bottom line was that when I came back to the United States and accepted a junior faculty position at Johns Hopkins, I already had experience, skills, and confidence far beyond my years. So when the position of director of pediatric neurosurgery opened up the following year, I was given the job—at the unheard-of age of thirty-three. That never would have happened—and much of what happened in my career after that never would have happened—if I hadn't taken the risk, accepted the uncertainty, and moved away with my pregnant wife to do "down-under" brain surgery for a year.

The decision to return to Johns Hopkins after that year was also something of a risk. A number of people who counseled me about other options believed I was making a foolish mistake staying in academic medicine rather than testing the far more lucrative waters of private practice. One person who offered me a position at another Baltimore Hospital even warned me that I would never be happy or fairly treated in such a "racist" organizational environment as Johns Hopkins.

In my year of internship and five years of residency, I never felt victimized by institutional bias or prejudice, nor did I see any evidence of anything I ever viewed as a culture of racism. I had always been happy at Hopkins, and that person's concern of unfairness was discredited the very next year when I was offered, despite my youth, the position of director of pediatric neurosurgery.

Financial considerations did become an issue sooner that I would have guessed, however, but not in the way I or anyone who had advised me ever expected. By the end of my second year in academic medicine at Hopkins, I was disillusioned as much by my concern about departmental finances as I was about my own personal compensation. I was informed there wasn't enough money budgeted for me to have my own secretary; I had to share one with other docs. Neither was there enough money for me to have my own computer; I had to share that as well.

Factor into that my salary, which was far below the industry standard for neurosurgeons, and it wasn't surprising that despite a terrific work environment, the opportunity to tackle difficult cases, and the great reward of helping so many people, I couldn't help feeling like maybe I was missing out on something professionally.

I began to put out feelers, looked at a few other opportunities, and was eventually offered the opportunity to join a private practice group in Texas that would have paid me about six times what I was making at Johns Hopkins.

The decision seemed like a no-brainer. So I submitted my letter of resignation and began to make preparations to move to Texas. But my letter of resignation was never accepted by the head of the neurosurgery department. In fact, Dr. Donlin Long, who had been a respected mentor of mine since I'd arrived in Baltimore for my internships, came marching into my office accompanied by the chairman of the neurology department. They wanted to talk about my letter, which they deemed "ridiculous."

"Of course there's enough money in the budget for you to have your own secretary," they told me. "And of course you should have your own computer." They even proposed and persuaded the dean to approve an incentive program that would tie salaries to the number of cases and the amount of money brought into Hopkins by my caseload.

Although I hadn't intended my letter to be a bargaining chip, it turned out to be a great one. Suddenly all of my concerns were addressed and my problems solved.

Still, there remained an element of risk. I'd be giving up a degree of independence and greater financial potential that private practice might offer. At the same time, that felt like an acceptable risk because

I believed that, for some reason I didn't yet understand, God wanted me to stay in academic medicine.

Looking back, I see so many different ways that decision has paid off.

———

Perhaps the greatest benefit in staying at Johns Hopkins has been the privilege to work on some amazing cases. Many of them—like the Bijanis and the other conjoined-twin cases, the hemispherectomies such as Maranda's, and desperately complex cases like Bo-Bo's—presented some significant and memorable risks all their own.

But I'll give you one more example here because it's the one that forced me to draw on all of the risk-analysis skills I'd developed up to that point, all of the lessons I'd learned about facing and taking risks, and condense them all into a simple formula that I have used personally and professionally ever since.

Denise Baca came to Johns Hopkins all the way from New Mexico. She was thirteen years old and in *status epilepticus*, which meant she was having constant seizures and had been having them for more than two months. Unable to control her breathing because of the seizures, she had undergone a tracheostomy and hadn't been able to speak for several months.

A few years earlier Denise had been a normal, healthy child. Since the seizures had begun, she'd been to doctors all over the country as her condition steadily deteriorated. Most of the experts agreed that the primary seizure focus was from the Broca's area (the speech area) and the motor cortex, the two most important sections of her dominant hemisphere.

The experts had told her parents, "There is nothing that can be done for her." But then a family friend read one of the articles written about Maranda Francisco and called the Bacas, who contacted us to ask if we would examine their daughter to see if she might be a candidate for a hemispherectomy.

Controversy immediately broke out at Johns Hopkins. Several neurologists thought it crazy to even consider the procedure for this patient. They had good reasons for their opinions. At thirteen, Denise was older than our previous patients; since her brain wouldn't have as much elasticity as our younger patients' had, she was more apt to permanently lose function. Her seizures were focused in particularly troublesome areas of her brain, making the surgery even riskier than usual. The constant seizures had certainly taken a toll, so she was in terrible medical condition already. For example, she had aspirated and was having pulmonary problems that presented surgical risk all by themselves.

Our most adamant critic predicted, "She'll likely die on the table just from her medical problems, much less from a hemispherectomy!" I knew the man was genuinely concerned.

But my colleagues Doctors Freeman and Vining and I (the three people directly involved with all of the hemispherectomies done at Hopkins up to that point) disagreed. We thought our growing expertise with the procedure earned us the biggest say about who was and who wasn't a candidate for the surgery.

Out of respect for those who opposed the idea, we held a number of conferences over a period of several days. Because of the controversy, we delayed the operation and took this particular decision slowly and carefully. We agreed our opposition deserved a fair hearing, but we insisted on having the final word.

Our primary critic went so far as to write a very strong letter to the chairman of the neurology department (with copies to the chair of neurosurgery, the hospital president, and a number of other folks). The letter stated that in his medical opinion, under no circumstances should Johns Hopkins consider this operation. And he spelled out his reasoning again.

Inevitably, some hard feelings developed. I managed to stay out of the conflict by refusing to take his arguments as personal indictments. I believed in our critic's sincerity and genuine concern about what was best for Denise and for Hopkins. He was entitled to his opinion. I just didn't agree.

Still, we didn't want to proceed and risk more controversy that might further affect the morale of the entire hospital. For days I prayed and asked God to help us resolve this problem, yet I couldn't see how it could work out.

Then suddenly the issue resolved itself. Our leading opponent left the country for a long overseas conference, and our hemispherectomy team decided to proceed with our plan while there would not be any loud outcries.

I explained to the Bacas, as I did to parents of other children needing the radical measure of hemispherectomies, "If we don't do anything, Denise is going to die. If we try this procedure, she still may die, but at least we have a chance."

Her parents clearly understood. They wanted to provide Denise with "at least a fighting chance."

The procedure itself went pretty much as we'd expected. But as was sometimes the case with hemispherectomy patients, Denise remained in a coma for several days. All we could do was wait. When she finally woke, she had stopped seizing. By the time she had recovered enough to go home, Denise was talking again. Weeks later she returned to school and began making steady improvements.

By the time our colleague returned from overseas, Denise was showing enough progress that there was no reason for him to continue his protest. The controversy blew over, and the outcome had a definite calming and quieting impact on what might have been even more controversial cases in the years to come. So the risk involved in the Baca case paid off in more ways than one.

The success of that case provided me a surprising benefit that I have profited from ever since and expect to continue profiting from for the remainder of my life. During those difficult waiting days after the surgery—not yet knowing the results of the surgery, whether or not the operation had helped Denise, who had been right about the course of action, or what the impact of the outcome would be on the patient, her family, the doctors, and the hospital—I did a lot of thinking about the risk I had been willing to take. How was it I came to the position I took? What made me so sure it was the right decision? When was any risk worth taking? How and when would I consider a surgical risk too great to take? And on and on.

I probably wrestled over the reasoning of this case more than others because I realized if something did go wrong, I'd need to be able to defend my decision to go ahead with what had admittedly been a risky surgery. The critics would want their say. So I kept rolling the questions around in my mind, looking back at my decision process from every angle. Then I began to compare the risk analysis I'd done in the Baca case with other risks I'd faced. What had I learned about my decision-making process? How had I learned to handle risk?

That's when I came up with the four questions for my Best/Worst Analysis (B/WA) formula:

- What is the *best* thing that can happen if I *do* this?
- What is the *worst* thing that can happen if I *do* this?
- What is the *best* thing that can happen if I *don't* do it?
- What is the *worst* thing that can happen if I *don't* do it?

You're probably looking at the questions, shaking your head, and thinking, *Is it that easy?*

I believe it is, and we're going to use the remainder of this book to look at examples that will help you understand how this simple risk-analysis approach can be applied in our personal and professional lives — and how the same prescription could be applied to some of the most complex and troubling issues facing our nation — and our world — today.

Four Simple Questions
to Help Assess Any Risk

Not long after Denise Baca's case, the same four basic Best/ Worst Analysis questions served me well in dealing with the risk presented by the very difficult and memorable case of Christopher Pylant.

Doctors had diagnosed a large, complex brain-stem tumor when Christopher was four. Everyone who saw the boy gave the same discouraging prognosis. His condition was terminal; the size and the location of the growth made it inoperable. When the parents finally brought him to Johns Hopkins to seek another opinion from me, I examined all of the radiological studies and had to concur. The tumor appeared so extensively entwined throughout the brain stem that I saw no way to operate without doing devastating or fatal damage to the boy.

From that first appointment, I was impressed by the spiritual faith of Christopher's family. His parents came right out and told me they believed God had led them to Johns Hopkins where they would find a neurosurgeon who had a strong Christian faith and would be able to help their son.

As respectfully and gently as I knew how, I told them that perhaps I was that neurosurgeon they were meant to see, that I did have a strong personal faith in God and would gladly do anything I felt was possible to help their son. But perhaps the best help I could offer was to reassure them that they had done everything they could for their son and that they now needed to leave him in God's hands.

The Pylants' obvious reluctance to accept that explanation bothered me. I'd certainly confronted parents struggling with denial before. But the fervency of their request that I reconsider my verdict was somehow different. *Couldn't I do something*—anything—*for their son?*

I was torn. I had great empathy for these anguished parents. My own son was Christopher's age. Not only did I believe in a powerful God, but in my short medical career I had already seen cases that could only be explained as answers to prayer. Still, I knew I couldn't justify taking action simply because the parents had faith that I should. I needed some logical basis, some rational justification for pursuing a dangerous operation. So I had to do some soul-searching: *Is there any possibility that this is something other than an invasive malignant tumor of the brain stem? Is there any possibility we could all be mistaken? Should I go after this thing?*

Eventually I came back to those same simple questions:

What's the worst thing that could happen if we operate? We would confirm the fatal diagnosis by finding a horribly malignant and advanced brain stem tumor. There also was a chance Christopher could die on the operating table from the trauma of such a dangerous and delicate surgery.

What's the best thing that could happen if we operate? We might find something different from what we expect based on the scans and then have a chance to do something that could make a difference.

What's the worst thing that could happen if we don't operate? Doing nothing would mean he would slowly but surely deteriorate and eventually die.

What's the best thing that could happen if we don't operate? Based on what I knew, there was no "best thing" that could happen if I didn't do anything. Christopher was going to die.

Thinking through all four questions, I quickly realized the answers to three of them were virtually the same. That helped crystallize my thinking—only one option presented any chance of a positive outcome at all. But was it enough of a chance?

I decided there was nothing to lose by proceeding with at least an initial exploration, and that's what we did. Unfortunately, after doing a frozen section (an ultrathin segment of tissue that could be quickly examined under a microscope), we found that we did have a horribly malignant-looking tumor consistent with what all the scans had shown. I don't know that I had ever been so disappointed to be proven right.

I was quite discouraged after closing the patient up and sharing the devastating news with the parents. What came as a pleasant surprise, however, was the child's response and recovery. Christopher did not show any of the potential ill effects following the operation. In fact, he actually seemed to improve after the decompression we had achieved in the process of opening up the back of his skull and relieving some of the pressure the growing tumor exerted on the crowded brain stem. *This is quite odd!* I thought. So I ordered another MRI.

On this new image it seemed there might actually be a plane *between* the tumor and the brain stem. *Could the brain stem have been so tightly compressed that it had been impossible to distinguish between it and the impinging tumor in all of the previous scans?*

All I was certain of was that now, after just a little decompression, we could see what looked like a tiny sliver of clear boundary between the tumor and the brain stem, reason enough to decide we should go back in one more time to re-explore the possibilities. That news delighted the parents, who remained absolutely confident we would find something other than an infiltrative malignant tumor.

The sweet-and-condensed version of the story's conclusion is this: further exploration revealed the tumor was severely constricting the brain stem and would have continued to cripple and eventually kill the boy. But it had not yet penetrated into Christopher's brain stem itself. By working tediously and carefully, we tugged away, teased out, and excised every possible bit of tumor. With nothing encroaching on his brain stem, Christopher soon made a tremendous recovery and eventually grew up, pursued higher education, and became a minister — a happy ending that would not have happened if I hadn't done a rudimentary B/WA to help me weigh the risk and decide my course of action.

I want to point out, however, that even the most careful execution of the B/WA does not guarantee a storybook outcome. Just months after the Pylant case, a child came to Hopkins from Ohio with a remarkably similar MRI scan and equally concerned parents who weren't ready to accept their previous doctors' bleak prognosis. Naturally I thought back to the case of Christopher Pylant and took considerably less time before doing another Best/Worst Analysis and reaching the same decision to at least explore the lesion.

This time, however, the tumor did turn out to be a malignant primary tumor of the brain stem. I removed a good portion of it to relieve some of the pressure, but I could not get to it all. So the tumor kept growing, the patient continued to deteriorate, and she eventually died.

This is not to say that the Best/Worst Analysis failed us in this case. The four-question device served us quite well, actually. As it turns out, the best thing that could have happened in doing something was that we did not hurt her. And we did not. We actually may have given her a little more time with her family. The best thing that would have happened if we did nothing is that she would have continued to regress and died anyway. But in that case, the parents might not have felt that they had done everything and perhaps would have always had some lingering doubt. The worst thing that could have happened if we had done something was that we could have injured her severely or accelerated her demise, which would not have been a dramatically different outcome. And the worst thing that could have happened if we did nothing was that she would have continued to regress and died, as she did.

Even when the Best/Worse Analysis doesn't result in a particularly positive outcome, you are unlikely to have a worse outcome because you did the analysis, and what a B/WA does guarantee is that you consider the various possibilities in a reasonable, logical manner before making any uncertain or risky decision. That has to improve the odds that you come up with a happy solution — or at least with a reasonable and defensible course of action that will minimize the risk of regrets.

That same four-question B/WA served as an invaluable decision-making tool in what turned out to be the most critical — or at least the most life-changing — case of my medical career.

When Josef and Theresa Binder came to Johns Hopkins in early 1987 seeking help for their sons, Patrick and Benjamin, I immediately knew surgery would pose a greater risk than any professional challenge I'd ever faced. These boys had been born healthy in every way except one—they were twins conjoined at the back of the head. All of the European medical specialists the Binders had consulted had advised against surgery because they believed it would require sacrificing one of the twins.

Yet the Binders refused to give up. The first time we met, Theresa admitted that ever since the twins' birth, she had "lived with a dream that has kept me going. A dream that somehow we would find doctors who would be able to perform a miracle." I recount that miracle at length in *Gifted Hands*; you can read the medical details and a full account of the surgery there. Here I want to focus primarily on the decision-making process I went through.

No one had ever successfully separated occipital craniopagus twins because of the extreme complexity of the vascular connections in the back of the head. The handful of times it had been attempted, one or both children died. Such a surgery wasn't merely *risky*, it meant venturing into uncharted territory.

Less than eighteen months had passed since the Denise Baca case, so my personal Best/Worst Analysis framework wasn't exactly second nature yet. But I immediately asked and tried to answer the four basic questions:

What is the best thing that could happen if we operate? If we succeeded in separating the twins, they (and their parents) finally would have a chance at leading normal lives.

What is the worst thing that could happen if we operate? Because of the extreme complexity of such an unprecedented surgery, there was a very significant risk something could go wrong and one or both boys could die or suffer severe brain damage as a result.

What is the best thing that could happen if we don't operate? The boys would remain attached and for an indeterminate number of years might enjoy relative good health—at least as good health as they could have without ever being able to walk, crawl, sit, or turn over. They couldn't even turn and see each other.

What is the worst thing that could happen if we don't operate? Given that most craniopagus twins have or develop any number of medical issues that keep them from living to adulthood (which is what fifteen years later made the Bijani twins unique), the chances were high that eventually one or both of the boys would develop life-threatening complications. And when one died, so would the other.

These first reactions to the four questions helped focus and direct my thinking, but this case came with so many complex and complicating factors that I realized a desperate need for additional input to flesh out the answers and then make the subsequent decisions with any sort of confidence. I needed a lot more knowledge and a boatload of wisdom before proceeding further in the Binder case.

But where was I to find that additional knowledge *and* wisdom needed to address such a difficult medical challenge? What's the difference between them? How do I know when I have enough of each to make the right decision? And why do I even think there is a "right" decision? Those are all crucial questions to contemplate before embarking on an unprecedented medical procedure—or before making any uncertain or risky decision, for that matter.

In an attempt to keep my prescription as simple as possible, I'd like to suggest an easy-to-remember strategy for acquiring the knowledge and wisdom necessary for decision-making in our dangerous world. Just think

- Who?
- What?
- Where?

- When?
- How?
- Why?

Answering these familiar queries in the context of the four basic Best/Worst Analysis questions will sharpen the focus and refine the accuracy of any risk analysis process.

Let's demonstrate the application of these questions in the Binder decision:

Who?

I gained helpful insight by identifying those *who* would be most affected by any decisions made in the Binder case, and then I revisited the four B/WA questions from their points of view.

For example, the parents' perspective:

What's the best thing that can happen if we operate? A successful separation would fulfill the deepest wishes of the parents; plus it would simplify the Binders' family life in an almost unbelievable way. Just caring for their children and taking them places were huge challenges, to say nothing of the heartache of watching the boys struggle in vain to achieve the most basic developmental milestones.

What's the worst thing that can happen if we do operate? The worst thing would be adding more heartache if one or both boys died or suffered serious brain damage during the surgery.

What's the best thing that can happen if we don't operate? Without surgery the boys might remain healthy enough so the family could successfully love and care for them, learn to accept their limitations and challenges, and be able to celebrate and enjoy whatever developmental achievements the boys experienced, for as long as the boys lived.

What's the worst thing that can happen if we don't operate? The worst thing was the likelihood—maybe sooner rather than later—of complications from the boys' conjoined condition or from their severely restricted lifestyle, leading to deteriorating health and eventually death.

Of course, I also did a Best/Worst Analysis from the boys' viewpoint—which actually carried more weight than the parents' viewpoint, but the parents' perspective did need to factor somehow into the ultimate decision.

Who else might be affected? Consider for a moment other craniopagus twins in the future. For them, the best thing that could have happened in the Binder case would have been a successful separation that could be copied the next time. Even an unsuccessful operation could have resulted in valuable lessons learned that could improve their odds. There was no upside for any future conjoined twins if we didn't operate, a possible downside again being the lost opportunity to advance medical knowledge and learn something new and useful to apply in a future separation procedure.

Because I'm a scientist interested in furthering knowledge in my field, I couldn't simply dismiss the future. Still, since no other craniopagus twins had yet made an appointment for what I believed at the time would be a once-in-a-lifetime experience for me, my first concern needed to be the Binders.

At some point, however, I also had to consider a Best/Worst Analysis from my own perspective. I recognized that deciding to do the operation not only gave the family their only real chance of a positive outcome, but the "best thing that could happen" for them might also be the "best thing" for Hopkins and for me. A successful operation would certainly be a huge feather in the cap of our department of neurosurgery.

At the same time, the worst that could happen, from my personal perspective, might be a significant risk to my own reputation. I was still only thirty-five at the time, just a couple of years out of residency, though I was already chief of pediatric neurosurgery at what was arguably the leading medical research and training hospital in the world. I'd achieved my fifteen minutes of fame with the hemispherectomy procedures and another fifteen minutes of fame for some success with intrauterine surgery by implanting a ventriculo-amniotic shunt to correct hydrocephalus in an unborn twin baby. Not only was my personal career off to a great start, but Hopkins was making a name for itself as a strong new force in pediatric neurosurgery. A high-profile case like the Binders', if it turned out badly, could be a serious professional setback for me—a blow from which it might be difficult to recover.

Identifying *who* would be affected and considering their different perspectives helped with the Binder decision.

What?

What did I need to know in the Binder case? Everything possible! Therefore I read anything and everything I could find on previous cases of conjoined twins, paying particular attention to what went wrong and what complications arose. I also noted any similarities and differences between earlier attempts and the Binder case to consider what might be done differently. Then I consulted other knowledgeable people on some of the ideas I was beginning to consider.

Here's where learning plays an important role—not just what I studied in the past, but what I was willing to learn now. I wanted to know as much as I absolutely could about twins conjoined at the head.

I've noted over the years that when I'm considering an action or an idea that seems particularly challenging or risky, there are usually an abundance of people who can come up with a long list of reasons why it won't work and why I shouldn't consider it. Not in this case. Instead of finding naysayers, people kept turning up who would say, "Boy, this seems like a good idea. I think you're onto something. *What* can I do to help?" Then they would introduce me to other people willing to help who also offered good ideas of their own.

Where?

At least three applications of *where* have to be considered in making decisions:

- *Where are you going?* (your goals)
- *Where are you now?* (your skills, your abilities, your thinking, and your attitudes)
- *Where will you start?* (your preparation)

In the Binder case my ultimate goal was to help the boys and their family by finding the safest way to separate them. So that answered the question *Where are you going?*

In answer to *Where are you now?* I came to the conclusion, after considerable and careful study, that my Hopkins colleagues and I had the skill required to pull off this surgery.

I also knew that answering the question *Where will you start?* would involve an enormous amount of preparation. So our surgical team at Johns Hopkins spent five months getting ready, including five three-hour dress rehearsals in which we practiced and refined the procedure with life-sized dolls attached at the head with Velcro. We assembled a team of seven pediatric anesthesiologists, five neurosurgeons, two cardiac surgeons, five plastic surgeons, and, equally important, dozens of nurses and technicians — seventy people in all. It was going be one crowded and well-choreographed operating room, because we literally had to determine *where* everyone would stand.

When?

Often the timing of a Best/Worst Analysis affects our conclusion. Had I been practicing medicine twenty years earlier and the Binders had come to me, I probably never would have considered such a surgery. The history of separation attempts was too discouraging. But the intervening years had brought enough new techniques to improve the odds that I was willing to weigh the options.

I also recommend that you do a B/WA again whenever you think something has changed significantly: a year later, at a different point in life, or maybe after pondering some of these *who, what, where, when, how,* and *why* considerations. Times change. So do circumstances. Sometimes those changes will affect your Best/Worst Analysis, modifying your thinking — maybe even reversing your decision.

Here's one memorable example of this sort of timing from my childhood. When we lived with our aunt and uncle in Boston, my brother, Curtis, and I often played in a nearby park where we imagined our own mountain-climbing and Wild West adventures as we scrambled up, over, and around the large rock formations that were that park's most distinctive physical feature. If that park still exists today, I'm sure those rocks are fenced off to protect children from getting hurt and the city from getting sued. But in the late 1950s, we played on those rocks without ever seriously considering any risk. Until one afternoon ...

I don't recall whether someone had dared me or it was just a personal challenge I'd set for myself, but for whatever reason, I found myself traversing the face of a rock wall on a precariously high and narrow rock ledge. With one hand jammed firmly in a crack, I plastered my body as tightly against the rock as I could while slowly easing myself forward and feeling for someplace to hold on with my other hand. Suddenly a chunk of ledge gave way beneath my feet, which left me dangling by one hand and listening to the broken rock hit the ground far below.

Just an arm's length ahead, the remaining ledge looked wider and stronger, but I needed another handhold to reach it. From where I was hanging, I could see another crevice I thought I could reach with my free hand. The trouble was, I could see a thick spider's web stretched across the opening. I've told you how I loved animals. What I haven't told you is that I absolutely hated spiders. They terrified me. And I'd seen some humongous wolf spiders with webs just like this one among the rocks of this park. There was no way in the world I ever would have imagined daring to stick my hand in a nest of wolf spiders. Then I looked down. My profound arachnophobia and the risk of being bitten paled in comparison to the serious harm I realized I would suffer from a fifty-foot fall onto the rocky ground below. I needed a handhold in that crevice. So I stretched, gained a solid grip, swung my feet onto the ledge, and quickly scampered safely off that rock wall.

Different times, different circumstances, different decisions.

How?

You don't have to address *who*, *what*, *where*, *when*, *how*, and *why* in any particular order. They may need to be viewed simultaneously because they sometimes complement each other or need to be combined. In the Binder case, for example, the *when* answer made all the difference in answering the *how*.

To inflict as little damage as possible to Patrick's and Benjamin's brains during surgery, I came up with a rather audacious three-part plan that involved the combination of hypothermia, circulatory bypass, and deliberate cardiac arrest. The babies' temperature would be lowered to slow their bodily functions. A bypass would circulate the boys' blood through a heart-lung machine to keep it oxygenated. And for a time, at the most crucial juncture of the operation, to better control the loss of blood, we would intentionally stop the boys' hearts. Never before had all three techniques been used simultaneously in a pediatric neurosurgery case, so I talked to a lot of experts about how best to pull it all off. My conclusion was that at this point in time, each of these procedures was familiar enough to my surgical team that we could safely and effectively combine all three.

Arriving at this particular *how* conclusion changed my risk-analysis equation entirely. We now had what looked like a workable strategy that gave us a reasonable hope of success.

Why?

I find it's almost impossible for me to do an effective B/WA without considering *why*. Deciding how to respond to any risk nearly always requires me to examine, and often reexamine, my reasoning in light of my motives, which involves my personal values. Those values are what I weigh carefully against my analyses and conclusions. This requires I actually have values, know what they are, and have practice applying them in my life.

In the Binder case, I had already considered the risk from various parties' perspectives. From my own perspective there was enormous potential risk to my reputation if we experienced a negative outcome. My personal value system, however, made it relatively easy to discount any worries about my reputation and focus more on my patients' perspective. My spiritual faith (I'll talk more about that later) greatly influences my value system. Jesus' Golden Rule, "Do unto others as you would have others do unto you," and other biblical admonitions to "put others ahead of yourself" usually give me clear direction in how much weight to lend to various perspectives, especially my own.

My experience has confirmed the wisdom of so much of what the Bible teaches. In my career I have seen how often ego and selfishness are the root of conflict in people's lives. Too many people are more concerned with their reputations and what other people think than they are about the best course of action or what risks they really ought to take.

It all boils down to your values. If your priority is to look good in front of people, your life will take a different direction than if your priority is to use the talents God has given you to make a positive difference in the world. Such values will influence what risks you choose to take.

You'll remember that my decision to risk involvement in the controversial Bijani case came down to a sense of obligation (my values). After doing an initial B/WA on that case and deciding there was too much possibility of *worst* and little hope of *best*, I decided not to get involved. What changed my mind was the realization that I had knowledge, skill, and experience to bring to that case that could improve the odds of success. Not joining that case would have left me feeling like those in Jesus' Good Samaritan parable who ignored the beaten man on the side of the road and walked right on by. I couldn't do that. So I changed my mind and signed on to take part in that case.

Truth be known, the *why* factor plays a pivotal role in every risk I choose to accept. After all, Jesus once said, "Whatever you do for the least of these, you do for me." Most of the children I see in my office face serious medical risks. They and their families are hurting, helpless, and often hopeless by the time they get to Johns Hopkins. They certainly qualify among "the least of these." Because of my personal value system, because I know *why* I do what I do, I'm usually more than willing to take a risk in treating them.

———

I took that risk with the Binder twins, and my B/WA paid off in a huge way. Twenty-two hours after the surgery began, the surgical team walked out of the operating room. One of the staff doctors walked up to the boys' mother and asked with a smile, "Which child would you like to see first?"

A few months later, Theresa and Josef Binder returned to Germany with their beloved sons, ready to begin living a very different life.

By then the media coverage surrounding the case had made me something of a celebrity. I began to receive referrals on challenging cases from doctors around the country and around the world. Suddenly I was in great demand as a speaker. My life, too, had been changed forever by the outcome of that case.

When I look at the world today, I see a lot of risk-related decisions being made, but I wish more of them were made on the basis of a Best/Worst Analysis.

For instance, *Good Morning America* did a feature on me and wanted to see some of the early influences in my life. I took them back to elementary school, where the students called me "dummy," to meet Mr. Jaeck, the dapper young science teacher who had held up the obsidian and was so impressed by my knowledge about it that he invited me to start coming by his room after school to help with the laboratory chores. He further sparked my interest in science by allowing me to feed and take care of the school's lab animals: a red squirrel, a tarantula, a Jack Dempsey fish, some crawfish, and more.

I showed up with an ABC camera crew in my wake to find a bald and somewhat rumpled Mr. Jaeck still teaching. He and I enjoyed a short reunion and reminisced for a while; then I wanted the video crew to see the wonderful collection of creatures in his lab. He shook his head sadly and said, "We don't have animals in our science lab anymore because of the risk that one of the students might get bitten or scratched. The school system can't afford the liability."

I couldn't believe it! Well, I *could* believe it. I just didn't want to believe it because I hated to think of generations of young students missing out on the very thing that sparked my interest in biology and kept feeding the dream that led to my becoming a medical scientist today.

The authorities who made such a lamentable decision seemed to have considered only one risk-analysis question: *What is the worst that can happen if we continue to let students study and care for live animals in our biology lab?* A student could get hurt and a family could sue the school.

But they seem not to have asked, *What's the best thing that could happen if we let students study and care for live animals in our biology lab?* Our science program will be more engaging, students may become interested in biological sciences, and so much more. They did ask, *What is the best thing that can happen if we get rid of the animals?* We reduce our potential "liability" by removing a "risk" that has never been a problem, and maybe we give our paranoid insurance carriers one less reason to raise the rates. But apparently they didn't ask, *What is the worst thing that can happen if we get rid of the animals?* We never know how many at-risk students like Ben Carson might lose out on the excitement and inspiration they need to achieve their potential in school and in life.

Ask only about worst cases, and I understand why, in our lawsuit-happy culture, school authorities would make a knee-jerk decision to exile the animals. Ask all four questions, however, and it would be hard for most people not to at least come up with a different and more reasoned policy.

If we set as our priority "the removal of all risk," we'll soon have sterile, stagnant, and unstimulating learning environments. How does that risk compare with the danger of a squirrel scratching someone's finger? Do you think this might be a relevant question to consider at a time when countries like India and China have far surpassed us in the number (and the percentage) of college graduates in the sciences and technology every year?

You see how a simple B/WA can apply in so many circumstances? Here is another, far less serious personal example:

A few years ago I received a phone call from Hollywood asking if I would be interested in making a cameo appearance in a big-screen comedy. They wanted me to perform as a surgeon separating conjoined twins played by Matt Damon and Greg Kinnear.

"Those guys are adults," I replied. "I'm in pediatric care."

They said that didn't matter.

"Where are they attached?" I wanted to know.

"At the liver."

"But I'm a neurosurgeon."

They said that didn't matter either.

I was laughing already and immediately doing a quick, partial B/WA:

What's the worst thing that could happen if I do this? The biggest risk I saw was to my image as a scientist who is serious about my calling. I take seriously my role as a successful doctor and as a Christian to inspire and model an example for young people. So I wouldn't want to compromise my moral or professional standards. There might also be some criticism from people who thought it wasn't appropriate for someone in my position to participate in the project. I could see a lot of reasons to say no.

So what's the best thing that could happen if I do this? I wasn't sure how to answer that. I needed more "what" information, and I had to bring my values to bear by asking, *Would I just do it for the sake of doing it? For the fun or the perceived glamour of being in a movie?* The answer to that was no. *But would I do it if there could be some significant benefit gained?* Perhaps.

That led me to say to my caller, "Okay, I'll look at the script, and if it's not too outrageous, I would consider being in your movie *if* you would do the world premiere in Baltimore as a fund-raiser for two nonprofit organizations I have founded—our Carson Scholars fund, which celebrates and encourages academic excellence, and Angels of the OR, an endowment fund used to assist those facing surgery without adequate insurance coverage."

They agreed to consider my proposal. I looked at the script, which was admittedly silly but didn't seem too outrageous. I then agreed to appear as myself in the movie *Stuck on You*, and the moviemakers agreed to hold the world premiere in Baltimore.

We ultimately raised almost half a million dollars from the event. I didn't get much flack about the movie; people were more intrigued than critical. So the benefit far outweighed the risk, as I judged that it would when I finished my B/WA and made the decision to do the movie.

One day, just weeks before completing the manuscript of this book, I received a timely email from a wildlife biologist who studies endangered Hawaiian monk seals for the National Marine Fisheries Service in Honolulu, Hawaii. He and his colleagues had heard an interview I'd done on National Public Radio in which I had spent maybe thirty seconds describing my basic B/WA template for making critical decisions in serious medical cases. "Strange as it may seem," he wrote, "it occurred to us that exact framework could be used to structure our logic with regard to a biological phenomenon affecting the monk seal."

The problem was this: In one of the six breeding atolls for this species in the Northwestern Hawaiian Islands, Galapagos sharks were devastating the population of nursing monk seal pups. The situation had gotten so bad the biologists began to think the only way to preserve the endangered seals was to take the drastic measure of culling the predatory sharks (which were abundant in those waters).

Just talking about killing twenty active predators was controversial because the waters in question were part of a federal refuge where all species were awarded special levels of protection. It is not a decision that these conservationists found easy to make—until they applied the four simple B/WA questions.

They emailed to ask my permission to include my questions, and they credited me in a professional scientific journal article they had written and tentatively titled "Galapagos Sharks and Monk Seals: A Conservation Conundrum."

After spelling out the basic problem, the article concluded:

> Ultimately, our analysis centers on a determination of the relative benefits and risks from action versus no action. Our logic can be conveniently structured within a simple framework of four questions:
>
> - What is the best that can happen if we apply the intervention?
> - What is the worst that can happen if we apply the intervention?
> - What is the best that can happen with no intervention?
> - What is the worst that can happen with no intervention?

Optimal results from the intervention would be successful elimination of all active and persistent predators from the pool of Galapagos sharks, thereby enhancing the survival of pre-weaned pups to a level commensurate with that at other sites (>90%)....

The worst that can happen with the intervention is that 1) we significantly reduce the population of inner-atoll Galapagos sharks so that ecosystem functioning is disrupted by the removal of a top-level predator, or 2) we succeed in eliminating the 20 sharks targeted for removal, but the predatory behavior continues at an unacceptable level because the pool of active predators is continually replenished by new individuals becoming familiar with a novel source of vulnerable prey. We have investigated the first possibility using the *EcoSim* model and found that the removal of 20 sharks has a nearly imperceptible effect on the dynamics of the ecosystem....

The best scenario with no intervention is that predation eventually subsides naturally. The only condition where we believe this is likely is if cohort sizes (or pup density at each islet) declines to the extent that foraging efficiency and energetic returns from persistent predation drop below the critical (and unknown) threshold. Alternatively, we might apply effective non-lethal deterrents that would eventually reduce predation risks, but these deterrents have yet to be identified....

Finally, *the worst that can happen without the intervention* is that the predatory behavior becomes so widespread that it affects every pupping area in the atoll, and possibly spreads to other breeding areas in the NWHI. Predators are capable of severely impacting prey populations.... Such a scenario could severely impede the possibilities for recovery of the subpopulation and perhaps the species.

Examining this set of responses, it is evident that the risks associated with the intervention are relatively minor as compared to the possible benefits from successful intervention. Further, the risks from non-intervention are large. When the options are evaluated within this framework, the case for intervention prevails.

The scientist who contacted me about this offered an encouraging endorsement of my B/WA idea when he added at the end of his note, "I know there are many volumes written about formal decision theory in the face of uncertainty, but we find your simple structure very appealing."

So do I, because it works in all kinds of situations.

Faith Is a Risk— Whatever You Believe

FAITH, BY DEFINITION, IS A RISK.

Even attempting to start a serious discussion on the subject often seems like a big risk. Are the risks of faith worth it? Is talking about faith too risky?

To answer those questions, I'll tell you about a keynote address I delivered at the National Science Teachers Convention in Philadelphia a few years ago. My subject? Evolution versus creationism—a risky, hot-potato topic to raise in front of some fifteen thousand public school teachers and administrators.

I started my talk by sharing an abridged version of my own personal journey—retracing my path from an at-risk childhood to my role in some of the challenging medical cases I've been privileged to work on. I made sure to pay tribute to Mr. Jaeck and other public school science teachers whose instruction, encouragement, and personal concern inspired my own interest in science. I lamented the fact that the liability fears had banned the lab animals and robbed the students now attending my old school of the chance to be inspired the way I had been. I also expressed concern over recent surveys showing that students in the United States scored twenty-first out of the twenty-two most educated countries in the world when it came to science and math.

I talked about the incredible capacity of the human mind and the tragedy that so many fail to harness the brain's awesome potential. I touched on some of the factors that contribute to that failure to utilize this most amazing God-given resource, including the peer pressure

associated with political correctness, which often limits our willingness, even as objective scientists, to have a thoughtful, rational discussion about evolution versus creationism.

So that's what I set out to do, starting at the macro level by talking about how much astronomy has learned about the mind-boggling
vastness and impeccable order of our universe. Today we can predict
the exact course and arrival time of a comet seventy-five years in the
future. Just think about the amazing precision that requires!

Naturally we ask how this came about. Some scientists believe it
all just happened as the result of a big bang that launched everything,
setting our earth spinning on its axis, at just the right speed, at precisely the right distance from the sun so it wouldn't be incinerated, yet
close enough not to freeze, with other planets in their orbits and other
galaxies positioned perfectly to keep harmful rays from destroying our
planet and us. I told my audience, "I just don't have enough faith to
believe all that happened by random chance."

I've never understood how the same scientists who propose the Big
Bang theory also accept the second law of thermodynamics (entropy),
which asserts that things naturally tend to move toward a state of dis-
organization, not organization. Yet much of the Big Bang theory rests
on the belief that after all this stuff around us (matter) just happened
to come out of nowhere in a giant explosion, instead of spreading
and growing more disorganized, somehow it assembled and organized itself into an awe-inspiring pattern of planets and orbits and
solar systems and stars and galaxies that reach to infinity and move
in a celestial choreography that is at once beautifully mysterious *and*
mathematically predictable. How does that jibe with the second law of
thermodynamics? I've talked to Nobel Prize–winning physicists who
spout hypotheses that amount to nothing more than a bunch of astro-
physical mumbo-jumbo before eventually admitting, "Well, we're still
learning. There's a lot we don't understand." I've yet to find anybody
sure enough to give a convincing explanation.

I suggested to the science teachers that many people accept the Big
Bang on faith, despite evidence for or against it. But tell me, I asked,
where did the very first living cell come from? Darwin built his entire

theory of evolution on the premise that the cell is the simplest, foundational building block of life.

The electron microscope and countless other contemporary tools have only begun to show us how incredibly complex a cell truly is. You have a cell membrane with lipoproteins phasically interposed with positive and negative charges that can allow certain types of molecules to pass through or not, a very complex nucleus and nucleolus, endoplasmic reticulum with ribosomes on it that are able to understand and replicate genetic patterns, and Golgi apparatuses that generate energy. We haven't even begun to discuss genes, the intricate communication patterns of DNA, or any number of additional subcellular ingredients and their functions. If cells are the *original* starting point of life, how did all of those complex interrelated parts and processes come to be?

But let's just concede that somehow, mysteriously, the first cell came about. Where did the great diversity of other cells come from? Darwinism holds that all life evolved in a gradual, progressive, step-by-step process from the simple to the more complex. So how did the earlier, simpler, single cells all get together to form more complex multicelled organisms?

Forget whole organisms. Let's consider a single eye. How did a rod cell just sit there for millions and millions of years until a cone cell could develop? Then how did multiple rods and cones join together into an intricate visual-sensory apparatus, embedded into the retina as part of a complex neurovascular network, which converts images into electrical information to be passed through the neural network along the optic nerve and reinterpreted in the occipital cortex of the brain as a recognizable image? Even before you get to the retina, what about the pupil? Where and how did it develop in isolation — because there would be no purpose for it without those other things. Nor would there be any purpose for the iris without the pupil and the anterior chamber. There would be no purpose for the cornea, no purpose for the short ciliary nerves, no purpose for any of it without all the other stuff.

Did each type of cell develop on its own and then sit around and wait for a couple of billion years in the hope that some perfectly compatible cell type might come along to finally make it not merely relevant but indispensable as part of an elaborate system that itself complements even more complex systems that are in turn part of the larger organism? How does that jibe with the "survival of the fittest" premise, in which function is a key factor in deciding what genetically useful characteristics are passed on and ultimately which organisms last another generation? Are we then to believe that specialized cells survived for millions of years, fit for no real purpose, until other specialized and completely worthless and unfit cells came along, which also survived for untold eons, to one day combine with them in anticipation of filling some future need that would take millions of more generations and evolutionary steps?

Believing that the origin of life can be explained by Darwinian evolution requires more faith than I have. I told the science teachers, "Evolution and creationism both require faith. It's just a matter of where you choose to place that faith." From what I know (and all we don't know) about biology, I find it as hard to accept the claims of evolution as it is to think that a hurricane blowing through a junkyard could somehow assemble a fully equipped and flight-ready 747. You could blow a billion hurricanes through a trillion junkyards over infinite periods of time, and I don't think you'd get one aerodynamic wing, let alone an entire jumbo jet complete with complex connections for a jet-propulsion system, a radar system, a fuel-injection system, an exhaust system, a ventilation system, control systems, electronic systems, plus backup systems for all of those, and so much more. There's simply not enough time in eternity for that to happen. Which is why not one of us has ever doubted that a 747, by its very existence, gives convincing evidence of someone's intelligent design.

So what are we to make of the human body and the human brain, which are immeasurably more complex, more versatile, more amazing in a gazillion ways than any airplane man has ever created? Aren't they even stronger evidence of intelligent design? That, I told those science teachers, is why evolution requires more faith than I can muster.

On the other hand, I told them, if we consider the possibility of a Creator, it's really fairly simple to believe and understand how such a complex, intelligently designed universe could come into existence. In fact, it's easy to imagine an intelligent designer making creatures with an impressive ability to survive by adapting to their environment.

In contrast, Darwin, who has a very interesting "religious" history, goes off to the Galapagos Islands. When he sees some finches with thick beaks compared to all the other finches in the world, Darwin looks for some sort of an explanation. It turns out there had been several years of severe drought in the Galapagos resulting in a shortage of usual food for the finches. Consequently, the only finches to survive were the ones with thick beaks strong enough to crack open the hardest of seeds to ingest enough nourishment to survive and breed. Very shortly the only finches left on the drought-stricken islands were thick-billed finches and their offspring who inherited that valuable trait.

Darwin termed the phenomenon "survival of the fittest," which he argued could explain life's diversity no longer as impressive evidence of the existence of a powerful and creative God, but as the predictable result of the more rational and scientific process of "natural selection." He then extrapolated his finch findings to make natural selection a cornerstone of a broader evolutionary theory by which he could explain the origin of life, man, and the universe without having to further credit or consider the existence of a creator God.

In Darwin's paradigm, the adaptability of the finches was a clear sign of natural (that is, godless) selection and thus strong evidence for evolution. But in another paradigm, it could be a sign of a wise and intelligent Creator who gave his creatures the ability to adapt so that every environmental change that came along wouldn't wipe them out.

It comes down to which paradigm you are willing to accept. As I told the teachers, both paradigms take faith.

For me, the plausibility of evolution is further strained by Darwin's assertion that within fifty to one hundred years of his time, scientists would become geologically sophisticated enough to find the fossil remains of the entire evolutionary tree in an unequivocal step-by-step progression of life from amoeba to man — including all of the intermediate species.

Of course that was 150 years ago, and there is still no such evidence. It's just not there. But when you bring that up to the proponents of Darwinism, the best explanation they can come up with is "Well ... uh ... it's lost!" Here again I find it requires too much faith for me to believe that explanation given all the fossils we have found without *any* fossilized evidence of the direct, step-by-step evolutionary progression from simple to complex organisms or from one species to another species. Shrugging and saying, "Well, it was mysteriously lost, and we'll probably never find it," doesn't seem like a particularly satisfying, objective, or scientific response. But what's even harder for me to swallow is how so many people who can't explain it are still willing to claim that evolution is not theory but fact, at the same time insisting anyone who wants to consider or discuss creationism as a possibility cannot be a real scientist.

By the end of my talk, I had made it clear that I believe we have these enormous brains with the ability to process so much information for a purpose — because we were made in God's image, not in the image of an amoeba. I also pointed out that if we're truly smart, we'll use our brains and challenge our students to use their brains not only to learn the facts of science, math, history, literature, and all the other disciplines, but to think about what we believe and why — and then be willing to risk some objective discussion.

I don't know when I've ever gotten a more encouraging reaction to a speech than the overwhelming response I received from those science teachers. (I think a standing ovation from fifteen thousand people qualifies as overwhelming.) Many educators came up to me afterward or wrote me later, saying how much they appreciated my raising this subject. They wanted me to know I'd said many of the things they really believed but never felt they could risk saying. Some even said that after hearing me speak out, they had determined to be more open about what they believe.

I found their feedback particularly heartening because it confirmed for me the value of the B/WA I'd conducted beforehand, as I'd considered whether or not to take the risk of discussing evolution versus creationism at a National Science Teachers conference.

I had asked myself all four of the basic B/WA questions:

What is the worst thing that could happen if I do talk about my beliefs? The audience probably wouldn't throw tomatoes or boo me off the platform, but they could write me off and say my thoughts were absurd or that my talk was just another example of how Christianity is weakening and destroying society. Then my whole talk could be used as a wedge to drive people who might already disagree even further apart.

What is the best thing that could happen if I speak out? A large number of people might find their courage to talk about what they truly believe. It might help open objective discussion.

What is the best thing that could happen if I don't talk about this already controversial topic? Everything goes on pretty much as is and nothing changes.

What is the worst thing that could happen if I don't address this issue? At the very least, I would lose a wonderful opportunity to show many members of the scientific community that belief in God is not anti-science.

Even that initial Best/Worst Analysis convinced me there was little to be accomplished by not taking the risk of talking about evolution versus creationism. That *best* chance to encourage more open discussion greatly appealed to me, and after weighing some of the *how* and *why* factors, I felt confident I could lower the odds of the *worst* things happening.

So I decided to take the risk. And I'm glad I did.

What Were Those *How* and *Why* Factors?

Over the years I've learned a few things about how to talk about my faith in ways that don't offend but seem to intrigue people. I always begin any speech with a summary or some part of my personal story. I find that when an audience understands a bit about who you are, where you come from, what you've been through, and how you came to the ideas and the values you have, they are more inclined to listen to you explain why you believe the way you do.

Whenever I do touch on the subject of faith, I find the best policy is to talk about it in terms of its effect on me personally, as opposed to what I think it should mean or do for someone else. Frankly, I'm convinced this strategy is the reason my books have slipped under the radar so that they are read and reported on by thousands of students in public schools around the United States every year. Even though there are clear and regular references to faith in all of my writings, they are always in the context of my personal experience. I don't try to proselytize. I am sensitive to the fact that other people may have different beliefs. I would never presume to bludgeon someone with my faith, nor do I argue that my beliefs are the only ones that are *right* and that others are *wrong.* (Even though I have strong convictions about *truth.*) But when I talk about faith, I always present it as *my* faith and explain how and why it came to be my faith and what it has done for me.

One of the challenges for people of faith who fervently believe in a creator God is not to come off as totally closed-minded and unreasonable when dealing with those who don't believe. In the scientific community, a dismissal of Christian thought is often not so much hostility to the idea of God as hostility to the attitudes that accompany that idea. A holier-than-thou demeanor and a refusal to respect or even listen to someone else's point of view actually present a risk to both sides.

So why take the risk of talking about faith at all?

When I started doing interviews after the first hemispherectomies, and especially after separating the Binder twins, invariably the subject of faith came up. I easily could have said, "That is a private issue and not relevant to the discussion." That would have been the safest way out, and most interviewers would have been glad to move on to another subject. But that just didn't seem right to me.

I didn't even need to do a formal B/WA to come to that conclusion. Given the values I embrace as a part of my deeply held spiritual beliefs, I chose to take the risk of talking about my faith for some fairly simple reasons. Jesus clearly instructed his followers that a crucial part of their Christian life was living out his teachings in everyday life and sharing the good news of faith with others. Not being willing to talk about my faith would mean disregarding his specific teaching.

But my reasoning went beyond that. I believe God has a specific purpose for me—and for every other person to whom he gives the gift of life. From the time I was eight years old and first believed God wanted me to be a doctor, I have recognized that my life is not my own. The path has not always run straight; on occasion I have wandered off in search of my own way. But God has guided me and intervened so many times that I would be dishonest and ungrateful *not* to acknowledge his role and influence in my life.

I also believe that God's plan for me includes the remarkable platform I have been given to speak, write, and be held up as an example for many young people around our country. Because I never sought out or expected such opportunities, I have to conclude they are more God's doing than mine. If that's true, it only follows that God must want me to use the platform not so I can be comfortable and play it safe, but so I can try to make a difference. For me, that's a risk worth taking.

In fact, my B/WA helps me realize one of the *worst* things about playing it safe is how that displays not only a lack of honesty and gratitude on my part, but also a failure of trust. Playing it safe would send a message all its own—that I don't truly trust God with my life; that I don't believe he is able to direct and guide people, events, and circumstances according to his will. Such a message would be false, because I remember what Proverbs 21:1 says: "The heart of the king is in the LORD's hands. As the rivers of water, He turned it wheresoever He will"—which says to me that if the Lord has the power to control kings and rivers, surely I can trust him with the details of my life. I don't have to tread lightly when it comes to talking about, or living my life by, my faith in him.

Let me be quick to reiterate a point I touched on earlier. If I'm not careful, confidence, like firm convictions, can come across as arrogance. Which is why I constantly watch my attitude and try to be sensitive in what I say, where I say it, and even how others might feel about it. I've run into some Christians who contend that no matter where or what the circumstances, believers must declare, "Jesus is the way!" But if you're speaking at a Jewish synagogue, that's just not a smart approach. In fact, there aren't many situations in which I think an insistent *I'm right and you're wrong!* approach is ever effective.

People who think they aren't doing their Christian responsibility or fulfilling Jesus' Great Commission unless they preach an in-your-face message are just not looking at the big picture. It doesn't matter whether your approach turns off a hundred people or a hundred thousand. What good have you done? In the bigger picture, the ultimate goal, the real instruction Jesus gave his followers, was to *attract* others — not to *repel* them.

That's also why I try never to argue with people, insisting they're mistaken or inferring there must be something wrong with them because they don't agree with me. It's actually because of the strength of my beliefs that I feel comfortable approaching any discussion about faith with an open-minded willingness to consider any truth.

Hey, if we call ourselves scientists, let's not automatically close our ears and our eyes to things just because we don't understand them. When we see something that can't be proven by scientific evidence or explained in a way that makes sense, let's at least be objective enough to calmly discuss the subject in the light of different theories and consider how each one best addresses the issue. I find when I make that kind of an appeal, people who disagree with me are not nearly so hostile, and they often actually seem to hear and think about what I have to say.

Even so, I admit that one of the risks faced by anyone willing to talk about his or her spiritual faith publicly is the danger of being misunderstood and stereotyped by people who have only the most superficial understanding of faith. I remember doing an NPR interview fairly early in my career. The interviewer said, "I understand you are a very religious person." I immediately corrected her, explaining that I'm bothered by the fact that organized religion has, historically, at times been used in the wrong way to control people. For that reason, I said to the interviewer, I don't consider myself a "religious" person at all. I am, however, a person of enormous faith. I have a deep, personal, ever-growing relationship with God, which guides my thoughts and actions.

Over the years, I have made this point time and again, that there is a distinction between having a religion and having a faith that allows me to enjoy a personal relationship with God. Millions and millions of people have been turned off and sometimes even hurt through regrettable interactions with "religious" groups. Those people need to understand that the essence of Christian faith is not so much a connection to any organized group of people as a personal relationship with a single person — Jesus.

I'm not big on religious tradition. I have no problem with other people who find great inspiration and meaning in rites or ceremonies, but religious ritual has never done much for me. What does mean a lot to me is regular communication with God.

I know all that sounds presumptuous to some people. They wonder what makes Christians so egotistical as to suppose the all-powerful Creator would have a relationship with them. But people need to understand that this unbelievably good news of a personal relationship was God's idea in the first place and that this privilege, according to the Bible, is available to everyone, not just a special few.

One of the most encouraging examples of this for me is King David. If anybody was ever a slime ball, it was David. He lied, he cheated, he murdered, he committed adultery. You name it, he did it. And yet the Bible describes King David as "a man after God's own heart."

How can that be?

The answer can be found in Psalm 51 when the wayward king goes to God in remorse to plead, "Create in me a clean heart, oh Lord, renew a right spirit within me. Cast me not away from thy presence and take not thy Holy Spirit from me [even though I'm a slime ball — Carson Paraphrased Version]. Restore unto me the joy of thy salvation." David knew from experience about the joy of communing with God. It's not something you can logically explain, but when you're in harmony with God, you experience a certain joy, whether you live in the Taj Mahal or in a broken-down ghetto apartment. That relationship satisfies and upholds you, and that's what David understood.

So there he was, this king of Israel. He had wealth, power, and honor, but he knew his selfish and wrongful actions had separated him from God. He had lost that warmth of their close relationship — of God's salvation — and he wanted it back. He was willing to plead, beg, do whatever it took to be restored to God's good graces. And God took him back, to be acclaimed forever as "a man after God's own heart."

David's story gives me hope because it tells me that having a personal relationship with the Creator of the universe does not require me to dot all the i's and cross all the t's and be picture perfect in everything. I don't even have to be "religious." It just means that I seek after God and try to grow and strengthen and maintain my relationship with him as the most significant and central motivation in my life.

Although I certainly consider that relationship *special*, it doesn't make *me* special or in any way better than anyone else. On the contrary, it constantly reminds me that I'm as imperfect as anyone. So the privilege of having a relationship with and serving the Lord and ruler of the entire universe actually humbles me and forces me to recognize and acknowledge my weaknesses.

That's the kind of attitude I think God wants from us as the starting point of a relationship. I believe it's also the truth he wants his followers to keep in mind as we share our faith with others. When we do, the chances are better that they will listen.

Living Your Faith
in an Uncertain World

LET ME TELL YOU ABOUT A TIME WHEN I WASN'T SURE I WANTED TO explain what I believed—in front of the most formidable audience I ever faced. Talking to fifteen thousand science teachers about evolution and creationism didn't compare, nor did the opportunity to address the most powerful leaders of our country who attended the President's Annual National Prayer Breakfast when I spoke there a few years ago.

My most formidable audience was the ultra-prestigious Academy of Achievement. They had invited me to take part in a panel discussion on the subject of "Faith and Science" during their annual International Summit. The prospect gave me serious pause. The membership of that organization is imposing. Every living former president of the United States had been inducted, along with numerous other heads of states and Nobel Peace Prize recipients such as Poland's Lech Walesa and former Soviet Premier Mikhail Gorbachev. The Academy also honors high achievers in

- the arts—from Maya Angelou to John Grisham, from Quincy Jones to Stephen Sondheim;
- business—from Disney's Michael Eisner to Jeff Bezos, the founder and CEO of Amazon.com, and Fred Smith, the founder of Federal Express;
- public service—Archbishop Desmond Tutu of South Africa and consumer advocate Ralph Nader are both members, as was the late Rosa Parks;

- science and exploration—from the late economist Milton Friedman to Everest conqueror Sir Edmund Hillary (I can't even count the number of Nobel Prize winners there are in medicine and the sciences); and

- sports—whose achievers include such athletic luminaries as Dorothy Hamill, Willie Mays, and John Wooden.

Did I really want to discuss my spiritual beliefs in front of such an august assembly? My years of membership in the Academy had provided some wonderful experiences, and I had made a lot of friends whose opinions, goodwill, and respect still matter to me. But did I want to risk all that to share honestly with them my views on faith and science? How much of a risk might it be?

My Best/Worst Analysis was similar to the one I did before the National Science Teachers Convention in Philadelphia, but the stakes felt higher this time. The possibility of embarrassing myself in front of all those Nobel scientists seemed a potentially worse *worst* than being written off by a group of public school science teachers. Still, the same positive potential—the chance that this opportunity could open objective discussion and might help others find the courage to talk about what they truly believe—also seemed like a better *best*. That wasn't so much because I thought anything I said would change the thinking of the Academy's distinguished members, but because we invite as guests to our summit each year three hundred or so of the next generation's best and brightest (Rhodes Scholars, Fulbright Scholars, White House Fellows, and the like) who might benefit from hearing that belief in God doesn't have to be anti-science.

So I decided to accept. The experience proved to be every bit as challenging and interesting as you might expect. One of the other panelists was Dr. Donald Johanson, the noted paleoanthropologist, who is famous for his claims that the fossilized specimen he discovered in Africa named "Lucy" represented an extinct species from which the human race descended. In the course of our discussion, he made what felt to me like a pretty condescending remark when he asserted that "true scientists" base everything they do and decide, upon facts, unlike those people who choose to depend on God. So when it was my turn to speak, I made the point that "true scientists" often overlook many, many gaps in what they purport to be fact as they sit on their high horses and declare their devotion to factual truth, when in reality some of their own theories require a great deal of faith to accept.

At that point Don Johanson jumped out of his chair to interrupt me with his protests. I responded as calmly as I could that "I wasn't speaking about anyone in particular, only making a general observation based on my experience. But if the shoe fits ..." Laughter rolled through the audience before I went on to say that religion and science both require faith, that the two disciplines don't always have to be mutually exclusive, that people have to choose where to put their faith, and that choice doesn't make you superior to those who believe differently.

I don't know if I got my point across to my fellow panelist, but the feedback I received over the remainder of the conference convinced me that some people were listening. George Lucas, the filmmaker, made a point of telling tell me he agreed there should not be so much hostility and controversy over the subject. "We can see God's reflection in everything he created," he said.

But the most affirming responses came from the young graduate students who came up to thank me for what I said. One young man from Oxford even told me, "I've always been an atheist. But I am now very seriously thinking about changing that belief."

That seemed reason enough to risk *talking* about faith.

But *why* risk faith in the first place?

For me the *why* is tied not only to a *personal relationship*, but to *personal experience*. I've already talked about how I've seen for myself, time after time after time, the powerful, positive impact personal faith has had on my life. At a particularly vulnerable time in my childhood, it provided me with a dream and a sense of calling that gave me hope for the future. When Mother sought wisdom about what to do with her at-risk sons, who were in serious danger of wasting their potential, the answer God gave her absolutely turned our lives around. As a teenager when I cried out in desperation for help with my out-of-control rage, I found emotional strength and healing.

College presented a very different risk of faith. Attending a secular, elite (okay, snobby), East Coast university where religion—unless it involved some kind of exotic and mysterious Eastern belief system—was not considered cool made my faith a subject of curiosity to many of my fellow students. That I attended choir practice and church every week seemed foreign to most of them. Yet over time several Yale friends came to church with me in an attempt to figure out what I was so devoted to. It was because of my faith commitment that I invited Candy to come to church with me, our friendship grew, we fell in love, and we eventually married. So my faith, even in college, had a profound effect on my life—and, I can honestly say, on others.

My roommate Larry Harris (who attended church with me) and I raised enormous amounts of money on campus for our church's missionary work. After obtaining permission to solicit donations, we would sit in front of the various residential college dining halls with colorful posters showing people in Africa, India, and elsewhere and telling how the money we collected would be used. Lots of people on Ivy League campuses in the early 1970s would talk about our responsibility to help poor and disadvantaged people around the world, but nobody else was providing such an easy opportunity for students to actually give. Of course, a lot of Yale kids came from wealthy families; our solicitations appealed to their sense of obligation, maybe even some guilt. We raised thousands of dollars for missions.

But I was motivated to do all of these faith-related activities because of a personal relationship that was so real to me. I felt no matter where I was, no matter what situation I was in, I could speak to God and know he would hear. I saw so many things happen that were just too far beyond coincidence when I prayed. (I tell about a number of those things in *Gifted Hands*.)

My faith presented a new sort of risk during medical school—the time issue. Med school students study from morning to night, and often from morning to morning. There was so much to learn, and there were never enough hours in the day. Yet I still spent every Friday evening at choir rehearsal; then I took off all day Saturday for church services and socializing with my church friends. That meant being away from my studies for more than half of every weekend. I followed the same routine even before our big comprehensive exams. Was that a risk? Absolutely! Some of my classmates thought I was nuts.

"You're going to do what?" they would say. "We have a test on Monday!"

"I'll be ready," I'd reply. And I would be. It wasn't a problem. In fact, while others were cramming, cramming, cramming, I had the opportunity to relax my mind. I think it gave me an advantage, and the risk of faith paid off again.

I've already told a few stories about some of the risks I've taken with medical cases over the years, but this is probably where I need to address the risk I take by trying to incorporate my spiritual faith and my values into my professional practice of medicine. Here's my current B/WA of this issue:

What is the worst that could result from trying to integrate my faith with my work? I can envision a number of possible worsts: patients and colleagues alike might think I'm nuts and treat me accordingly. I could be ostracized professionally and not be able to build or maintain a thriving practice. If my colleagues don't accept me, I could become a social outcast. If the wrong people take offense, I could even lose my job.

What is the best that could happen if I integrate my faith with my work? The best thing that happens if I exercise my faith in my profession is that I can be the same person at work as I am in all of the other areas of my life. I can base my professional decisions on the same values I live by in the rest of my life, which means I can feel totally in harmony with the will of God, attempting to use the talents he has given me in appropriate ways to uplift others and to uplift him by leading the type of life and living an example that would draw others to him. That harmony can give me a sense of settled calm, and such peace is an invaluable asset for a pediatric neurosurgeon making life-and-death judgments under pressure on a daily basis. Going in with calmness and assurance certainly makes a huge difference when performing intricate, life-threatening surgical procedures under the most severe time constraints.

Having the same primary motivation at work as I have in the rest of my life—the desire to please, love, honor, obey, and represent God to the best of my ability—also makes many of my professional decisions a lot less nerve-racking. If I only have to please God, I can let a lot of other anxieties go. For example, I don't waste a lot of emotional energy worrying, "What does this colleague or that boss think? What does he or she expect of me? How is that group going to react? What do these people want?" It's a lot easier to perform for an audience of One.

What is the worst that could happen if I don't try to integrate my faith with my work? I would soon become at odds with myself. Life would feel unbalanced and disjointed. Everything I do would seem hypocritical because there would be a cognitive dissonance in the recesses of my mind. I'd be miserable until I chose which diverging path I was going to take. Sooner or later I'd be forced to decide—either risk my faith or relinquish it.

What is the best that could happen if I don't lead a life of faith at work? For me there is no *best* scenario in this case. The *best* would be pretty much the same as the *worst*.

I actually didn't do a Best/Worst Analysis when I first made up my mind to incorporate my spiritual faith into my medical practice, though it might have made the decision easier, since it clarifies the relevant considerations. Still, revisiting that decision today in terms of a B/WA encourages and reinforces my beliefs.

Integrating faith and work is a difficult call for some people. They might have to pay a great price in terms of criticism, opposition, injustice, and more. But I think much (though by no means all) of the negative reaction people receive stems from the same sort of attitudes we discussed in the previous chapter, when they display insensitivity or use poor judgment in discussing their faith.

I'm reminded of a young medical resident who called me one day to ask for my support in protesting her dismissal from her surgical residency program. There had been complaints from patients about her practice of praying with them before surgery. I told her that I was sorry, but I couldn't support her. I didn't think as medical authority figures we had any right to impose our faith on patients. Many, if not most of my patients' families, know of my personal faith, and I have no problem talking about it if they ask me. I don't hesitate to tell the parents of my young patients the day before a surgery that if they will say their prayers that night, I will be saying mine and I believe we'll all have less to worry about the next day as a result. And I have gladly prayed with many of my patients and their families — but only at their request. That is very different than deciding to pray with them whether they want to or not. I hoped the resident learned the difference and showed a little more restraint the next place she went. There is something to be said for wisdom or discernment, and we can all reduce the risk of living out our faith at work if we use a little of both.

What we can't do is remove all risk from faith. If we could prove the existence of God beyond a shadow of a doubt, believing in him would no longer demand faith. So I realize this idea of pursuing a personal relationship with a God we can't see or touch, whose existence can't be proven scientifically, may seem a risky proposition to many people. Making that relationship the central motivation of your life, the foundation of your most basic values, and the inspiration of your life goals may seem an unreasonable, terrifying, even paralyzing risk.

I find that risk a lot more acceptable, however, when I realize that my personal relationship with God came at great risk to him as well. In fact, according to the Bible, God took the initial risk at creation by granting humankind free will to choose to believe and obey — or not. Then he took an even bigger risk in sending his own Son to earth to live and die to give us a clearer idea of how we could have a personal relationship with him and what that relationship could be like.

Knowing that he isn't asking us to risk anything for him that he hasn't already risked for us makes it easier for me to accept the risk inherent in some of the Bible's hardest teachings:

- Do unto others as you would have others do unto you.
- Greater love has no one than this, that he lays down his life for his friends.

- If anyone would come after me, he must deny himself and take up his cross and follow me. For whoever wants to save his life will lose it, but whoever loses his life for my sake will find it.

My natural reaction to instructions like that is *Whoa, now! That kind of faith requires one whopping big risk!*

Whether I consider that an acceptable risk is a matter of experience and perspective. Looking back over my life, I'm aware of some short-term costs. Have there been inconveniences? Of course. Have there been things I might have liked to do but didn't because of my faith values? Absolutely. Did I wonder if I was missing out on some things? Sure. But I will tell you this: I honestly don't regret a single time that I ever took a risk for my faith.

Some people of faith pay a terribly high toll for taking a stand. Because I'm out in public doing a lot of speaking, I hear from other scientists who tell me they share my Christian beliefs but don't feel they can be public about them. It's just too risky to go against the politically correct conventions of the scientific community. But I can't help wishing more of them would take heart and remember the rallying cry of the apostle Paul when he wrote in the eighth chapter of Romans, "What, then, shall we say in response to this? If God is for us, who can be against us?"

That's precisely the kind of encouragement I needed when the Academy of Achievement asked me to participate in another panel discussion of the same topic in 2006. With the memory of the positive response from the year before, I didn't have to think twice.

If anything, the second panel was even more formidable than the first. I shared the platform with three eminent scientists: fellow believer Dr. Francis Collins, the director of the Human Genome Project, one of the largest research undertakings in the history of science; Dr. Daniel Dennett, who synthesized cutting-edge research in such fields as neurology, linguistics, computer science, and artificial intelligence to construct a model to explain his theory of the evolutionary neurological basis of consciousness and religion as a "natural phenomenon"; and Dr. Richard Dawkins, whose defense of evolutionary theory throughout his career has earned him the moniker "Darwin's

Rottweiler." He aired his criticism of religious faith and the role of religion in history in the television documentary *Root of All Evil?* and he had recently published his book titled *The God Delusion.* So I felt pretty sure I knew where he'd be coming from.

This panel discussion proved every bit as entertaining as the one the previous year. When one of the others referred to evolution as a fact and pointed out some of the similarities between different species as evidence, he seemed a bit shocked when I spoke up to say I don't believe in evolution and I believe it is possible for two objective individuals to look at the same "evidence" and come to very different conclusions. For example, I suggested a scenario in which life in our world ended and millions of years passed before explorers from another galaxy visited Earth. Somewhere in their exploration they did some excavating and uncovered a Volkswagen Beetle and a Rolls Royce. The aliens at first noted the differences, but then they realized each had an engine and a transmission that served much the same function. Should they logically conclude that the more complex specimen must have evolved from the simpler model? Might it be just as reasonable to infer that the same thinking creator of the first one saw that his basic design for a system of locomotion — an engine and a transmission — could be improved and made a more sophisticated version for the second vehicle? Sometimes the conclusions we arrive at depend entirely on the suppositions we start with.

I reminded the panel and our audience that I spend a lot of time and energy dealing with the human brain and nervous system. The more I learn, the more impressed I am with its complexity. I also deal with children and have reason to consider the wonders of human potential. I've come to the conclusion that there is an added development, an extra dimension, a deeper sense that distinguishes human beings from all other creatures. I call it spirituality.

I admitted it was impossible to scientifically prove the existence of God. But I agreed with Francis Collins, who reminded our other two colleagues that it's impossible to prove a negative. "How then," he asked them, "can it be said with certainty that there is no God? That seems like the strongest kind of fallacy. Agnosticism I grant you is a more intellectually honest approach. Strong atheism, to say that 'there can be no

God, and I know that's the case,' falls apart on the altar of logical debate
... and really ought to be considered as its own form of blind faith."

Daniel Dennett responded to that by saying, "I don't know anyone
who would assert what you call strong atheism."

I was surprised to hear that, as was Francis Collins, who replied
incredulously, "You don't? *The God Delusion?*" referring to the title
of Richard Dawkins's book. A lot of people chuckled.

I said to Collins, "I think maybe we've made a convert."

The resulting laughter around the room was so loud that I don't
think many people heard Dawkins sputter, "This is ridiculous!" He
then went on to argue that by our reasoning he supposed even a "flying spaghetti monster is *possible*" — at which point Dr. Collins and I
laughingly told him we were agnostics on that point.

I pointed out that "as sophisticated as we are, with all of our MRIs
and our PET scanners, we have yet to discover the origin of a thought. We
don't know the origin of a feeling. We can talk about electro-physological
responses, but we cannot take it to the next level; we cannot put that in a
box. I think that's one of the things that makes us different." I admitted
that I couldn't *prove* my belief that this is evidence of a creator God. But
by the same token, the other members of our panel couldn't *prove* their
theory either. It was all a matter of how much faith we have and where
we place that faith. I said, "I simply don't have enough faith to believe
that something as complex as our ability to rationalize, think, plan, and
have a moral sense of what's right and wrong just appeared."

Near the end of our session, a member of the audience asked us
how much of what we believed or didn't believe was a result of our
personal experience. I readily admitted, "Experiences are clearly what
have given me my faith in God." I referred to once being an angry
young teenager who tried to stab a friend. Angry, that is, until I had
an experience one day and I began to recognize that there was a power
beyond myself. I explained that when I began "to connect myself with
that power, my life completely changed. Some people say that's balo-
ney. You have to experience it yourself."

Dr. Dawkins took issue with that when he said, "I don't think *my*
personal experiences are of the slightest interest to anyone. I care about
what is true. That means I care about evidence. My personal private
experience is not evidentiary."

I didn't have a chance to respond to that comment, but in thinking about it since, I beg to differ. While I would never claim my experience is all there is to know about anything, I would argue that my own personal *experience* is one valid and convincing form of evidence. What is a scientific experiment if not a controlled *experience* in which the scientist records his personal observations, results, and conclusions? If enough people repeat the experimental experience with the same results and come to the same conclusions, then the scientific community considers that evidentiary. All of us, scientists and laypeople alike, learn from experience. Personal experience is not the same as truth. But it can be evidence that points us toward the Truth.

Everyone on the panel was given fifteen seconds to "summarize" the discussion on faith and science. I think we all laughed at the absurdity of that request.

I took my fifteen seconds to challenge the audience: "Ask yourself the question, if there is a God, what is the risk of not believing in him versus believing in him? If there is no God, what is the risk of not believing in him versus believing in him? Ask yourself those questions tonight while you are in bed."

Richard Dawkins informed the audience, "Dr. Carson has just invoked what is known as Pascal's Wager. It assumes that the God who confronts you when you reach the pearly gates is indeed a God who cares passionately about whether or not you believe in him. If I were God, I would not care so much about whether someone believed in me [here Dawkins changed perspectives from I-God to I-person as he continued] but whether I was a good person, and whether I was an honest person, and whether I spent my life honestly seeking the truth. And as Bertrand Russell answered when someone asked him, 'What would you say if you found yourself confronted by God?' If God challenged you and asked, 'Why didn't you believe in me?' Bertrand said he would reply, 'Not enough evidence, God, not enough evidence!' "

So Dawkins concluded, "I think any God worth worshiping would respect that far more than someone who believes in him just because it was the safe option to do so."

I think my respected colleague was right in suggesting that there ought to be better reasons to risk believing in God than because it's the *safe option*. I think there are.

He was also right in accusing me of borrowing Pascal's Wager, but I felt it was applicable for that audience and perhaps even more appropriate here in this book. Blaise Pascal, the French mathematician/philosopher who is widely considered the father of risk analysis, was something of a playboy dilettante before he changed his lifestyle and entered a monastery to grow closer to God. When asked to explain the transformation, this brilliant man, who had spent much of his life trying to construct a workable mathematical formula for quantifying probabilities, came up with his own Best/Worst Analysis—Pascal's Wager. While I would hope this isn't anyone's only rationale for faith, it's a good place to start for anyone considering whether or not to take the risk of personal faith. You do the B/WA.

If there is a God and you believe in him, you know the best is yet to come. If there is a God and you totally reject the idea to lead your life in a contrary way, the eternal risk to you is incalculable. If there is no God and you believe in him, the worst that happens is you spend your life with some increased endorphin levels thinking you're believing in a good thing. If there is no God and you don't believe in him, there's no serious consequence either way.

I believe—and so did Pascal—that when you sit down and think about it in that way, it makes a lot more sense to put faith in God than not to, if only because you have much more to lose if you're wrong and he does exist than if you're wrong and he doesn't. As I told one of the other panel members at the Academy of Achievement, not believing in God doesn't make you a bad person, just as believing in God doesn't make me a good person.

We all have the choice. But only when someone takes the risk of faith can he or she truly begin to experience the best consequence and the best rationale I know for belief in God. That's the privilege of a personal relationship with the Creator of the universe, who wants to offer his wisdom and guidance to help us deal with all of the other risks we face in our dangerous world.

12

Navigating
Professional Risks

IN EARLIER CHAPTERS I'VE TALKED ABOUT THE RISKS INVOLVED IN A number of my surgical cases, but I have faced other career issues where difficult decisions required some thoughtful risk analysis.

You recall the risk I took by ignoring the advice of my first-year advisor, who suggested I drop out of med school or consider taking a reduced load. Well, my subsequent choice of neurosurgery as a specialty, a decision made during my third year of med school, also entailed a measure of risk. For one thing, I didn't get a whole lot of encouragement in that direction either. I don't know whether that was cause or effect, but neurosurgery obviously wasn't a field very many people of my racial or economic background pursued. In fact, there had been only eight black neurosurgeons in the world at the time.

I had to weigh the risks of investing so much time and effort preparing for a field that might present particular challenges for me. While I hadn't yet formulated my Best/Worst Analysis template, I did consider some questions that helped me do a thoughtful pro-versus-con assessment.

After a long string of academic successes, did I want to risk substantial embarrassment if I failed to make the grade in what was considered by many to be the most demanding of all medical specialties? How hard might it be to win the confidence and earn the acceptance of the medical community and potential patients? I saw a lot of uncertainties that could present problems.

On the positive side, I could see great benefits. With its complex anatomy and unlimited potential, the human brain fascinated me like nothing else we covered in med school. I could imagine no greater dream than to become a neurosurgeon.

It's difficult to put a value on fulfilling one's highest aspirations. To improve the lives of others, to not only give them longevity but improve their quality of life—you can't put a value on that either. Those things certainly justified a significant risk.

Then I had to consider yet another benefit, that by taking this less-chosen path, I could become a role model for others. That may have been the *best* and most appealing reason for risking a choice discouraged by so many people.

Obviously my sense of values was a significant influence in my decision. The timing—the *when* factor—played a role as well. If there had been more substantial risks than the ones just mentioned—for example, if it had been thirty years earlier and I'd been living in the South—the risk might have outweighed the benefits, and I might have chosen a different career path.

In chapter 8 I referred to the time early in my career when the budgetary constraints of academic medicine prodded me to seriously consider the more lucrative opportunities of private practice. But financial considerations were not the last or only factors that forced me to weigh the risks of staying where I was at Johns Hopkins.

For a junior faculty member, I had an unusual career. Because of the remarkable cases I had the privilege to work on—first the hemispherectomies, then the separation of the Binder twins—I had become extremely well known not only in the United States but around the world. My growing reputation within my profession led to an increase in the number of referrals and in the complexity of cases I received—which were both challenges I welcomed. But the accompanying renown came with its own totally unexpected consequence.

The media coverage, with all its interviews, was a novelty at first, and I decided to enjoy the experience while it lasted. During the wild media frenzy following the Binder case, I assured Candy that "all this will die down eventually and our lives will return to normal." But the combination of my noteworthy professional achievements and my background story of overcoming poverty and hardship made for what a lot of folks evidently thought was an appealing human interest feature in its own right. Many media accounts of the twins' remarkable medical story were accompanied or followed up by biographical background stories about me. Soon I was inundated by calls from individuals and groups clamoring for me to "come and speak to help our cause" or "share your personal story to inspire the youth with whom we work."

Since one of the primary motives for choosing my career direction in the first place was the desire to be an encouragement to and a role model for underprivileged young people from backgrounds like mine, I welcomed the invitations to speak for schools, churches, and other organizations around the country. But the more I spoke, the more invitations poured in.

The responses I received from young people were gratifying. So many junior high, high school, and even college students wrote to tell me how my sharing the lessons I'd learned—about peer pressure, the importance of reading and education, and the overcoming of hardship—had given them hope to pursue their own dreams. To realize I could make an impact like that just by recounting my own life experience was a humbling thing. How could I not accept all of these opportunities to speak and perhaps make a significant difference in young people's lives?

But all of those speaking engagements required time, energy, and travel—on top of a career in academic medicine that came with its own innumerable demands. Patients and a heavy surgical caseload were merely the tip of the professional iceberg. Surviving in an academic environment, let alone advancing and succeeding, also required conducting research studies, participating in national organizations, and publishing articles in professional journals.

For a time I managed to balance the dueling demands of my career and public life, but I soon realized my private life was slowly being crowded out in the process. Friends and colleagues warned me if I didn't give up my outside interests—meaning my fledgling speaking career—I would never have any hope of advancing through the ranks to become a tenured full professor.

I felt I couldn't continue to be pulled in so many different directions, but how to choose? To make such a crucial and complex decision, I had to evaluate the entire spectrum of competing interests and af-filiated risks. I could tell myself that my values demanded I make my family a higher priority than my career or my public speaking, but that didn't help me know how to balance the professional-versus-public opportunities before me. I didn't want to risk the chance to succeed in the career that had provided me the public platform I now enjoyed, a career I believed God had led me into as a means to help others, a career thus deserving my best efforts.

I recognized that there was a risk to me, to my career, to my suc-cess, and to my calling if I didn't ever achieve the pinnacle of academic achievement—as a tenured full professor. But there was also a regret-tably dire price to be paid if I turned my back on the innumerable young people in this country and other countries who never achieve their potential for want of a little inspiration and the example of one person to show them the way.

Weighing these risks in light of my beliefs and my values, I real-ized my obligations to others should be greater than my obligations to myself. So I decided I wouldn't worry too much about professional advancement or becoming a tenured professor. But even after I tried to take myself out of the picture, I was still left feeling an obligation to patients to whom I could offer lifesaving medical help and a compet-ing obligation to the multitudes I might help through my speaking by providing encouragement and guidance.

Did these conflicting opportunities truly represent diverging roads? Did the two options have to be mutually exclusive? I didn't think so. I wanted to believe there could be substantial overlap, but I didn't see how I could make it all happen.

Since I believed God's guidance and provision had brought me to this point, I asked him to open the doors he wanted me to walk through and to give me wisdom in how to proceed. And I believe he did.

One insight he gave me was that I could use all the travel time to my speaking engagements to greater advantage. In that unpres-sured, unstructured downtime on airplanes, at airports, and in motel rooms—away from the usual daily pressures and interruptions—I could keep abreast of the literature, write research protocols, draft articles, and review work done by collaborators. With creative planning I could often take Candy, one or more of our boys, my mother, or sometimes the entire Carson family on trips to interesting locations we might never have visited otherwise.

With some new, combined goals in mind, I decided not to give up my speaking career after all, and I'll be forever grateful I took that risk. For by taking maximum advantage of my travel time (as well as the help of individuals who were brought into my life as a result), I found it was possible to speak an average of twice a week and still further my medical career.

For most of my career, I have performed an average of 450 brain surgeries a year (neurosurgeons in private practice usually average around 150) while doing the requisite research and publishing often enough in professional journals to eventually be named a tenured full professor in four disciplines: neurosurgery, oncology, pediatrics, and plastic surgery.

Ironically, an unforeseen result of my decision to speak to young people was that my public visibility eventually negated any financial sacrifice I'd expected to sustain by staying in academia. Demand for me as a speaker motivated me to join a speakers' bureau to help manage, prioritize, and maximize my public appearances. I also began writing books. Eventually I found myself appointed to a number of large corporate boards. Altogether my "extracurricular" activities added up to a better financial situation than I might have expected to attain in private practice.

But the greatest confirmation for me that I made the right decision to combine the two career directions is the more than one hundred thousand letters I've received from people throughout America and around the world. Every week, almost every day, young people write to tell me their lives were changed by hearing me tell my story, by reading one of my books, or by seeing an interview on television or in some magazine and realizing they too have a brain and thereby the ability to define their own lives.

If that's the only legacy I leave, I'll be very happy, and all the risks will have been worth it.

I never could have maintained my medical career at Johns Hopkins or done so much public speaking if I hadn't taken yet another crucial risk near the outset of my career. At that time, my caseload had grown to the point that I was at the hospital late almost every night, spending inordinate hours dealing with patient problems. When I wasn't in the operating room, I was on call 24/7 for questions or concerns that arose for any pediatric neurosurgical patients at Johns Hopkins.

I soon realized I was going to burn out if I kept up that pace. So I started thinking about ways to spread the burden, and the idea of hiring a physician's assistant became very appealing. PAs were expensive, but our growing pediatric neurosurgery program was bringing in enough money (this was before insurance companies decided they should use Medicare and Medicaid as their base for paying) that I had enough funds available to hire a terrific PA, Carol James, who has been with me throughout my career. Carol quickly gained the confidence of my patients and has proven invaluable. So as our program expanded, I hired another PA, then another, until today we have four. They make it possible for me to see and treat more patients — a value that did not go unnoticed by the hospital. Eventually our administration began to ante up the means to pay for our PAs, so I no longer had to pay for them out of my own personal clinical budget (which was ever shrinking as insurance companies began to decide when and how much to pay in a relatively arbitrary fashion). More colleagues began hiring their own PAs as everyone realized how valuable they could be. Since the enactment of the eighty-hour work week limit for residents, our PAs have shouldered a much bigger part of the burden for patient care.

I don't know what I would do without my PAs, though there was a time when I was afraid I would find out. It was perhaps one of the most critical professional risks I have ever encountered. In fact, I became so discouraged I seriously considered quitting medicine altogether.

Throughout the latter years of the 1990s, most health insurance companies were steadily reducing their reimbursement level (the percentage of the surgeon's fee they would cover for their clients) to the point that I simply didn't have the money to pay the people working for me. I went from five full-time employees down to three. Morale was terrible. Friction in the office skyrocketed because the remaining staff were terribly overworked. (You have to realize my team has always been overworked, routinely putting in twelve or more hours a day. I couldn't ask them to do more, yet they did.) With an ever-growing workload falling on fewer people, I realized it was only a matter of time before it would be impossible to sustain the quality of care I was used to providing.

That simply was not an acceptable risk. No matter how many Best/Worst Analyses I did, I couldn't see any *best* outcome to this dilemma. I had done everything I thought I could do; the rest was out of my control. That was when I decided that quitting medicine would be preferable to compromising the level of care I could offer patients.

But before I followed through on that decision, I sought additional wisdom. I talked to a number of CEOs of large companies and people in responsible leadership positions around the country, acquaintances and friends I'd met through the Academy of Achievement, the Horatio Alger Society, and other places over the years. As I listened to these advisors, one suggestion kept cropping up—that I simply quit dealing with insurance companies or Medicare and accept only patients who could pay out of pocket. I can't say the idea didn't appeal to me. I'd be able to use all of my talents and time to care for patients and never again have to hassle with the all-powerful and capricious insurance industry that has assumed control of health care in America.

But I didn't think I could do what people were suggesting for one reason—I will never forget how much of my own medical care as a child came through some form of medical assistance. I would feel like a hypocrite turning down patients in the same situation I'd once been in. Yet all of this counsel I received got me thinking.

Some of the most helpful input came from George Lucas, the Hollywood producer/director, a friend who was extremely encouraging to me. He listened as I described my dilemma. He even said he'd gladly do what he could to help financially, which I appreciated, but that wasn't what I'd been looking for. Neither had I approached him expecting specific advice about the issues plaguing health care today—he didn't know much about that. But since he's an immensely creative guy, I figured he knew something about professional risks and dreams, and I hoped he would have some wisdom to share. He did.

His most pertinent counsel had to do with the importance of using one's talents and not allowing minor interferences to derail one's mission in life. That challenging advice lifted my spirits enormously and prompted me to stop thinking so much about quitting and start asking what possible steps I could take to continue practicing.

I reexamined the dilemma from every angle I could think of. I knew *what* the problem was: insufficient reimbursement for surgeon's fees. *Who* was the biggest culprit wasn't hard to figure out either: more of my patients were insured by Blue Cross/Blue Shield (BC/BS) than any other company. That wasn't surprising, since BC/BS is the biggest health insurer in America, and because it is so big, it can set reimbursement rates for medical services nearly wherever it wants. The level also varies tremendously from state to state, so that doctors in a state such as Alabama receive a much better deal than those in Maryland. (For example, Alabama BC/BS will reimburse 80 percent of a neurosurgeon's fees, while Maryland BC/BS will cover only 28 percent of my fees.) To make matters worse, Blue Cross has decided that no matter where our patients come from (and people come to Johns Hopkins from all over), the company has the right to reimburse us at the (lowest) Maryland rate. In other words, BC/BS of Alabama would pay me at Johns Hopkins in Baltimore just over a third the reimbursement they would offer me for performing the same surgery in Birmingham.

I did some calculations and concluded that because we had so many BC/BS patients, the change in this one policy would solve my division's immediate financial crisis. So I called the head of Blue Cross in Maryland to see what might be done. After he said he couldn't help me, I then talked to the people at the company's national office to explain the circumstances and express my desire to continue to participate as a BC/BS provider and to ask if some adjustment to this policy could be worked out. It very quickly became clear to me that they had no motivation and thus no desire to consider any changes either.

So I made the difficult and seemingly risky decision to become nonparticipatory with Blue Cross. Going non-par meant I was no longer listed as a Blue Cross/Blue Shield–approved medical provider. Any

BC/BS patients who came to me for surgery would expect to pay my fees out of pocket, in advance.

I knew this decision presented a significant risk, but I had assessed that risk by doing a basic Best/Worst Analysis: What was the *best* thing that could happen if I went non-par and refused to deal with Blue Cross/Blue Shield? The best that could happen would be that I'd collect a large enough portion of my fees to maintain my current staff—even rehire a full staff—and we could provide a better level of care for our patients. The *worst* thing that could happen if I went non-par would be that more and more patients would decide they couldn't afford to come to me until my caseload shrank to the point that everyone would have to be let go—including me. Before it got to that point, I'd have to make a tough decision: either endure the embarrassment of going back to BC/BS bowing and scraping and asking them to put me back on their approved list—or quit medicine.

The *best* thing that could happen if I didn't take the risk of going non-par was that I might somehow manage to continue scraping along with fewer staff and minimally acceptable care. But it would be unpleasant and increasingly frustrating. The only other remotely viable option I could see if I didn't go non-par was to cut back even further on staff and severely limit our patient load. Then we would have to start telling people who called, "Sorry, we just can't help your child." The *worst* thing that could happen if I did nothing was that I would have to get rid of more staff and would not be able to do the things I felt God had called me to do.

After weighing the risk, I went non-par, and an interesting phenomenon took place. My patients with BC/BS had to pay out of pocket up front, but when they then turned that bill into their carrier, the company actually reimbursed them at a higher rate than Blue Cross had been reimbursing me. I guess they figured they needed to do so to appease and maintain their clientele, whereas before the insurance company realized they had me over a barrel. (Most doctors have so many Blue Cross/Blue Shield patients, the company could arbitrarily dictate terms, figuring we weren't going to deny care to their clients simply because we weren't getting properly reimbursed.)

Since they were getting reimbursed pretty quickly at a reasonable level, most BC/BS patients stuck with me. I tried to help by giving an automatic 20 percent discount to all Blue Cross patients so they'd be personally responsible for as little as possible, and I didn't turn my back on those I knew couldn't afford the difference between my discounted charge and what BC/BS would reimburse them. To assist folks in the most dire financial straits, I helped create a nonprofit organization called Angels of the OR (more about that later).

When I went non-par with Blue Cross back in 2001, I wasn't at all sure what would happen. But it worked out well—for patients and for me. Revenues soon climbed enough that we went back to full staff. We stayed as busy as ever and were able to provide quality care to all of our patients no matter their financial status.

These professional risks I've dealt with over the years are in some ways unique to my profession. Because I go to work every day to open the heads of children and operate on their brains, I'm well aware that my decisions and my actions will have serious implications for those kids and their families for the remainder of their lives. These difficult issues facing the health care industry today present their own special challenges to *any* medical providers.

But I'm not just a surgeon; I'm a teacher, and teaching is always a risk because you never know how a student will respond. It's risky for an instructor to teach a student pilot how to fly a jet, because at some point he has to turn the controls over. It's not much different teaching open-heart or brain surgery. It's so much easier to do it all yourself—so much faster, so much less stressful. But if everybody did that, nobody else would ever learn how to do it. And when the teacher died, the skill would be lost. So at some point, you have to take that risk.

If you do it right, you reduce the risk. A good teacher watches the skills and progress of his student and knows when he can trust that student. Some grasp the lessons quickly. I remember a particular resident who absorbed everything like a sponge. By the end of his junior resident year, he could do what a chief resident could do. I thought he had the technical ability to become perhaps the best neurosurgeon the world had ever seen. Unfortunately, he had a swimming accident and drowned. When you're working with and teaching human beings, you never know what's going to happen. That too is a risk you have to live with, no matter what you might be teaching.

My professional success as a surgeon and a professor of medicine at Johns Hopkins has afforded me numerous invitations to sit on national corporate boards. I currently serve on two, the Kellogg Company and Costco Wholesale Corporation. With all of the problems and bad publicity surrounding the financial dealings of Enron, WorldCom, Tyco, and other big-name companies in recent years, I've had to weigh the risks of sitting on any corporate board today, both the risk of embarrassment and the potential financial exposure involved. But participating on corporate boards has introduced me to some extraordinary people. Plus I've learned a great deal about finances, corporate structure, and people management—information I've been able to apply in my own profession and to help improve the two charitable organizations I've founded.

The more I've interacted with colleagues on these corporate boards and other people in different fields, however, the more I see that every career has its own distinct challenges. I don't think I have ever talked with a highly successful person in any profession who hadn't known, faced, and overcome tremendous risks. I'd like to share two quick examples.

I think first of George Lucas, whose father had planned for him to join the family retail business. But that wasn't George's dream. He went to film school and envisioned a career in moviemaking. His creativity was never in question, but you can't eat ideas or pay the rent with dreams. He lived for a time as a typical starving artist, wondering where his next meal would come from—until he finally swallowed his pride and went back to his dad to ask for a loan. His father graciously advanced him the money he needed to get by, but he clearly believed the time would come when George would come back and work with him in the family business.

After transforming an award-winning student film he'd made into his first feature film, *THX 1138*, a fairly lucrative offer finally came for George to make another movie. The pay would have taken off a lot of pressure—and he was tempted by the offer—but that movie wasn't his dream either. He'd had some discouraging feedback on a manuscript he was working on at that time, but he believed in the idea and wanted to put all of his energies into that. So he kept pushing that project until he finally scrounged up the necessary financing to make it. And the low-budget *American Graffiti* jump-started his stellar career. He took what he made from that, sold his house, and invested all his money for the next several years in an even wilder idea. *Star Wars* not only changed his life, it revolutionized the film industry.

From the beginning, George Lucas dreamed of being an independent moviemaker who made his own pictures his own way—without lawyers or investors or industry executives telling him what he could or couldn't do. So by continuing to take the risk of rolling over his own profits from one movie to the next, he built a legacy and a business empire worth billions of dollars today.

He is quick to say that success for him has never been about the money. It has always been about the freedom to follow his dreams and pursue his passion. It has meant substantial creative and financial risks, but if he didn't take the risks—if he took an easier path and did what everyone else did, or what his father expected him to do—he doubted he would ever be happy. And that was a risk he wasn't willing to take.

I can't think of successful people I've encountered over the years without remembering the late A. G. Gaston. I had lunch with him several years ago at Tuskegee Institute when he was ninety-five years old. I knew something of his fascinating life story, so I came right out and asked him, "Mr. Gaston, how in the world did a black man like you become a multimillionaire living in Birmingham, Alabama, in the 1940s?"

He said, "It was simple. I just opened my eyes, looked around, and asked, what is it people need? And then whatever it was, I did."

He realized a lot of older black folks at the time worried about whether their family would be able to afford a nice funeral for them when they died. Whether it was a rational concern or not didn't matter.

It was how people felt. So A. G. Gaston began going door to door telling people if they would pay him a quarter a week, he would guarantee them a $600 funeral when they died. It wouldn't matter whether they lived to be a hundred or they died the next week; as long as they continued to pay him twenty-five cents each week for his funeral insurance, he would guarantee them a nice service when they died. A lot of people took Mr. Gaston up on his offer, and he used that weekly cash flow to build his own insurance company. He soon founded a bank and then diversified into ownership of hotels and other properties as he built a business empire that he eventually used to provide significant funding for the Civil Rights Movement in the 1960s. A. G. Gaston knew something about taking risks. He was quick to identify vision, both literal and figurative, as a key ingredient of his success. "*I just opened my eyes....*"

In talking to people like George Lucas and A. G. Gaston, I've come to the conclusion that the single most important determinant of the level of success a person achieves in any career is how he or she deals with the risks that career presents.

Think for a minute about those people who've had the greatest influence and impact on history. Consider their actions. Their character traits. Most of what made them special involved risk.

Creativity requires risk. So do exploration and innovation. Anyone who thinks outside the box is taking a risk. Leadership brings many risks. Courage is exercised in the face of risk. Investments involve risk. Decision-making always means a certain degree of risk.

Consider Columbus sailing into the unknown. Our founding fathers signing the Declaration of Independence. Lincoln introducing the Emancipation Proclamation. The Wright brothers at Kitty Hawk. Eisenhower on D-day. John Kennedy during the Cuban Missile Crisis. Rosa Parks on the bus. Greatness in any endeavor is often measured in terms of the risks a person faces. Heroism is earned in the face of risk. Success is defined by risks taken and overcome.

No matter what our professions, we will know risk. We have to use our brains to decide which ones are acceptable and how to approach them. And a careful Best/Worst Analysis is always a good place to start.

I don't believe, however, that the most important measure of a person is his or her career. True greatness isn't so much what you do as who you are. Which means the personal risks we face in everyday life may be even more significant than the professional ones.

My Personal Risks
in the Face of Death

A LOT OF PEOPLE HEARD ABOUT THE HEALTH CRISIS THAT RECENTLY put my life at risk, but few knew that was not my first up-close-and-personal encounter with cancer. Since my previous experience played such a significant role in how I responded this last time, I need to give you the background.

My residency training at Johns Hopkins designated a period of time for doing basic research in my field. My growing interest in brain tumors and neuro-oncology at that time led me to do a research project requiring the creation of an animal brain tumor model that I could image and then treat. Scientists had long known that if they could achieve consistent results working with small animals, their findings would translate into new cures and better care for human patients suffering from similar diseases. But earlier work using mice, monkeys, and dogs had presented problems. Dog models produced inconsistent results, monkeys were prohibitively expensive, and mice or rats (while cheap enough) were so small we couldn't operate on them. Nor did you get good images of their brains with CT scans or MRI equipment.

The challenge for me was to find an affordable model that produced consistent results and was large enough for me to image and operate on.

I eventually discovered that by using pieces of an extremely virulent type of tumor called VX2, we could overwhelm the immune system of New Zealand white rabbits and successfully grow tumors wherever we wanted by injecting the animals with the cancer. The resulting brain tumors grew at a consistent and predictable rate (an essential criterion

for the research I needed to do) until the rabbits fell ill and died between twelve and fourteen days after the injection.

We were able to observe and record the growth rate of each tumor
by the use of CAT scans and magnetic resonance imaging (MRI), but
we had to take the rabbits to Germany for the MRIs because the process was so new at the time and we didn't yet have the technology
available at Johns Hopkins. We did, however, use some of the first PET
(positron emission topography) scans at Johns Hopkins to image the
brain tumors on these rabbits.

One day in the lab, in the process of injecting cancer into a rabbit's
brain, my hand slipped and I accidentally inoculated my own finger
with the VX2 carcinoma. I had no idea what effect this might have on
a human being. I did know how easily this particular line of cells could
overcome the immune system in other small creatures, so I assumed
this could be a serious problem. Sure enough, within a matter of days
the injection site began to turn colors and nodules began to form on
that finger. But it was the lesion that began growing in my throat that
sent me to see a physician. When I explained what had happened and
showed him my symptoms, he was sufficiently alarmed to recommend
I check with an oncologist.

I had done enough research to realize that no one had any idea
how the human body would react to VX2, which meant there was no
established treatment protocol. I wasn't particularly keen on becoming
an experimental subject in someone else's research, so I began thinking
and praying about my alternatives.

At the time, I happened to be reading a very interesting book called
Back to Eden about natural healing remedies. So I turned to the cancer section and was impressed by what I read about the medicinal
properties of red clover tea. When I shared that information with my
wife, Candy went out and purchased all of the red clover tea she could
find in the greater Baltimore area. She brewed it by the gallon every
day, and as I drank it incessantly over several weeks, the discoloration
and nodules on my finger, and the lesions in my throat, went away.
I will never know for certain whether, or how much, that tea naturally suppressed the cancer's growth. I did know that because VX2
was a *xenograph*, meaning it came from another species, my own im-

mune system would be inclined to attack it ferociously, so anything that would have boosted my natural immune system might have been enough to do the job. And I wasn't about to discount the role prayer might have played. What I did know for certain—whether it should be attributed to the tea, my own immunity, prayer, or some combination of all three factors—was that once I started drinking the tea, the cancer stopped progressing and quickly dissipated.

Did I take a risk by pursuing a natural remedy rather than undergoing a more traditional regimen of chemotherapy or radiation treatments? Yes, I took a risk. But I will hasten to add that I chose that route knowing that any traditional approach in my case would have been entirely experimental. No one had any experience treating this cancer in humans. There were no real experts to consult.

If there had been, if a number of other people had previously been injected with VX2 and were successfully treated with chemo or radiation, I would have elected to rush right out and start those treatments. As it was, I didn't feel my experimental approach would be any riskier than someone else's. And if I had not seen improvement immediately, I would have quickly sought other opinions from the best medical experts I could find and then done whatever they thought I needed to do to aggressively treat the cancer.

Fortunately, it never came to that, and regular annual checkups for the next twenty years showed no further indication of cancer whatsoever. So what happened to me in the summer of 2002 came as a real surprise.

Unlike a lot of people, including many doctors who should know better, I've always been diligent about having my PSAs checked and doing all the things you are supposed to do. I'd actually had my annual physical just a few months earlier, so I wasn't particularly concerned when I first noticed that I had some degree of urinary urgency. I'd been blessed with a camel bladder at birth; normally I could spend ten hours standing in the OR with no problem. Now I would have to break scrubs and go to the bathroom. *Something is different here*, I realized.

So I consulted my friend Dr. Pat Walsh, chief of urology at Johns Hopkins and probably the most famous urologist in the world. I explained the symptoms and asked Pat, "What do you think is going on?"

"Oh, you probably have a little prostatitis," Pat told me. "Let's give you an antibiotic."

I took the antibiotic, but the symptoms persisted. So I went back to Pat, who said, "Maybe you have a little prostatic hyperplasia. Why don't we give you some Flomax."

I took the Flomax. Nothing changed. *Maybe something is more seriously wrong,* I began to wonder.

To be cautious, Pat suggested, "Let's repeat your PSA. I know it was fine a few months ago, but let's check it again, just to be sure."

This time it came back slightly elevated. Nothing dramatic, just a little above normal.

"I think we should do a biopsy," Pat told me.

I had the biopsy done at Johns Hopkins by Dr. Alan Partin, the man who developed the Partin Tables (which is how prostate cancer is officially staged). I asked him to call me the minute he knew the results, but Alan tried to reassure me by saying, "Your chances of prostate cancer are maybe 18 percent." So I didn't stay up all night worrying.

The next day I was in surgery when Alan called the OR. A nurse held the phone up to my ear while I was operating, and that's how I got the news. Not only did I have prostate cancer, but the biopsy indicated a very malignant and aggressive form.

Somehow I was able to put that out of my mind and finish the operation.

Not until I was driving home that day did it hit me. I remember thinking, *Wow, my life may not be anywhere near as long as I thought it would be.* I began to think of all the people I was going to be abandoning: my wife, my three sons, my mother, my colleagues, my patients. I thought of things I'd started that I wouldn't be able to finish. What about my plans for expanding the Carson Scholars Fund? And Angels of the OR?

I was immediately scheduled for an MRI to make sure the cancer hadn't metastasized (spread elsewhere in my body). If it hadn't, I would be a candidate for surgery.

When I came out of the MRI machine, I saw no radiologist waiting to reassure me that everything looked okay. I considered that a bad sign. As I was leaving, the technician handed me an envelope containing my scans and said, "I thought you might like to have a copy."

I carried them to my office and stuck the film up on the lighted scan board mounted on the wall. My heart sank as I saw the series of lesions up and down my spine. I quickly double-checked the patient's name on the film. Unfortunately, it was mine.

I sank down in my desk chair and thought, *I really am going to die from this.* Carol, the physician's assistant who'd worked with me for twenty years, came in and asked, "What did it show?" (All day she'd been saying, "You know it's going to be negative.")

"It's there on the board," I told Carol. She headed over to look and then walked back toward my desk with the longest face imaginable. There was nothing left for her to say.

Somehow the word got out, because the very next day an area radio station reported that I had been diagnosed with cancer, a malignant brain tumor, they said. The subsequent flurry of follow-up reports in the local media claimed I had lung cancer, or colon cancer, or pancreatic cancer, or kidney cancer. You name it, I had it. I was dying. Or I had died already. One woman even called my office to say, "I heard Dr. Carson was dead. I want to speak to him!"

It was amazing! The news was immediately everywhere.

I had been hoping to keep the whole thing quiet, start treatment, and move on without anyone making a big deal of it. Clearly that wasn't going to be possible.

The *Washington Post* called. Their reporter told me they had been planning to do a series on me. "But *now that the timetable needs to move up*, maybe we could focus on the cancer." That seemed to be one way to clarify all of the rumors flying around, so I agreed to an interview.

For three days running, major articles appeared in the *Washington Post*, and many other news organizations picked up the story. I found myself doing a bunch of national television programs and radio programs about it.

But what I remember better than all the hoopla was getting up early on the Fourth of July. (I'd had the MRI just a couple of days earlier.) As I walked around our farm in the early morning light, I noticed how peaceful and beautiful everything looked. I heard the birds singing, and I thought, *I've really taken so much for granted in my life. I'm just going to enjoy all these beautiful things that God created.* I had always wondered how I would react when I was facing death, and I had such an amazing peace.

All of a sudden, very few things mattered. I began to appreciate life much more. I began to appreciate my loved ones much more. I began to appreciate God much more. I kept reassuring myself and those closest to me. *God doesn't make mistakes. So if I'm supposed to die, there's a very good reason for it. I'm not going to question him. It's okay.*

I confess, the thought of leaving my family behind was difficult to deal with. Sometimes I would wake up in the middle of the night and hear Candy sobbing. That was heart-wrenching.

Still, I had to face the reality of my situation. At best, I figured I had only five years ahead of me, and it promised to be a painful time—particularly the final year or so. I told the boys they were going to have to do all the heavy work from now on; I would no longer even ride the lawn mower. I was going to have to start using elevators. With the lesions where they were on my spine, it would be easy for me to get a compression fracture. A serious enough injury could mean I'd be a paraplegic.

I'd started thinking about all the changes I would have to make.

I planned to work until the pain became unbearable. Hopefully I could practice three or four more years, but long before the end I would need to start winding down—getting people's care transferred. I would try to keep speaking as long as I could. I felt I'd been given a new message to share; I was in a strong position to help other people realize how important it is to be vigilant about their health, to discover these things before something bad happens.

My case was unusual. Normally with aggressive forms of prostate cancer, your PSAs are significantly elevated, but there's an unusual variety where you can have advanced cancer without elevated PSAs. I had that variety. But if it could happen to me, it could happen to anyone. All the more reason for everyone to take good care of themselves and carefully monitor their health.

———

On a positive note, I was almost overwhelmed by the outpouring of goodwill and concern. In the wake of my diagnosis, I received mailbags full of cards and letters from across the globe—from janitors who worked at our hospital, from families of former patients, from President and Mrs. Bush—all saying they were praying for me. I believe the Lord heard those prayers. In fact, I suspect he got tired of hearing about me!

Six days following the MRI, after multiple consultations and second opinions, I received the wonderful news that the abnormalities that had shown up on the scan looking like cancerous lesions were actually congenital anomalies of the bone marrow, a completely benign condition. My prostate cancer had not metastasized after all.

In fairness to our chief of neuro-radiology at Johns Hopkins, when he'd looked at my scan a day or two after the MRI, he expressed doubts that the spots along my spine were cancer. But he wasn't 100 percent sure. So I started checking with other people until I reached an expert in metastic disease who confirmed the bone marrow anomaly and told me, "Many people get fooled by that. What looks so much like cancerous lesions is not."

So I was a candidate for surgery after all, if that was the route I chose to take. There were actually a number of treatment options available, each with its own risks. The decision would not be easy.

The surgical option carried the risk of nerve damage that could result in urinary incontinence and sexual dysfunction. But it also had the highest rate of success. Pat Walsh, who'd been my friend for twenty-five years, had pioneered the surgery. He's the expert people come to from all over the world for a radical prostatectomy, and I knew he'd take good care of me.

I also considered traditional radiation therapy. It wasn't quite as certain a cure, but it would not carry the same risk of nerve damage.

Then there was proton beam therapy—a newer technology available in only a few places around the country—which many people felt showed real promise for dealing with this kind of cancer.

The chief of radiology at Loma Linda in California called to offer their proton beam treatment. He even extended an invitation to stay in his home. "We have a guest suite that will be private and quiet. We'll get you in right away for treatment."

The various medical options were laid out, but they weren't the only possibilities I had to consider. Along with all those cards and letters I received, people were sending me teas, grasses, herbs, tonics, pills—you name the natural remedy and I got it. Other people sent literature and books with suggestions for my healing, and I read quite a bit of the material.

What really caught my attention, though, were glyco-nutrients. I read the background material and talked to a physician who had been in charge of some of the scientific studies behind glyco-nutrients and was going around the country giving lectures about them. So I read some of his work and reviewed other studies that had been done, and he sent me a whole case of the product. I decided to try it.

Within a week of starting a glyco-nutrient regimen, my symptoms completely resolved. I began to wonder if I might have another red clover tea situation on my hands. I gave serious consideration to forgoing the medical options, using glyco-nutrients instead and changing my dietary habits and seeing if that cured me. But I decided to do my risk analysis again at that point as I weighed the choice between surgery and what looked to me like a promising natural remedy.

The *best* thing that could happen if I went the traditional medicine route and had the surgery would be the permanent removal of the cancer. As long as the tumor was contained, the odds of a complete cure and a normal life expectancy were very good. Of all the medical options, it promised the lowest likelihood of recurrence.

The *worst* thing that could happen if I opted for surgery would be the risk of nerve damage that could leave me incontinent or impotent. Because of the expertise of the surgeon, however, the odds of suffering that nerve damage didn't seem high. Either way, if the cancer was contained, the tumor could be effectively removed, and I'd be cured of the cancer and should have a normal life expectancy.

The *best* thing that could happen if I opted for the natural dietary treatment is that I might be able to manage (perhaps even cure) the cancer *and* avoid any risk of nerve damage that had to be considered with the surgical option.

The *worst* thing that could happen if I chose to start a glyco-nutrient regimen would be that it might not arrest my cancer. While I was impressed enough by what I learned from my study to think the natural treatment had a reasonable chance for success, the odds for survival and longevity probably weren't as good as with surgery.

In part because of my previous experience with natural healing, I was still feeling torn. It wasn't until I looked again at the Best/Worst Analysis from an entirely different angle, and considered how my decision could impact *others*, that I found real clarity in my thinking.

When I asked, "What is the worst possible impact on other people if I decide against surgery with the idea of taking glyco-nutrients and reforming my eating and health habits?" I didn't like the answer. My case had already garnered so much public attention that I feared some cancer patients who were familiar with my story would say, "Dr. Carson didn't go with traditional treatments for his cancer, so I won't either. I'll take a natural healing approach like he did." The problem that scenario presented was that even if glyco-nutrients worked for me, others might not be so diligent with their dietary changes and their use of the nutritional supplements as I would be. So because they thought they were following my example, some people might possibly lose their lives. That was a risk I didn't want to take. (Indeed, using risk analysis to consider the implications of any decision, not just for one's self but for other people, is something responsible people should always do.)

I also had to consider what my decision would say to others about my colleagues and the place I work. If I'm in the institution with the number one urology department in the country, if I have access to the absolute best that traditional medicine has to offer, and I opted not to take advantage of it, what message would that communicate to the public?

When I got through with the analysis, I concluded that it made the most sense, for a variety of reasons, to have surgery. But I was in no hurry once I learned there was no indication the cancer had spread. We had a long-anticipated family vacation to Hawaii planned for August, so I wanted to put off any surgery until November, which would give me time to readjust my busy schedule.

But Pat Walsh, my urologist and my friend, told me, "You can put off the surgery until then if you want, but I have a feeling we might all regret it if you do." That was his gut feeling, not mine. But he was my doctor, so I decided to go with his instincts.

We scheduled the surgery in early August, as he suggested. It turned out that the cancer was within one millimeter of breaking through the capsule. If we had waited until November, it might have been too late. The cancer may well have metastasized by then.

Instead, Pat was able to completely resect the tumor and spare the nerves. My PSAs dropped to undetectable, which is the goal of therapy. I went back to work less than a month later cancer-free, anticipating a long and healthy life (although realizing recurrences are possible). But I'm well aware that if I hadn't been vigilant, if I hadn't paid attention to a relatively subtle change taking place in my body, my personal circumstances might be very different today.

In fact, sometime after my surgery, another doctor, the same age I am, approached me and confided that as a result of his first physical exam in fifteen years, he had recently learned he had prostate cancer. His PSAs were sky-high and the cancer had metastasized throughout his body. There could be no surgery for him. Radiation and hormone treatments were his best option, but that was basically nothing more than palliative care that might buy him three to five more years. He went out and bought himself a very expensive car—a model he'd always wanted.

At the same time my heart went out to my fellow physician, I couldn't help thinking, *That could have so easily been me.* And I felt grateful that I hadn't taken foolish or unnecessary risks with my personal health.

Yet many people do. A lot of people who should know better do. A lot of very smart people do.

Many careful, thoughtful, responsible individuals who would never think of embarking on a two-week traveling vacation without asking their mechanic to give the family car a quick once-over, without buckling the kids into safety seats, and without taking along a map of their route, nevertheless expose themselves and their families to much more serious peril because of huge risks they take with their health.

Too many people tell themselves, *I'm feeling good today, I'm healthy. Therefore I really don't need to pay that much money for health insurance. I can go without it for another two, three, four, five, six, ... ten years.* But something happens and leaves them in the lurch financially. Or because they don't have insurance that covers it, they aren't getting regular checkups, and something fairly common and treatable isn't detected until the condition is so advanced that medical science can't correct it. Then the quality of the rest of their lives is severely compromised.

Is that a risk worth taking? Do a quick Best/Worst Analysis for whether or not to carry health insurance. There are many *worst* scenarios unless you bite the bullet and do it. Yet how many people are willing to spend thousands of dollars on a Disney World vacation, then think they can't afford health insurance? How many people develop physical symptoms they know they probably should have checked out but then decide not to go to the doctor because they have a $25 co-pay?

Since I've just talked about my own experience with prostate cancer, let me ask: How many middle-aged guys out there know they really ought to be screened for prostate problems and have regular PSA tests, but don't because they'd rather not learn they have a problem that might necessitate surgery with the accompanying risk of potential nerve damage, impotence, and so on? Hey, guys, let me share what is evidently a too-little-known medical fact—there is a 100 percent chance of impotence if you're *dead*!

Far too many people, including a lot of doctors, use an asinine value system when considering what risks they are willing to take with their health. Please take the time and make the effort to do a serious B/WA on this subject. We're talking about your life.

I'm sorry if I come across as preachy on this subject, but my own up-close-and-personal experience with the risk of cancer has had a lasting impact by changing my perspective on so many things. I've maintained much of that heightened appreciation for the world around me that I experienced so vividly in those first days after my diagnosis. Walking around my property today, I still notice the subtle variations in the grasses and the colors of the wildflowers. I really listen to the arias of songbirds now, even as I watch the animal variety show taking place on various stages around the property. Squirrels cavorting around the trees. A herd of deer grazing peacefully in my neighbor's pasture. A red fox skulking through the trees at the edge of the woods. My dog bounding happily around me, oblivious to it all.

But it's not just nature that I have a deeper appreciation for. My experience has also given me a heightened appreciation for the people in my life. I know it has resulted in added understanding for my patients and greater empathy for all that their families are going through. If anything, it has given me a greater sense of dependency on and trust in God as well.

It has made me more determined than ever to wisely and carefully weigh a wide variety of other personal risks that I (and most people) encounter in everyday life. A number of which we'll consider in the next chapter.

Taking Yourself Out
of the Middle of Decisions

I HAD NEVER SOUGHT ANY ELECTED OFFICE IN MY LIFE UNTIL JUST A few years ago when the president of Yale University asked me to run for a position on the Yale Corporation board, the governing body of the school. When I was an undergrad on campus in the early seventies, we all thought of the Yale Corporation as a bunch of stuffy, old, rich white men. So it came as a bit of a surprise to be considered for membership in such a group.

I knew I should feel honored, but I needed to think about whether I really wanted to have my name placed on the ballot. One reason I'd never run for an elected position was that I had never relished the idea of losing—so by never running, I avoided that risk. In this case, since my two opponents on that ballot would include the president of one of America's largest and most prestigious universities and an experienced business executive who headed a rather significant company, I figured I didn't have a chance.

In weighing my decision, I did my usual Best/Worst Analysis.

What's the best thing that could happen if I run? Win or lose, I would know the honor of serving the school that provided me the educational direction of my life.

What's the worst thing that could happen if I run? I could suffer the embarrassment of loss.

What's the best thing that could happen if I don't run? I could avoid that embarrassment.

What's the worst thing that could happen if I don't run? I could disappoint those people I respected who felt I should run, and as a result I might never get such an opportunity again.

In the end I decided that the risk of losing, and any sense of embarrassment that went with it, should not determine my decision. So I swallowed my pride. There would be no real shame in losing an election in which the entire Yale family from around the world was invited to vote. Most of them didn't know me anyway and would probably make their ballot selection based mostly on the brief bios supplied for each candidate. If they decided on one of the other men, I wouldn't need to take that as a personal rejection. Both of the other candidates were extremely well qualified, and I probably would have voted for them myself.

So I agreed to run. In the end — *surprise, surprise!* — the Yale alumni elected me to represent them on the Yale Corporation board.

I felt bad for the other two worthy individuals who had lost, but I was excited about my opportunity to sit at the big table for the next six years to share my opinions and help make decisions about how to improve the educational experience at my alma mater. I consider my term with the Yale Corporation to be one of the most significant honors of my life, and it wouldn't have happened if I hadn't been willing to thoughtfully consider and accept a little personal risk.

That whole experience reinforced an important truth that I've seen validated many times over the years. It's this: Once we manage to remove our egos from the equation, many of the most commonplace and unsettling personal risks we face in life become a lot less personal and no longer seem to be much of a risk after all. That discovery frees us up to better concentrate on dealing with the real risks presented by truly important issues.

I've developed a simple means of remembering and applying this lesson in a variety of personal-risk scenarios. I call it "Taking Myself Out of the Middle." I've found this to be one of the most useful strategies for facing and reducing risk in my life, and it dovetails nicely with the kind of B/WA we have been talking about — particularly in the area of relational risks. Let me give some examples.

I first began to understand this principle in the wake of my angry attempt to stab my friend when I was a young teenager. I've already told how that incident terrified me into some desperate soul-searching and a life-changing appeal for God's help with my temper, and how my discovery of all those verses about anger in Proverbs convinced me that the Bible offers practical resources for living. Coming to grips with my temper also involved this important revelation — that one of the main reasons I was always angry was because I was always in the middle of the equation. But if I could somehow just step out of the center of the situation, I wouldn't get angry.

This was an invaluable insight, because I was one of those people who thought he had a lot of rights. Of course, the more rights you think you have, the more likely someone is going to infringe upon them. So even before the stabbing incident, I would get into fights and injure people. As I mentioned, one day I split a guy's scalp open when I hit him with a padlock. Then there was the time I got so angry that I started to hit my mother before my brother jumped in and stopped me. That's how irrational I would become.

Where I lived, angry explosions were often viewed as an accepted, expected, macho thing. You get angry, you kick down a wall or punch in a window, and it makes you into a big man. It wasn't until I backed off enough to take myself out of the center that I realized reactions like that were not signs of strength, but rather indications of weakness. Such reactions meant I was letting other people, the environment, or circumstances control me, and I decided I didn't want to be so easily controlled. But if I took myself, my rights, my ego, my feelings out of the center, I couldn't be.

From that point on, whenever I faced a potentially upsetting situation, I found it interesting — kind of fun even — to pull back and watch people try to make me angry. I sometimes made a game of it, and I discovered once I was able to take myself out of the center of the equation, to look at things from other people's perspectives and not feel that all the rights belonged to me, the things that could make me angry were suddenly few and far between.

What might have seemed at first glance to be like a risky strategy — this taking myself out of the center — actually made life a lot *less* risky.

Knowing that no one else had the power to make me angry was, in fact, an empowering feeling. It still is.

This strategy isn't just for those with anger issues. It's a useful tool in the broader and often risky realm of interpersonal relationships. Ask yourself, why are some people so shy? Why are some people so lonely? For many the answer is that they are afraid to take the risk of reaching out to others because they imagine how bad they will feel if those people reject them or respond in a negative way. That fear becomes a more powerful deterrent than the loneliness they feel.

As a person who is naturally reserved, I constantly tell myself to be friendlier, more outgoing, to take the risk of reaching out and interacting with other people. My natural inclination (my comfort zone) is simply to sit quietly in a corner and read or think about some philosophical issue. I am not particularly gregarious. But when I do a B/WA on the risk of interacting more with people, the answers make the decision a lot easier.

What's the worst thing that could happen if I'm more outgoing? I could have my feelings hurt by others' responses. I could be misunderstood.

What's the best thing that could happen if I make a regular attempt to connect with others? I could develop more friends and deeper relationships. Perhaps I could even be seen in a more positive light—as a warm and friendly person.

What's the best thing that could happen if I don't make more of an effort to be outgoing? I'll feel more comfortable, and I can content myself with my life and the relationships I have now.

What's the worst thing that could happen if I don't make an effort to connect with others? I could be perceived as unfriendly. I could eventually become a recluse and never develop the interpersonal skills I'd like to have, and so on.

So far these B/WA questions have centered on me and my perspective. They bring a new focus to my thinking and force me to realize that the issue is much deeper than my personal comfort level; it's actually about the kind of person I want to be. When I start thinking in those terms, my personal values come into play and help me determine how I want to deal with this particular risk.

But what happens if I go a step further and try to take myself out of the middle of the equation? What if I now ask:

From others' perspectives, what's the worst thing that could happen if I'm more outgoing? They could misunderstand me or my motivations for making an overture.

From others' perspectives, what's the best thing that could happen if I make a regular attempt to connect with them? They could see me in a more positive light—as a warm, friendly, approachable person. Others might be more interested in being my friend.

What's the best thing that could happen, from others' perspectives, if I don't make more of an effort to be outgoing? The best they could hope for is the status quo.

What's the worst impact on others if I don't make an effort to connect with them? I may fail to help those I encounter in life who are lonely and hurting, or who need some help or encouragement I might have to offer. I could gradually become a less caring, colder person whom others won't be willing to approach.

By taking myself out of the middle of the equation, I've found that it's a lot easier to overcome the natural reserve that makes it seem so uncomfortable, so risky to reach out to others. As I've worked at stepping out in these areas, I have learned that except for a very few people who are deeply wounded individuals or have pathological personalities, almost everyone appreciates a person who acts friendly and outgoing once they get over their suspicion and uncertainty about what I might want from them. If I am consistently warm and outgoing, the suspicion levels drop quickly and other people will almost always respond in kind. So the risk isn't as great as it seemed.

Here again a real key is to try to keep myself out of the middle of the equation and consider others' perspectives. Instead of focusing on what makes me comfortable, I try to consider what might put them at ease. The truth is, they will almost certainly feel more comfortable if I'm friendly and outgoing than if I'm reserved or stiff. And soon, so do I.

What about those people who don't respond when I say hello or who don't want to shake my hand when I offer it or who rebuff my overtures in some other way? Instead of dwelling on my own feelings of rejection, I try to identify with and feel for the other person who is being cool for some unknown reason. Perhaps they have suffered some deep emotional wound, are for some reason preoccupied with some serious concerns of their own, or are simply too insecure to accept my attempt at friendliness. If that's the case, their reaction shouldn't discourage me from making such attempts but should instead increase my resolve to reach out to them.

While my simple taking-myself-out-of-the-middle strategy has helped me become a more outgoing person, I acknowledge that my wife has been an even bigger factor. The first thing I noticed when I met her, and one of the things I've come to love and appreciate most about Candy, is her wonderfully warm way with people. Many people are outgoing, but Candy is always out there. When my natural tendency would be to avoid the risks of relationships by staying home and reading, my wife seems to embrace those risks in the same way she naturally draws other people into meaningful relationships. Many of the most wonderful friendships we've developed over the years have happened primarily because of her natural manner of reaching out. She has shown me the tremendous rewards that come from taking relational risks, and what I've learned from my wife about relationships goes far beyond the risk of friendship. She has taught me even more about the risk (and rewards) of love. And when you think about it that way, love truly does present the greatest relational risks of all.

In chapter 8 I gave a summary account of my meeting my wife, our courtship, and the early days of our marriage. What I didn't say was that before meeting Candy, I'd dated a few girls. But before things ever got serious enough to demand any real emotional vulnerability, I had always pulled back, and the relationship seemed to fizzle out. When I finally recognized that pattern, I made the conscious decision to try to cultivate the next potential relationship instead of resisting it. It just so happened that very next relationship was with Candy. I wouldn't call what I did a thorough B/WA, as I wasn't yet thinking in those terms at the time. But I did do something of a risk analysis.

What might be the downside of trying to cultivate that relationship? I'd suffer the pain of disappointment or rejection if it didn't work out.

The upside of taking the risk? I might find my soul mate, get married, and live happily ever after.

The best that could happen if I don't? I could end up a happy bachelor all my life if I don't eventually cultivate some relationship.

The worst result if I don't? I could end up a lonely, bitter person who regrets missing out on marriage and family.

Thinking about my situation in those terms not only made my decision an easy one, but gave me the determination to take the risk and do whatever it took to develop that relationship.

If ever that take-myself-out-of-the-middle strategy is of value, it's in marriage. In fact, I'm not sure any marriage can survive, let alone thrive, without each spouse learning and applying this principle on a regular basis. Anyone whose primary attitude and concern about their marriage is *What is it doing for me today?* is destined for divorce or a life full of disappointment.

I know that in a day when pop psychology preaches the preeminence of self—self-awareness, self-image, self-confidence, self-fulfillment, self-sufficiency—any suggestion of downplaying or submitting one's self might sound not merely *risky*, but emotionally dangerous and irresponsible. But it works. Candy and I have been married more than thirty years now, and I can tell you the risk was well worth it.

Of course, I realize many people have taken the risk of love and experienced great pain and heartache as a result. Indeed, any kind of love—romantic love, an altruistic love of others, or a love for God—involves risk, perhaps greater personal risk than anything else in life. But those who are unwilling or unable to take the risk of love end up risking something far greater because they miss out on the greatest rewards to be found in life.

I think at least part of my understanding and acceptance of the take-myself-out-of-the-middle strategy as a valuable relational tool resulted from some of my mother's teaching, especially her wisdom regarding what many people probably think would be some of the most difficult and risky relationships in America over the past couple of generations—interracial relationships.

While my brother, Curtis, and I tried to spare our mother by not telling her about some of the bigotry we encountered growing up, she knew better than we did about the attitudes we would have to deal with if we were going to have the kind of success she expected of us. "Even if you walk into an auditorium full of bigoted, racist people," she told us, "you need to remember—you don't have a problem. They are the ones who have the problem. Because when you walk in, they are all going to cringe and wonder if you're going to sit next to them. You can just sit wherever you want."

Mother was telling us in different words, *Take yourself out of the middle. Realize they are the ones with the problem, so let them worry about it.* That became a philosophy I've tried to carry through life. If someone has problems with how I look, that's too bad. Even if their attitude impacts me, it's their problem, not mine. By taking myself out of the middle, I find I don't have to invest my energies in their problem. I can concentrate on more important issues and on my own priorities.

Sometimes by taking myself out of the middle, I've been able to knock down stereotypes and improve interracial relationships at the same time. When I was an intern and would walk into any ward for the first time with my scrubs on, one of the nurses would invariably say something like, "Oh, you know, Mr. Jones isn't ready to be taken down to the OR."

I could have taken offense at her assumption that I was a hospital orderly. Instead, I would smile and simply reply, "That's nice. But I'm not here to transport anyone. I'm Dr. Carson. I'm an intern."

The nurse would suddenly turn eighteen shades of red and awkwardly begin to apologize. I might have blown up and chewed her out for racist stereotyping. But chances were the only black men in scrubs she'd ever seen on her ward had been orderlies, so why would she think anything different? Her response might have been based solely on experience and might not have reflected any bigotry on her part at all.

I could have blown up and chewed out any nurse not giving me the respect my position warranted. He or she probably would have felt awkward, embarrassed, or even angry every time we met after that. But I found that when I responded to a nurse's gaffe and tried to set that person at ease by being cordial in return, I had a relieved and grateful friend for life. What's more, those nurses made it a special point to treat me with respect from then on—and I'm guessing they didn't make the same mistake with the next black doctor who walked into their wards.

I'm well aware that there are injustices in the world that need to be openly addressed; some rights are worth the risk of standing up for. In a post–Civil Rights era when we've all been hypersensitized to the gravity of individual rights, I realize that talk like this may sound foolhardy at best. But I have found that what sounds risky in fact protects me from the pain of some discrimination—both imagined and real. Rather than making me weaker and more vulnerable, it frees and empowers me to focus my attention on bigger concerns, and it often enables me to improve interracial relationships, one relationship at a time.

Those who have read my books *Think Big* and *The Big Picture* may remember that part of the simple advice I often give on how to succeed includes the following:

> Be nice to people. Once they get over their suspicions about why you're being nice, they will be nice to you. And you can get so much more done when people are being nice to you and you're nice to them.

If you're not a nice person, I challenge you to try it for one week. What day is this? Okay, look at your watch and note the time. From this minute, till exactly one week from now, be nice to everybody. That includes your spouse. Everyone you encounter.

What will that mean? That means not talking about people behind their backs. I know that's going to be hard for some of you. It means not talking about people in front of their backs. It means if you see somebody struggling with something, help them. It requires putting yourself in the other person's place before you begin to criticize.

If the elevator door is open and there is only one space left, let someone else get on. It means when you're driving your car and someone puts a blinker on, don't speed up; slow down and let them in. It means speaking to people in the morning. When you get in the elevator say, "Good morning." Once people get over their initial shock, they'll be happy to talk with you.

Because that's what we are created to be—social beings. Humans are not meant to be isolated individuals who are always suspicious of everyone else. We're meant to be loving, relating, interacting creatures. Which you will soon discover if you try this experiment. You'll also find that being nice gets to be contagious if you do it.

Like friendliness or love, niceness can seem to be a huge relational risk—until you get used to it. Being nice can be difficult because it requires making yourself vulnerable, and most of us like to be in control. Whenever you try to be nice and make that first overture toward others, you have automatically surrendered control to them. Now they are the ones who get to react to what you have done. If they respond negatively, you can be hurt.

A lot of people are not willing to take that risk. Even though someone might be a generally friendly person, when he sees someone he doesn't know on the elevator, he is not going to say hello because, well ... what if the other person doesn't say hello back? What if that stranger thinks he's a weirdo?

Let's change the scenario. Suppose you're the only survivor of a plane crash in the desert. You are searching the horizon for some sign of civilization, wondering which way to start walking, when you spot a stranger coming toward you across the sands. Will you say hello? *Of course*—and you'll say a whole lot more than that. You're willing to take that risk because you realize you have much more to be concerned about than what strangers are going to think about your speaking to them.

My point is this: the perceived "risk" in being nice is often the result of being overly concerned about your ego. If you can take yourself out of the equation and put your ego concerns into perspective, you'll find it much easier to be nice and to reach out to others. If you stop and really think about it—which is what a thoughtful B/WA and the taking-yourself-out-of-the-middle strategy force you to do—you may quickly conclude that your own ego worries could and should be a lower-priority concern in most situations. Also, you'll undoubtedly find you can move through life more easily and more effectively if you don't have to worry about what everyone else is going to say and do—and its impact on you.

I encounter difficult, unhappy, even disagreeable people almost every day as I confer with the parents and grandparents of my young patients. It would be easy to dread or even resent those unpleasant interactions, but I have to stop and realize why these people are so testy. This is their baby, and something bad has happened to him. By the time they have been referred to me at Johns Hopkins, it's usually something seriously bad. *That's* what has them so scared, upset, and irritable. They aren't really angry at me.

Taking myself out of the middle helps me realize that most people who are ugly toward others don't really mean to be. They usually act that way not because they're inherently nasty, but because they are hurting. Some days I decide, *My goal in this next hour is to make someone who is grumpy feel better.* I make it a challenge. Try it yourself sometime. I think you'll find it adds an extra, fun dimension to your day.

Another example of how being nice works: I absolutely despise the attitude of some surgeons who yell at people and throw things. I've known doctors who never seem to be happy unless they have some nurse in tears or the resident shaking in his shoes. They seem to think they increase their stature by making other people feel smaller. They don't realize how much more effective niceness can be.

If you make a habit of being nice and develop a reputation as some-one who is pleasant to work with, whenever you need something, or appear the least bit disappointed in something, you have people fall-ing all over themselves wanting to try to solve the problem. If they've learned you are someone who doesn't easily get upset, you only have to get the least bit upset or frustrated about something for people to realize it's important. Whereas the person who is always blowing his top gets ignored after a while, just like the little boy who cried wolf.

Here again, the simple strategy of being nice—which is, in fact, one way of taking yourself out of the equation—only *seems* to be a precarious proposition. In my experience it has proven to involve such little risk because it pays off in multiple ways. That shouldn't surprise those of us who profess to be Christians. (Here's where faith and val-ues factor in again.) The appropriate wisdom is right there in the Bible for us to see and understand and use. Even the Ten Commandments, which could be considered God's basic rules for reducing the risk in any and all relationships, have a lot to say about keeping ourselves, our actions, our thoughts, and our desires out of the center of life's equa-tion. Often Christians use the Bible to support a proper alignment of life priorities: God first, others second, self third. Jesus had his own input on this idea with his teachings on the Golden Rule, the first being last, and the importance of servanthood. Taking yourself out of the middle of the equation is also a good description of what's required if we are going to commit ourselves to Christ and let God have central control of our lives.

Once we as Christians take ourselves out of the center of every situation, taking relational risks by reaching out to others ought to become second nature. At the very least, an authentic Christian faith ought to serve as real motivation to make better relationships our high-est priority. Wherever you stand in regard to faith, understanding the importance of relationships, being nice, and taking yourself out of the middle of every equation are invaluable lessons to learn and apply in all areas of life, including one of the most important relationships we'll ever enjoy in life—which we'll talk about in the next chapter.

15
Parenting Perils?

COULD THERE BE A MORE PERSONAL, LESS PREDICTABLE, HIGHER-stakes task in life than parenthood? Handing the car keys to your teenager and watching him or her pull out of the driveway for that very first solo outing has to make every parent's late-night top-ten worries list.

I will forever remember our third son, Rhoeyce's, earliest days behind the wheel. No sooner did we allow him to begin driving himself to school than he totaled the car by plowing into a tree after losing control while rounding a sharp curve on a rain-slick road. When I saw the car, I found it hard to believe anyone had survived the crash. Fortunately, Rhoeyce was fine.

Candy and I faced a potentially painful and difficult decision: we had to decide what consequences our son should face as a result of the wreck. We thought about telling him, "It's obvious that you're not ready to drive yet," and revoking his driving privileges. But he had already meekly accepted responsibility for his mistake, and he hadn't been speeding or deliberately driving in an irresponsible manner. He'd had little experience driving under rainy conditions, and he simply misjudged the effect that would have on his ability to control the car on a curve. While that was indeed a serious mistake, it was an understandable one for someone with his lack of driving experience.

We lectured him on the importance of staying alert, concentrating on the details of driving, and always trying to anticipate what could happen in any situation so that he could react early enough to avoid an accident. We also told him that everyone makes mistakes but that it was important to build on those lessons to make himself a better driver in the future.

Rhoeyce never seemed to resist our warnings. He acted appropriately sobered by his brush with death. Not only did he acknowledge his culpability, but we could tell how bad he felt about the car, the expense, the inconvenience, and the scare he gave us. So we decided, in part as a vote of confidence in our youngest son, to let him continue driving one of our other family cars.

A couple of weeks later, Rhoeyce rear-ended a vehicle that stopped suddenly in front of him. Once again he was neither speeding nor driving recklessly, but he obviously made another serious misjudgment in not leaving himself enough room to stop. And it *was* his second serious accident in less than a month.

Naturally some very earnest discussion took place in our home about the consequences of this latest offense. What you might not have expected was Rhoeyce's reaction. He announced he didn't want to drive anymore, that he'd be fine with someone driving him wherever he had to go.

I have to admit, at the rate he was going through family vehicles, that seemed like an appealing option. Considering the seriousness of Rhoeyce's mistakes, revoking his driving privileges, for however long, seemed a justifiable response. And because he was so willing to accept that consequence, it also seemed like a simple solution. The punishment would certainly fit the crime.

But if ever a situation required some careful risk analysis, this was it. So Candy and I discussed the issue thoroughly.

What is the best thing that could happen if we don't let Rhoeyce drive? We might well improve the odds of keeping our son alive long enough to reach adulthood.

What is the best thing that could happen if we let him continue to drive? He could learn from these two experiences, become a very competent and safe driver, and maybe even develop some new self-confidence in the process.

What is the worst thing that could happen if we suspend his driving privileges? He could lose so much self-confidence that he would choose never to drive, might not learn the lessons of responsibility that come with driving, and, in either of those two cases, severely limit himself for the rest of his life.

What is the worst thing that could happen if we allow him to drive? He might have another accident and be killed.

That quick and simple B/WA certainly focused our thinking on the stakes involved, but we needed to consider a lot of secondary factors to arrive at a decision we could feel good about. I realize that some people might look at this B/WA, weigh the two accidents, and conclude that any risk of being killed has to trump everything else and makes the decision simple: don't let him drive. But here's where values, knowledge, and added perspective need to come in.

Rhoeyce's life was indeed my ultimate concern. But given my own values, and particularly my high regard and consideration for human potential, I see anything that might thwart that as a serious life threat as well. So we needed to factor in what we knew about our youngest son. Growing up in our household, often overshadowed by (and always in the footsteps of) two high-achieving older brothers, Rhoeyce had become a quiet, laid-back, and reserved young man. Reluctant to exercise his considerable talents to voluntarily take on responsibility, he seldom asserted any real leadership among his peers. So when I considered the B/WA questions from his perspective, I became concerned about how our decision would affect him. The accidents had already done a number on his self-confidence; that any teenage male would voluntarily announce his willingness to have his parents or siblings drive him where he needed to go convinced me of that. If we now told him we had concluded he wasn't ready to assume the responsibilities that come with driving, how would that affect his psyche? In effect we'd be saying, "Your brothers were ready at your age, but we don't think you are." What would that do to a kid whose basic personality had already been shaped in such large part by his own lifelong, unavoidable comparisons of himself with his older siblings? Might this be a final nail in the coffin, ending any prospect of his maturing into the self-assured, potential-reaching person we always hoped he would be? That would be a pretty significant *worst* in my book.

As is often the case, none of the B/WA answers could be answered with absolute certainty. Even saying the *best* that could happen if he didn't drive was that we'd protect him and keep him alive was no sure thing. He could be killed in an accident when someone else was driving. And when it came to the *worst* that could happen if he continued to drive (that he could have another wreck and be killed), steps could be taken to reduce the likelihood of that.

Finally, after much discussion—trying to weigh all of the risks, looking at our options from every perspective, and considering all of the relevant factors—we decided Rhoeyce needed to be responsible for getting himself to and from school and anywhere else he needed to go. We instructed him again on the importance of complete concentration when driving, the need to anticipate, and the value of caution. But we also explained our reasoning, assured him that we believed he had the skills and maturity to become a safe driver, and proved our faith in him by handing him the keys to yet another (older) family car.

I realize some people hearing about this decision may have thought that we were making a serious mistake, that Rhoeyce was not being held accountable, or that he was a spoiled youngest child. Other parents might have done the same B/WA and come to a different decision— for good reasons. A lot of subjectivity is involved in any risk analysis because everyone weighs factors differently. If Rhoeyce had been a cocky kid or hadn't been willing to accept responsibility for his own actions, I might have cut up his license myself. Certainly if he'd been speeding or if alcohol had been involved, there would have been very different consequences.

But subjective factors don't negate the value of doing a B/WA. We can't expect to identify *the* perfect response for every risky situation in which we find ourselves. What a B/WA does is force us to think in a manner that can help us reach an acceptable and reasoned decision in the most complex and emotionally wrought situations.

In Rhoeyce's case, I think we made the right call. That was five years ago, and he has never been in another accident; in fact, he's never even gotten a ticket. He's not only become an excellent, safety-conscious driver, but also matured into a more outgoing, responsible, and self-assured young man who is pursuing a nontraditional career path. He was confident enough to risk living on his own overseas for a time to experience a different culture and to learn a different language (Japanese) that he thinks will benefit him the rest of his life.

How different might our son and his future prospects be if we'd made the decision not to let him drive? There's no way to know for sure. I just know it wasn't a risk I wanted to take, and a careful B/WA helped us come to that conclusion.

Poets, psychologists, and pundits have often tried to describe the dual challenges of parenthood. You've probably come across the same images I have—how parents need to provide children with roots and wings, shield them then shove them, hold them tight until we learn to let them go.

However you describe it, parenting seems to demand of us two seemingly conflicting assignments: protecting and pushing. When our children come into the world as babies, they need our protection and care. But when it comes time for them to begin making their own way in the world, they may require encouraging, equipping, and sometimes even a healthy push to take off and live their own life. Both halves of our parental duty represent enormous responsibility and risk.

Adolescence, that troublesome transition time when our two primary missions overlap, may be the riskiest time of all for parents *and* children. If parents relinquish their protective role too early, there is enormous risk because kids won't have the judgment necessary to avoid the greatest dangers of life. But parents who wait too long or never shift to push mode may hinder the chance of their children's becoming independent, responsible, mature, and emotionally healthy adults. It's a precarious tightrope act parents must perform, with serious risks looming if we lean too much either way.

Before we consider those parenting risks, let me say this. What follows here, and anything I have to share on this subject, reflects these basic personal convictions:

- Parenting is the most important job most of us will ever have.
- No parent can protect a child from every risk our dangerous world holds, and we shouldn't try, because
- there is such a thing as acceptable risk,
- and the kind of risk analysis we've been talking about can be an invaluable tool for parents and kids facing a variety of common issues.

Greatest Responsibility

One of the biggest risks in parenting today is all the other parents who are not doing it. Too many biological mothers and fathers have abdicated their nurturing, disciplining, instructing, inspiring, and guiding roles by forfeiting them to day care, schools, churches, peers, media, or society at large. Such parental irresponsibility puts their children and their children's future at risk.

As a society and as individual parents, we ought to do a B/WA on this crisis. What's the worst thing that's going to happen if we don't change this growing trend? The best? What's the best and the worst we can expect if we do? At least that would get us thinking and talking, which we might feel more compelled to do if we stop and realize that from our perspective as parents, we will probably have more influence on the lives of our children than on anyone else we encounter in life. Everything we know from psychology confirms that from our children's perspective, we are the most significant people in the world. Whether that's good or bad depends largely on what we do with that awesome responsibility.

No Risk, No Chance

The horrendous slaughter of five innocent young Amish girls in their little country schoolhouse made headlines during the last days I was working on this book. What made that story all the more shocking was the realization that if such a thing could take place in the peaceful, picture-postcard, Old World setting of Lancaster, Pennsylvania, it truly could happen anywhere. It was a terrifying reminder for many parents today that it's impossible to shelter children from all of the risks our dangerous modern world throws at us.

Although some people try.

Schoolteachers have coined a new term to describe those people: *helicopter parents*. They are the ones who are always hovering (literally and figuratively) nearby—watching, worrying, and waiting to swoop down and rescue a son or daughter from any and all perceived threats to his or her physical, emotional, relational, or spiritual well-being. Reports from those in higher education indicate an alarming number of these interfering parents continue the practice at the college level, calling "on behalf of" their college-age sons and daughters to appeal test grades, to work out schedule conflicts, even to register complaints about interpersonal conflicts with a roommate. College administrators are shaking their heads in dismay over this troubling new trend toward increasingly inappropriate parental intrusion into their young adult children's college experience.

Recently our pediatric neurosurgery department at Johns Hopkins received a request that I attributed to that same overly protective mentality. We were asked by a safety group whether we'd be willing to say that kids riding tricycles ought to wear helmets. As far as I know, there has been no recent surge in the number of serious head traumas sustained by preschoolers falling off tricycles. Yet these proponents of helmets argued such a requirement would help young children develop the habit of wearing helmets so that when they graduated to a two-wheeled bike, it wouldn't seem like such a foreign concept.

I couldn't believe the range of opinion and serious discussion this issue prompted among members of our department. Some argued that helmets would obviously reduce the chances of serious injury; others eventually conceded, "It's probably best just to go with the helmet recommendation, because if we don't and someone gets hurt, they can say, 'You were the ones who didn't think tricycle riders needed to wear helmets.'" As the argument shifted focus from the risk for kids riding trikes to our own legal exposure if we didn't recommend helmets, the discussion moved from what's logical to what's litigious.

My sentiments on the subject paralleled what I say in my post-op visits with moms or dads who instinctively want to wrap their child up in an egg crate to prevent any additional injury during recovery. I say to those parents, "You have to let kids be kids. There may be a few reasonable things you can do, but for the most part you're not going to be able to stop them anyway.

"If you try too hard, if you're overly protective, you could make them into paranoid, ineffective individuals. And that's not going to be satisfactory for either you or them. Human beings, especially little ones who haven't yet had the characteristic stifled, are natural explorers and highly motivated by a terrific sense of curiosity. If you want to picture a miserable person, imagine a child who has no curiosity about anything—who is so wary of getting hurt that she sits there like a lump of clay. What a horrible existence!"

So in our trike-helmet discussion, I sided with the folks who argued *against* wearing helmets and instead advocated allowing children to become accustomed to the idea of taking reasonable risks to foster their adventuresome spirit. In my B/WA thinking, that's a pretty good *best* outcome for not wearing helmets. Combining that with my *worst* result of wearing helmets (I think it would be terribly sad to teach five-year-olds to be as wary of falling as a ninety-year-old should be) made it easy for me to settle on my position.

I've seen enough tragic head trauma in my career that I don't thoughtlessly dismiss the argument of those who say, "If we could prevent one child from suffering, we should." But where do we stop? More kids probably come into ERs every year with head injuries from falling off beds than off trikes. Do we next recommend children wear helmets when they sleep? While we're at it, why not recommend they wear goggles to prevent something from getting in their eyes? Maybe just order them little yellow bio-hazard suits to protect them from everything. But that might make it harder to ride tricycles without catching the pant legs in the spokes and risking a tear in the suit or a dangerous fall. On and on it goes, and the absurdity sometimes doesn't become apparent until you consider the extremes—which sometimes come to light in a *best* and *worst* analysis.

B/WA for Parents

Better risk analysis skills could benefit parents dealing with all manner of worrisome situations and trying to decide what's best for their children. Let's consider a few random issues as examples.

School Choices

For years I've publicly expressed concern about some of the current shortcomings of our American education system that I believe put the future of our children and our nation at risk. I've invested a lot of my own time and money trying to address the problem (more on that a little later), so I empathize with the dilemma facing parents trying to decide whether to opt out of public education altogether. This is definitely another of those parenting predicaments where various families facing the same issues come (for different reasons) to different conclusions about what would be best for their children.

The number of families who are homeschooling is skyrocketing. Private schools are also attracting more of our best and brightest. Many parents will tell you they chose these alternatives because they're afraid to send their kids to public school. They read stories like the Amish schoolhouse tragedy cited earlier, and they lose sleep worrying that some wacko with a gun will show up in their child's classroom one day.

A bit of careful risk analysis would indicate that particular fear isn't a logical basis for their decision. A child is at far greater risk of dying in an auto accident while driving the extra miles to and from a private school each day than of being killed in some Columbine-type incident. Far more kids get hurt and die at home, victims of a wide range of accidents, than are violently killed or injured at school.

So if fear of violence is your motivation, you need to rethink your B/WA. If you're concerned about the comparative quality of the education children are receiving today, however, that's a very valid concern to factor into your thinking. Consider this: 80 percent of American sixth graders cannot locate the United States on a world map. One in seven recipients of a high school diploma lacks minimal reading skills. (That could explain why 20 percent of U.S. adults can't understand the directions on a bottle of aspirin.) Odds that a U.S. high school graduate will be able to pass a seventh-grade arithmetic test: 50/50. (Which may explain why, according to the U.S. Department of Education, only half the adult population can make sense of a train or bus schedule.)

In my mind, facts like these indicate a far greater risk to our children and their future than any madman with a gun. So we need to be careful when assessing risks and making difficult parenting decisions regarding our kids to somehow make sure we apply rational thought processes. If we allow fear to trump reasoning, we all become victims.

The best way I know to avoid that is to make the effort and take the time to become informed and do a careful Best/Worst Analysis.

Spiritual Considerations of an Education

I talk to a lot of Christian parents who want to factor in spiritual concerns along with matters of safety and quality of education when considering the risks of where to send their kids to be educated. They try to weigh the advantages of a Christian education that incorporates the most important values of their faith against the risk of exposing their students to the non-Christian—and increasingly anti-Christian—values so common in a secular education.

During my final years of high school, many people in our church suggested I go to a Christian college. "You don't want to go to Yale," they warned. "You'll wind up being corrupted and terrible things will happen."

I didn't think that was a big risk, however, because I was solidly grounded in my convictions and beliefs. As it turned out, alcohol, drugs, partying, sexual promiscuity, and other common college-age enticements were never a serious temptation for me. With my personal radar warning system, there was no way anybody was coming close to me with any of that stuff. My spiritual faith and convictions grew deeper rather than weaker during my college years because of my involvement with a wonderful local church.

I'm not saying everyone should do what I did. The risks would be different for different people, so I think you have to make that choice based on a variety of factors. As a young person, you have to know yourself; as a parent, you have to know your children and what kind of relationship they have with God, as well as how easily they are influenced by others. All of those things are important considerations.

Bear in mind, I graduated from an urban public school before heading off to Yale. I'd been exposed to all sorts of temptations and peer pressure. Maybe if I had grown up in a more sheltered environment and college was going to be my first exposure to a broader world, the experience might have presented more of a risk.

Parents have to realize that somewhere along the line, our children have to exit any sheltered environment—family, home, church, school—we attempt to provide them. So it's vitally important for parents to spend what time and resources we have not merely to *protect*, but to *prepare* our children for all they will encounter when they venture beyond our limited and temporary defenses.

How do we do that? How can we prepare them to survive in a dangerous world full of risks—both known and unknown?

Three things we as parents can and must do come to mind.

Instill Right Identity

Risk-resistant young people require a solid sense of self-identity, because that's the bedrock foundation necessary for building strong character. So our most important job as parents may well be to make certain our children know who they are, what they believe, and where they are going.

What they believe is central, because beliefs and values shape and bring understanding to the rest of human identity, helping us see who we are (how we came to be and how we fit into this world) and where we are going (what our purpose and goals ought to be).

Parenting without providing our children a reasonable, workable, tested value system is like putting them alone on a sailboat somewhere off of Boston and expecting them to find their way to England—without a compass, a sextant, or GPS. What happens once a sailboat gets out of sight of land, when the wind changes and all you can see is ocean and sky in every direction? You are suddenly in big trouble. Your risk goes up enormously without a compass or some other directional system.

The same is true of life.

When we ship our kids off to college or launch them into the world, they need an anchor that keeps them from being blown hither and yon by every little wind that comes. They need reference points that will enable them to steer clear of dangers and maintain a course that will take them to their desired destination. Without a working compass, they will be either lost or dependent on someone (or everyone) else's reckoning. I don't believe God gave us such wonderfully complex brains to simply look at somebody else's compass or drift aimlessly through life without purpose or direction. Of course, if we want to provide a viable guidance system for our children, we have to have one of our own and be able to understand the value of those beliefs. If we don't, we're sending forth our next generation on a very risky expedition indeed.

My own faith values play a beneficial role in my parenting. What is true for me, and for a lot of parents who enjoy a prayer relationship, is that regular communication with God through prayer results in an added sense of confidence about enacting our values and ideals. That confidence comes through to others. Children can detect a lack of confidence, so if we hope to instill foundational values in them, it's important that we honestly project an assurance about what we believe. When I prayerfully go to the Lord seeking wisdom and direction, the settled feeling that results serves me and my family well. Plus, what I always tell the parents of my patients the night before surgery—that I've never known worry to help and if we all say our prayers, we'll have less to worry about tomorrow—I have found to be true in all manner of parenting situations.

Provide Tools to Use

Long before they reach the risky teenage years, kids are capable of learning and using a basic B/WA as a simple decision-making tool. You can make it a natural part of growing up. When they ask permission to do something, you can go through the questions with them as a means of helping them understand your reasoning for making a certain decision. Eventually, as you feel good enough about their answers, you can begin to let them make decisions for themselves. I think you'll soon discover kids can be smarter and wiser than we often give them credit for. Doing regular risk analysis with our kids will not only introduce them to a practical tool that will serve them well in the future, but also help us recognize, address, and reduce the risks they face today. It's a great way to open up discussion on a wide variety of topics.

We've all heard horror stories about sexual predators using the Internet to find unsuspecting victims. So when your eleven-year-old daughter wants to go online and set up her own site on MySpace.com, you would do well to conduct a B/WA of your own. Then help her answer the best/worst possibilities questions before making any decision.

Before kids leave for college, a few good B/WA discussions would be more effective than telling them to "just say *no!*" to any number of temptations. What's the risk of being alone in a dorm room with a member of the opposite sex? Do a B/WA on that. I've told my boys, don't be lounging around on a bed with a girl, even if you're just watching a video and even if all the other kids are doing it. Those are the kinds of things that get your guard down and make it easier to cross established boundaries into riskier territory. And those are the kind of commonsense insights our kids are more apt to arrive at on their own if we help them make a habit of doing a simple B/WA, because such analysis forces them to think. The vast majority of teenagers who get in trouble do so not because they are bad kids, but because they don't think.

Consider the true story of one sharp seventeen-year-old inner-city kid, an honor student, a competitive diver good enough to draw the attention of coaches at one prestigious East Coast university willing to offer him a full ride. One night he was riding in a car with his cousin, who had picked up a couple of gang-banger friends. They decide to cruise another gang's turf. To announce their presence, they hand this kid a shotgun and order him to fire out the window as they pass through the heart of their enemies' neighborhood.

If he does even the most cursory of B/WAs, the decision will be easy. *What's the best thing that can happen?* It's hard to even think of a *best* thing under those circumstances. *The worst thing?* Tragically, the *worst* thing imaginable is what actually happened. An innocent bystander, whom that boy claims he never saw, was killed. My coauthor on this book covered the young man's death-sentence trial in an Illinois court years ago.

If that kid had for one moment seriously considered the *best* and *worst* possibilities, there wouldn't even have been a comparison. Yet how many kids never stop to make that analysis? How many smart kids, by not thinking in the heat of one moment, end up ruining the rest of their lives?

Consider another sad case the cable news channels highlighted and rehashed for months during the time I was working on this manuscript. A bright and attractive teenage girl from a well-to-do suburban family goes with a big group of her high school friends on a senior class trip to Aruba. Their last night on the island, when the teens go to a popular local nightspot for a final celebration, the girl slips off alone with three young men and is never heard from again (as of this writing anyway).

The details of her disappearance are sketchy, and so far no one has been able to prove what happened to that young woman. But one thing I'm pretty sure of—if Natalee Holloway had done a simple B/WA that night before she walked out into the darkness with three men she didn't know, none of us ever would have heard her name.

Allow Appropriate Risk

Newsweek ran a thought-provoking article several years ago about teenagers and risk, and its premise should be instructive to parents. The gist of the piece—supported by extensive quotes from psychologists, much anecdotal illustration, statistics, and research—was this: since risk-taking is an almost universal trait of adolescence, the wisest strategy for parents (and society) is to offer teenagers controlled, acceptable risk-experiences.

Their argument and advice made a lot of sense. Adolescence at best is an awkward transition time between childhood and adulthood, dependence and independence. It's also much longer today than it was in the earlier agrarian world, when a boy proved himself a man at the point when he could shoulder and share adult hardships, risks, and responsibility working side by side with his father in the fields. By the time he was a seasoned seventeen or eighteen, he was ready to start his own family. A girl became a woman by the time she reached child-bearing age; fourteen or fifteen was often considered old enough to marry. The transition from childhood to adulthood was so short that adolescence — at least as the distinct stage of life we now consider it — hardly existed. If it had, the trials and adversity of everyday life usually delivered testing and risks enough to challenge and content the most adventuresome youth.

Today those traditional determinations of adulthood — the establishment of occupation and family — are routinely postponed until after college. With the period of childhood innocence seeming shorter and shorter, we've created a new ten-or-twelve-or-more-years-long designation, a no-man's-land (or no-woman's-land) we term *adolescence*. Over the past half century or so, this new limbo-land life stage has become an extended period of awkward uncertainty for teenagers who are still driven by human nature to establish, discover, and prove who they will be and where they will fit into an adult world. How will they do that? By exploring, experimenting, practicing, and testing all manner of new experiences — and dealing with the incumbent risks is an essential part of the process.

The central conclusion of the *Newsweek* article was that teenagers, by nature, are risk-takers. The most troublesome and dangerous teen behavior — everything from alcohol and drug abuse, to gang involvement, to promiscuous sex, to reckless driving — is merely proof of the fact. But by providing teens more acceptable, controlled risks, parents and society can reduce the chances our kids will engage in such self-destructive behavior.

More of us might encourage our kids to participate in activities such as rock climbing and white-water rafting if we weighed the risks of that against the odds of our child's acquiring a sexually transmitted disease or becoming another teenage drunk-driving fatality. But there are many other acceptable risks that hold less danger to life and limb. Public performance of any kind—music, drama, dance, sports—presents some degree of risk for all who participate. There's always the risk of failure and embarrassment, and there's the risk of time and effort invested in practice. The responsibilities of an after-school job can mean mastering new skills with new risks in terms of time management. Church mission trips and service projects can get kids out of their comfort zones and provide a real sense of adventure and acceptable risk. Any novel activity that challenges and pushes the envelope of a teenager's experience and potential might fill the bill, but especially those in which the risk of failure and disappointment is every bit as real as the chance for success.

As parents we'll never be able to create a risk-free life for our teen-agers. But we can equip them to better deal with the dangers and uncertainties they will encounter for the remainder of their lives if we provide them with basic risk-analysis tools and encourage them to pursue and enjoy activities that expose them to acceptable risks.

Two quick stories. The first involves a carpenter who volunteered to go to the Mississippi Gulf Coast with a relief team from his church immediately following Hurricane Katrina. When his junior high–aged son wanted to go along, this father told his wife, "Everyone says condi-tions down there are terrible. It's complete devastation. What if some-thing happens, and he gets injured or catches some disease? I'd never forgive myself." But after they thought and talked a bit more about the *best* that could come of the experience and weighed it against the *worst* that could happen, this couple decided the risk paled in com-parison to the potential reward. Father and son went and had such a wonderfully memorable and meaningful time meeting and helping people in desperate need, that they went again a few weeks later and brought the mother and sister along for the experience. For them the acceptable risk was definitely worth it.

The second story involves another couple with similar family val-ues. These concerned, involved parents had a beautiful daughter in her last year of high school who wanted to take a special senior trip with three of her girlfriends. The four girls thought it would be a blast to go to Rio de Janeiro during Mardi Gras. I don't know what, if any, discussion took place (this was the year after the Holloway case), but the decision was made to let the girl go with her friends. They went, they came home safe, and as far as I know, nothing regrettable happened. But when I heard about it, my reaction was "No way! What were those parents thinking?"

That's the problem, I concluded. *They weren't thinking.* If they had done a good B/WA, maybe they would have made a different decision. They might even have come up with a more acceptable risk for their daughter than spending five days and nights in Rio with her teenage friends during Mardi Gras—unchaperoned.

That brings me to my final observation about parenting our kids in a risky world: the most useful weapon we have in this daunting task is the marvelous brain we've each been given. So the first order of business may be for us parents to use ours to teach our kids to use theirs.

16

Public Risk
(and the Beginning of Some Solutions)

You don't have to be a doctor to spot the symptoms — fear, frustration, stress, impotence, discouragement, even despair—rampant in American culture today. A quick review of the patient's history and pathology reveals even more reason for alarm. What we see all around us may be clear evidence of a serious societal overexposure to risk.

Probable cause? We live and work in a dangerous world.

The diagnosis? A new, or perhaps just mutating, human strain of risk disorder. It's usually a persistent, low-grade, chronic complaint, intermittently manifested in acute flare-ups triggered by sudden changes in environmental conditions and circumstances. The body's (anybody's or everybody's) inability to properly process risk is often accompanied by mild to moderate cases of risk aversion. Left untreated, the condition can result in serious, sometimes even total, paralysis.

My prescription? I'm tempted to say, "Take two risks and call me in the morning," but I know of no quick cures for this malady.

I believe, however, that the basic treatment plan we've been talking about in this book, the simple approach to risk I've found helpful in my life and work, holds promise. Based on my observations and experience, I'm hopeful that through the acceptance, familiarity, and mastery of risk in our professional and private lives, we will discover the incentive, the know-how, and the resources to tackle some of the most troublesome issues that threaten our broader society.

Let me describe two case studies in which I've seen this happen:

Educational Failings

For years I've regularly cited a 1992 survey measuring the ability of eighth-grade students in twenty-two countries to solve complex math and science problems. The United States ranked twenty-one out of twenty-two, barely beating out one nonindustrialized Third World country. Another study conducted six years later, comparing top American high schoolers with the "cream of the crop" in other industrial nations, showed U.S. students dead last in advanced physics, next to last in advanced mathematics, and close to the bottom in most other categories.

If you shrug off the significance of such survey results as artificial and alarmist, consider these more recent real-world statistics. In 2004, U.S. institutions of higher learning graduated a total of 60,000 engineers—40 percent of whom were foreign. Meanwhile, China produced 392,000 of its own.

Don't you think maybe someone ought to do a B/WA on this issue?

What's the best thing that can happen if this trend continues? We will soon have to import a lot of technical talent to handle most of the high-tech jobs we have in America, or we will have to outsource more and more technical jobs to countries like India.

What's the worst thing that can happen if this trend continues? Not only might our economy be crippled, but our nation could soon lose the leadership position we have had in the world for the past century.

What's the best that can happen if we manage to reverse this trend? By regaining strength here, we are much more likely to maintain our position as the world's only remaining superpower and the accompanying platform from which we can better provide not only a strong diplomatic, military, and economic presence, but also an example of democratic values, humanitarianism, and moral leadership for nations around the globe.

> *What's the worst thing that can happen if we try to reverse this trend?* We fail and the same thing happens as would happen if we don't try to reverse it.

You don't have to think about this B/WA very long to decide that these risks merit serious concern. Though I love and respect the immense potential in the people of India, China, Korea, and other places, I feel we in the United States must find a way to maximize our intellectual talent because we occupy a special place in the world. Our nation is, in a sense, the child of every other nation. Since we are made up of people from all of the other nations, I believe we have a special obligation to help lead the rest of the world rather than just follow it. If our technological strength lags as we move through the twenty-first century, our resulting national decline will create a vacuum of leadership that can only exacerbate the growing instability we see in the world today.

My wife and I became so concerned about this issue that we decided to try something aimed at helping keep our nation in a position of leadership far into the future. To do so, we launched a national scholarship program—the Carson Scholars Fund—for young people that would emphasize their tremendous intellectual potential and their positive humanitarian qualities as well. A lot of advisors tried to discourage us. They told us there were already thousands of scholarship programs—that there was no way we would be able to distinguish ourselves in a meaningful way. They warned us that the vast majority of nonprofit scholarship organizations fail.

I refused to be discouraged. If I'd listened to all the people in my life who have told me something couldn't be done, I certainly wouldn't be where I am today—personally or professionally.

Candy and I considered the possibility of failure, but we believed the potential benefits far outweighed the risks. From the start we knew we had to work hard if there was any hope of succeeding. I must say that Candy was a superstar in putting together the infrastructure of an organization, paving the way for an excellent board of directors made up of some extremely smart people we'd gotten to know over the years.

We awarded twenty-five $1,000 scholarships our first year. By 2006, our tenth year, we gave out more than five hundred scholarships. The program has spread to sixteen states and D.C. and has honored more than 2,800 scholars. The program won the Simon Award for nonprofit leadership in 2005 and the Ronald McDonald House Award the year before that—both honors coming with substantial financial awards.

Despite the doubts of early advisors, our program has distinguished itself not just for what we do as a scholarship fund, but for how and why we do it. Our philosophy grew out of my awareness of world history and the recognition that those pinnacle nations that preceded us all began their decline to irrelevancy when they lost their moral compass and became enamored with sports, entertainment, and the lifestyles of the rich and famous. Convinced America today is heading down that same pathway, almost as if we're a civilization of actors reading and following a script, we determined to create a program designed specifically to correct this ruinous course.

Whenever I visited or spoke at schools around the country, I noticed all the trophy cases in the hallways honoring athletes. While there's nothing wrong with that, I wondered what might happen if every elementary, middle, and high school in the country made as big a deal over its top academic stars.

So that's what the Carson Scholars Fund set out to do. Not only do we honor our recipients every year at big regional banquets, but they are recognized before their peers at school with nice awards to take home, their names permanently engraved in the school display case, and a $1,000 scholarship.

One of the distinctives of our program is that we recognize and promote young people (starting in the fourth grade) for superior academic performance and a demonstration of humanitarian qualities as we try to make them role models for other children. Our thinking was that fourth and fifth grade is often when the divergence starts and many kids begin heading in a wrong direction. Most scholarship programs start too late to influence a great number of kids who are already so far down the wrong path they are never coming back. We've found that when we give $1,000 awards to fourth, fifth, and sixth graders in front of their peers, it is such a big deal that everybody sits up and takes notice. Suddenly, instead of being the class nerd or the class geek, they are now the big man or woman on campus.

Some of these kids win year after year as they progress through school. But every year, whoever wins the award serves as an honored role model, inspiring others to pursue higher academic achievements. By the time they graduate, our winners are so sharp most of them have won multiple scholarships from numerous sources. But their Carson Scholar Award will always be remembered proudly because it was often their first—the one that convinced them (and their peers) that they were really somebody special.

Not only do we hand each graduating winner a scholarship of $1,000 plus interest for each award, but we enjoy the satisfaction of knowing our involvement with them over the years has helped them achieve the role of leaders in their schools and has made a substantial impact on the kind of adults who will populate and lead our nation in the future.

As our program grows to a national scale, it is the intention of the board to create an army of bright young people (candidates must have a minimum 3.75 GPA on a 4.0 scale) who demonstrate significant community involvement. Then by networking this army together and initiating various opportunities for them in terms of service and employment, they, and the ripple effect they have had on their peers for years, will have begun to close the current academic achievement gap between America and the rest of the industrial world—particularly in science and math.

You may think the goal sounds impossibly ambitious. Complex issues like this often seem so daunting that most people won't even think about it. They feel overwhelmed by the magnitude. But in my mind that's all the more reason for something like the Carson Scholars program. I want to nurture future leaders who not only are bright but also care about helping other people meet the greatest challenges that face them. If we start fostering and developing leadership and achievement in young people now, we may yet produce an abundant enough crop of capable leaders to tackle whatever new challenges and risks America will face in the future.

High hopes to be sure. But we're already seeing promising results—not just in the increasing numbers of Carson Scholars, but in the individual quality of character already demonstrated by our recipients.

Andrew was a brilliant young high school student from Maryland who used to walk miles every day rather than ride the school bus and have to endure the cruel taunts of classmates who called him a "nerd" and a lot worse. But by the time he won his school's Carson Scholar Award three years in a row, had his name engraved on a large trophy displayed in the hallway of his school, and received the attention of the local media for those accomplishments, he became something of a hero throughout his school and his community. The first morning Andrew's younger sixth-grade brother climbed on the school bus, he made the mistake of walking all the way to the back to look for a seat.

"Hey, get out of here!" he was told. "Only eighth graders allowed back here!"

Then one of the older kids recognized him. "That's Andrew's brother! Hey, man! You can sit back here with us—no problem!"

A couple of years ago, I was thrilled to learn one of my med school "mentees" was a Carson Scholar back during her high school days in Pikesville, Maryland. She went off to college at NYU and came back to medical school at Johns Hopkins. Now she's a fourth-year student, and I've found it particularly rewarding to watch her progress.

Another of our first scholars finished MIT with a 5.0 average and is now employed by Microsoft. As he works his way up the ranks, who knows what may happen? He's already making contributions back to the Carson Scholars Fund.

That's all part of our strategy. We are connecting with extremely bright kids throughout the country, all of whom we expect to be not only successful, but thoughtful and caring people who will be inclined to gratefully remember and donate back to the Carson Scholars Fund—which will help sustain and expand it in the years ahead. Who could have better alumni than the best and the brightest?

We are finding a lot of corporate support, but in some schools the kids themselves are raising the money for the Carson Scholars Fund. It takes $25,000 given by or for any school to permanently endow the program and guarantee that every year one of its students will receive the Carson Scholar honor and the $1,000 scholarship. Some schools choose to participate on an annual basis, which requires only $1,500 a year. Quite a few schools have seen the benefits of the program and are now naming more than one honoree each year.

Another element of our program not only rewards the superstar students, but also directly impacts all of the students in a school. Because we know that 70 to 80 percent of students who eventually drop out of school are functionally illiterate, we're trying to address that issue as well. That's the reason our Carson Scholars Fund sponsors reading rooms in elementary schools. These are designated places, sometimes entire rooms, decorated in bright and inviting colors, furnished with kid-comfortable seating areas, and stocked with wonderful books that appeal to elementary school kids. We even offer a point/prize system for the number of books read, with the hope that those kids who need such motivation will soon discover the joy of reading and never again be at risk of becoming an illiterate dropout. And just maybe some of these kids who are considered the dummies of their class will find that reading will do for them what it did for me.

I'm particularly pleased that the Pittsburgh Steelers and the Indianapolis Colts have donated funds to establish our program at schools in their cities. I've told them it might be more meaningful when athletes are encouraging young people to accept an academic challenge to develop their brains than when I try to do it. Everyone expects a brain surgeon to preach academics. When football players give that same message, more kids pay attention.

I'm hoping we can partner with additional professional teams, not just in football but in other sports. Perhaps colleges as well. We'll take all the help we can get.

Despite everything the skeptics warned us about at the beginning, our recipients, their parents, and educators all testify to the fact that our program is already making a difference. So all of the time, effort, and money we've risked in this endeavor have definitely been worth it. (For more info on the Carson Scholars Fund, go to www.carson scholars.org.)

A True Medical Emergency

In chapter 12 I wrote about the risk I took by going non-par with Blue Cross. I was concerned about the effect of my decision on all those patients and their parents who are uninsured or underinsured—families like the one in which I grew up. We simply couldn't afford to pay for quality medical care.

When I first entered medicine and encountered patients with complex neurosurgery issues whose families didn't have adequate resources to cover our service, I would routinely say to my staff, "Just overwrite it." In other words, *We'll take care of it and just eat the costs.* As long as we didn't do that too often, no one in higher administration at Johns Hopkins raised any objection. But that was back in the days when hospitals actually had money in their budgets. That's no longer the case.

Now if I want to perform an operation on someone who has no insurance and no money, I can no longer tell the patient's family, "That's okay. We'll just write off the expense." My superiors will call a halt and tell me, "You may be willing to overwrite your fee as the surgeon, but can you overwrite the anesthesiology fee? The PICU's fee? This fee and that fee?" Of course the answer is no, I don't have the authority or budget to do that. What should I do, since I believe the practice of medicine ought to be a humanitarian thing and not a big-business thing? It just doesn't feel right to me that every time we see a patient, the first question we ask is "What kind of insurance coverage do you have?" But how do we find another potential payment mechanism so that the size of the bill no longer has to be an overriding concern?

Since we'd already had such great success with our nonprofit Carson Scholars Fund in addressing some of the most serious shortcomings in our educational system, what if we started another nonprofit to take on one of the thorniest problems in medical care today? What if we designed a new and different mechanism whereby anyone who really needed care could get it?

Before I would let myself think seriously along those lines, I had to do a B/WA:

What's the worst thing that happens if I try to do this? If it fails, I will end up investing time, effort, and money for nothing and regret that I didn't use those resources to advantage somewhere else.

What's the best thing that happens if I try to do it? We could meet a desperate need and at the same time make my job more rewarding and a lot more pleasant than it has been lately.

What's the best thing that happens if I don't try to do this? I manage to live with the status quo a few years longer and hope someone eventually finds an answer for one of the most troublesome developments in medicine today.

What's the worst thing that happens if I don't do anything? I burn out and retire early from the practice of medicine, frustrated by my inability to help the very patients who are growing up under the kind of hardship and stress that characterized my own early life.

One of the people I talked to when I got frustrated with the built-in hassles of health care was attorney Ron Shapiro. Ron represents many sports figures and is a terrific motivational speaker; he is also a great thinker and problem solver. He helped me establish (and was the first major donor to) a nonprofit fund that has since become known as "Angels of the OR" when our efforts were joined by long-time friend and colleague Dr. Cliff Solomon, who is interested in doing the same kind of thing for adults as I am for children.

We are continuing to work on establishing a fund we hope can demonstrate the viability of endowments in medicine. One reason universities continue to operate through good times and bad is their endowment funds, so our goal is to create an endowment large enough that we can just use the interest to help cover needy patients' bills. The principal would never decrease, and as we add to it, we will be able to take care of more and more patients.

We see a broader application that could better address the growing financial crisis in American health care today. I know it's a lofty goal, but if we can show how this works on a small scale, we can take this idea to Congress and say, "What about the concept of national endowments for medicine?" We could create a corpus, an endowment fund, the interest on which we use to pay the medical expenses of the neediest.

The numbers could work. Approximately one-seventh of our national economy today is health care related. What if we were smart enough to set aside just 10 percent of that each year to begin a national medical endowment? If we were wise enough and disciplined enough to risk doing that for ten to fifteen years, we would be talking a *corpus* of three trillion dollars. What could we do with the interest on that? We could easily take care of the forty-four million people who have no insurance and quite a few more than that. And if we continued to do that for another ten to fifteen years, we might be talking about a corpus large enough to fund American health care forever—without ever adding another dime to it. Not only would we provide for everyone Medicare and Medicaid now provide for (only better and without the complex rules and costly bureaucracy), but we would actually have what many think they should have—free, universal health care. Except it wouldn't really be free, just paid for. Once and for all.

The nonprofit structure (including legal and financial oversight) for Angels of the OR is in place. We've had several medical device manufacturers, some big corporations, and a few wealthy and nationally prominent people contribute so far. We expect participation to grow, but we have raised enough endowment money already that we hope to begin distributing funding by the time this book is published. Over the next few years, we'll see how the experiment works—and if the results are impressive enough to transfer to a national scale.

I am well aware this revolutionary idea would require considerable forethought and discipline, all-too-rare commodities in our American government where political leadership tends more to the reactionary than to the proactive. But we have some very smart people in this country, and I believe God has given us human beings this remarkable problem-solving potential for innovation, insight, and application. I'm optimistic that if we show at a local level how the endowments work, many bright people across this country (and maybe even enough smart people in Washington) will recognize the wisdom of such a plan to address a looming national catastrophe in health care.

Is this a pipe dream? Could such a reform really happen? Aren't too many politicians too beholden to too many special interests? Maybe. But I know for sure that the financial crisis in health care is going to grow geometrically worse as baby boomers continue to age over the coming decades—unless and until we are willing to take the risk of trying something different. (For more info on Angels of the OR, go to www.angelsoftheor.org.)

For reasons that should be obvious by now, I have great concern about the terrible waste of our nation's most precious resource—the minds of so many young people who may never reach their potential because they have neither the vision nor the encouragement required. As a surgeon, I live and deal with the financial dilemma in medicine every day, so it's not surprising that I would try to apply everything I've said about risk in this book to such personal hot-button subjects.

I'm sure you have special concerns of your own. What are you planning to do about those risks to our nation, its people, and our future? What's keeping you from doing so? Is it the risk you see in getting involved?

These are the kinds of questions I asked recently when I spoke to an audience of major investors at a swank California resort. The sponsor of this conference/retreat, the Northern Trust, a conglomerate of banks whose high-powered clients have at least $75 million or more to invest, invited me to tell about my life and share with their clients my own philosophy of philanthropy. Since these were just the sort of folks I hoped might be interested in one or the other of our nonprofit charities, I was more than happy to share a little of what I've learned through my own involvement with the Carson Scholars Fund and Angels in the OR.

The Risk of Caring—My Philosophy of Philanthropy

I didn't tell my Northern Trust audience, and I won't tell you, that there is no risk to caring or to giving—because there is. Caring deserves a thoughtful B/WA. Consider the societal issue you're most concerned about personally and ask yourself, *What's the best thing that could happen if I get involved and try to do something about it? What's the worst thing that could happen? What's the best thing that could happen if I don't get involved? What's the worst that could happen if I do nothing?*

Don't just focus the questions on the issue. Consider them from your own perspective—what are the best and worst implications for you if you get involved or if you don't? As you weigh the risks, be sure to factor in your values and their impact on your answers. Then answer the same questions from the perspective of the others impacted by this issue.

I confess that my own philosophy of philanthropy is driven primarily by my spiritual values and beliefs. My motivation is simple: Christ said, "Whatever you have done to the least of these, you have done to me." And there is nothing I wouldn't do for him because he has done so much for me.

I'm very much influenced by having grown up very, very poor and remembering how much I appreciated it when anybody who was better off did something nice for us. Having an opportunity to return the favor, to give something back to those in similar situations, is tremendously satisfying.

I also view philanthropy as an investment. We are investing in people, and when you consider how many go astray in our society today, it is heartening to believe you can play a role in somehow redirecting at least some of them. Through Carson Scholars we not only help keep kids heading in the right direction, but also better enable thousands to potentially become *very* productive members of society.

When you compare such tremendous returns on the initial investment, it hardly seems a risk at all. But I'm not suggesting that you should give in order to get. Your motives need to be pure, and giving with the wrong motives is risky. But philanthropy is especially risky when it only involves money. Sometimes it's far more rewarding to give of yourself, your time, and your efforts.

I learned this lesson early on with the Carson Scholars Fund, which we originally called "USA Scholars" in keeping with our national goal to motivate young Americans of all backgrounds to become future leaders and to better measure up to students in other countries. The kids, who wanted and needed a person, a face, to identify with, not just a country, started referring to themselves as "Carson Scholars." They wanted that name attached to the award.

Eventually our board convinced me to call it "Carson Scholars." I was uncomfortable with the idea of using my name at first. As time has passed, however, I've seen the positive reaction of people, particularly young people, wherever I go. *Oh, there's Dr. Ben Carson!* When I see how excited they are getting over something that is intellectual, as opposed to athletic or entertaining, I'm gratified by how much progress we are making.

As I indicated to the Northern Trust folks, the most meaningful philanthropy involves risking something of yourself—your time, your interest, your security, your future, your priorities, your reputation. You put all of these things at risk in order to accomplish what you envision as a greater good, but you have no guarantee. You can never be certain the recipients of your giving will use what they get in a way that will make you proud. So that too is a risk.

It's difficult for me to talk about philanthropy without acknowledging its connection in my mind with biblical teaching on the importance of tithing. That principle wasn't just for those with $75 million or more to invest—God asks all of us to give him a tenth of our best, however much we have.

For most of us, but especially people living close to the edge financially, the idea of giving 10 percent to God for the benefit of others is truly an act of faith and may seem like a substantial risk to our livelihood. Yet I can tell you I have never regretted tithing, nor have I ever known anyone who suffered in tithing, because God is true to his word and promises to bless our tithe.

I'm not saying what I know you've probably heard some people preach—that if you give your money, God will bless you by giving you wealth or some guaranteed monetary return of fortyfold or a hundredfold. I don't believe the Bible tells us that. What it does promise is a blessing—on us as well as what we give.

As often as not, our blessing may come in the currency of emotional satisfaction, a real enough reward that I often find more than generous. But at least two other advantages are to be gained as well.

Scientists are studying actual positive physical benefits that result from individuals' thinking about, serving, and giving to others. I suspect someday they will be able to measure an increase in endorphin levels or other chemical indicators of well-being that will document the reality of a phenomenon researchers have long recognized and termed "helper's high." I believe there are indeed physical, tangible benefits to be enjoyed from God's blessing on our giving.

There is also at least one very practical reward: when you are paying attention to finances, which you have to do to tithe because you have to know what 10 percent of your income is, you just naturally end up being more aware, more careful, and more deliberate about what you do with all of your financial resources. As the book of Proverbs says, there are benefit and blessing just in knowing the actual state of your plots, as opposed to having a general sense. The logical consequence of regular proportional giving makes you much more careful—in terms of both what you are spending and how you invest your money.

Experiencing that real, practical benefit, on top of the less tangible but still very real emotional and physical blessings, has made tithing a low-risk, no-brainer decision for me. I see the same principle applying to philanthropy. Giving may seem like a sacrifice, yet in the long run it's not. Somehow in God's economy, by giving to others, you will generally end up better off. So will the rest of the world.

I won't try to tell you that your giving or mine will cure all the world's ills. But I am convinced that any number of crises facing our nation today and tomorrow could benefit not just from our giving, but from a careful risk analysis and a leadership willing and able to understand, accept, and take appropriate risks.

In the following chapter we'll consider a few that come to my mind.

Even Bigger Risks

Not long ago, our list of patients had grown so long that I couldn't fit them all into that month's schedule. So I asked my physician's assistants to pare the list down by determining which patients I most needed to see. It was easy to check the charts and ask previous patients to wait a little longer for routine follow-up exams, but new patients required more research to know how urgent their cases really were.

That's how we found out about a little boy with a potentially serious neurosurgical problem who was scheduled for a first-time visit. When we called to speak to his mom for more information, the boy's aunt told us she wasn't available. After we explained our situation, the aunt said that the boy's mother was in a psychiatric facility and that she, the aunt, though not an official legal guardian, had assumed care of the child and planned to accompany her nephew to Johns Hopkins.

Because of patient privacy issues raised by the current HIPPA regulations, a red flag went up. We had to ask ourselves, can we still see this patient? We'd never had a case quite like this, so one of my PAs phoned the Johns Hopkins' HIPPA office. (Like other hospitals, we have a cadre of people who do nothing but explain, monitor compliance with, and enforce HIPPA regulations throughout the hospital.) The first person we talked to didn't know if HIPPA rules allowed us to see a minor patient accompanied by a relative who was not his legal guardian. So we talked to a HIPPA office supervisor who eventually sent us to the hospital's legal office, where the question kept getting passed up the ladder. The head of our legal office finally got back to us saying, "According to the regulations, we cannot see this patient."

In other words, regulations designed to protect patients' privacy were preventing us from caring for a patient whose life might be at risk. The real issue was not privacy but the health of this child. The artificial, imposed issue—the risk of violating HIPPA guidelines—trumped that concern.

Unfortunately, that's an all-too-common result of overregulating risk. Too easily we lose sight of our goal, getting so bogged down in micro-risks that we miss the macro-risks—some of which are inadvertently created by too-careful management of the micro-risk. It's like being so concerned that your baby, who's just learning to take his first micro-steps, doesn't fall too hard that you never notice the two of you are standing in the middle of a highway with a macro-truck barreling toward you at seventy miles an hour. This kind of thing happens a lot in medicine these days.

Here's another example. The original role of circulating nurses in the OR was to "circulate" around the room during an operation, keeping an eye on the medical team and the equipment, anticipating needs and problems, making sure that all of the details were in order, and keeping an experienced eye on the action as an extra safety precaution. But legal paranoia has resulted in so many regulations today that a circulating nurse no longer has time to move out of her seat. Instead, the circulating nurse's time is consumed by the checklists and paperwork that have to be filled out at every stage of the operation to create a paper trail to prove everything was done safely and properly in case the patient files a suit. Here again an imposed and secondary concern, abiding by safety regulations, trumps the original intent of actually providing safety.

Or consider the unintended consequences of legal judgments in liability cases against doctors—the patients' right to sue to protect them against the potential risk of medical malpractice. The specter of increased lawsuits, soaring settlements, and the skyrocketing cost of malpractice insurance today is driving some doctors out of the medical profession and discouraging a lot of bright young people from even considering a career in medicine today.

For example, there's the implication of liability on obstetricians who can legally be sued for birth-related injuries or conditions anytime before a child they've delivered turns eighteen. Knowing there is no way they could continue to afford malpractice insurance premiums on their retirement income, and leery of exposing themselves and their families to financial ruin in their golden years, many obstetricians are making the decision to quit delivering babies eighteen years before their planned retirement. As a result, society is deprived the services of some of our most experienced OBs in the prime of their lives.

Then there are neurosurgeons, whose average life expectancy already is ten years lower than the general population's. On top of job stress, there is so much increased financial stress and liability exposure that many areas of the country no longer have neurosurgeons who cover emergencies — a worsening problem over the last ten to fifteen years. In a lot of places, if you get in an auto accident, suffer a simple subdural hematoma, and are rushed to the nearest ER, you will quickly learn that things have changed. A few years ago, a neurosurgeon would have come in, operated, and taken it out. After some rehab, you would have been fine. But today you might die — simply because fewer neurosurgeons are on call for emergencies. Tomorrow a lot more people will die needlessly for this very same reason.

We've provided our patients with every right to sue, but in the process we've lowered their odds of living long enough to do so. That doesn't make sense.

Unfortunately, medicine isn't the only place this sort of thinking (or should I say, lack of thinking) occurs. Remember how the liability concern over the risk of students' getting scratched or bitten by the animals in Mr. Jaeck's science lab trumped what should have been everyone's primary concern — inspiring and fostering an interest in science among grade school students?

Or consider the more ominous issue of airport security. To avoid the risk of profiling passengers by sex, age, race, or nationality, our already-stretched-too-thin security teams are required to give the same scrutiny to little old ladies from Kansas traveling with their grandchildren as they do to single, twentysomething males in Arab dress carrying Middle Eastern passports. What is the primary concern here?

Perhaps it's time to do a B/WA on the risk of failing to identify and assess real risks — or maybe on the risk of failing to think.

The No-Money Risk

You must be able to think big before you can consider the risks inherent in something like a growing national debt—and you have to think even bigger to imagine addressing the problem.

So how's this for a big idea? Perhaps we could pay off our national debt if we did away with money altogether. Sound risky? Hear me out. (I've actually spoken to the president about this issue.)

Who is the fairest individual in the universe? The answer, of course, is God. What does the Bible say God requires of his people financially? A tithe. A percentage. Ten percent. He didn't say, if your crops all die, don't give me anything. He didn't say, when you have a bumper crop, give me a triple tithe. There must be something inherently fair about proportionality if God thought tithing was the way to go. For that reason I'm convinced any national model we use ought to be based on a proportional template. That's the bottom-line requirement.

But the real starting point is getting rid of money altogether. No more paper money, no more coins, no more credit cards. Identify everyone by a scan of their handprint and their retina and do all monetary transactions electronically. Then if we set a national tax rate of 10 percent (or 12 to 15 percent, if that's what it takes) on all financial transactions, the government would bring in 10 percent of the gross domestic product (GDP), which is certainly more than what is collected in taxes now—far more.

I know numerous glitches would have to be worked out, and some new safeguards would have to be put in place for this concept to work on such a massive scale, but some such system would have a number of positive effects.

The first would be psychological. Right now there are widespread issues with fairness—at every level of society.

I know billionaires who pay very little tax because they utilize every possible mechanism to avoid doing so. It's hard to blame them, because the government claims a disproportionately huge chunk of their income. But an across-the-board proportional tax on all financial transactions would do away with most of the incentives for corporations and very rich individuals to dodge taxes. No more need for complex and costly tax loopholes, sophisticated financial shell games, or banks in the Cayman Islands. There would no longer be the need to hide income. More money would stay in our country to be spent and invested here. And I believe most of the wealthy would gladly pay their share of a straight percentage they knew wasn't higher than everyone else's.

Right now, families making $50,000 to $200,000 a year, which includes a lot of the middle class, are getting clobbered percentagewise. They are having to foot a disproportionate amount of the tax bill and often end up paying a higher percentage of their income in taxes than the super rich in order to provide for those who contribute nothing to the pot—which doesn't really seem fair either way to those in the beleaguered middle class.

Then there are some people below a certain income line who have no tax obligations at all—which many folks seem to think is a wonderful thing. But if we're not careful, that can be a lot like patting someone on the head and saying, "There, there, you're so poor you don't have to do anything. We'll take care of you." I don't think that's a very good idea either, if for no other reason than what it does to people's self esteem. At least in that sense, the current system isn't really fair to the poor either.

A tax that is a functional percentage of all the transactions that make up the GDP would benefit all of us. Without penalizing the rich or patronizing the poor, we could easily take in enough money to quickly erase the national debt. If a situation arises in which we get into a war and we need more money, no problem. Since it's all done electronically, zap, you can just raise the rate up a couple of percentage points and not have to worry about running a deficit at all.

Some people say, "That all sounds well and good, but it hurts the little guy more than it hurts the big guy. A guy making only $10,000 a year has to give a good thousand, and that hurts him more than the guy who makes $10 billion and has to give a billion." Well, I don't see anywhere in God's plan where it says you have to hurt the guy who makes a lot to compensate. I mean, the guy just put a billion dollars in the pot! We should be happy because he's making it that much easier for the rest of us. Penalizing him for that is just totally distorted thinking.

Frankly, jealously makes people think that way, and jealousy is always counterproductive.

A functional tax on the GDP would provide the government with more than enough funding to cover its current obligations *and* to assist the struggling guy who makes $10,000 a year if, when, and how he needs some help. In the meantime he feels more invested in society and may even feel better about himself because he knows he's paying his fair share. He goes about his daily life knowing he's helping to pay for the roads he drives on, the schools his kids attend, the police officers who protect him—so he's just as much a contributing citizen as the next person. Not only is that good for his psyche, but it's good for everybody else. It could even eliminate a reason for those who do pay taxes to resent those who don't.

In addition to providing adequate revenue, the kind of system we're talking about would eliminate much of the bureaucracy needed to collect it, which would reduce the cost of government as well. If we got rid of money and made every financial transaction electronically, we'd increase the tax base by approximately 30 percent—the estimate of the cash transactions and underground economy that go untaxed now—which would allow us to lower the tax percentage by that much. Everyone from hot dog vendors on New York City street corners to big-time eBayers would have to pay the same percentage into the system, but they would all be treated equally. That new input might lower the percentage even further.

One more added benefit would be the crippling effect a moneyless financial system would have on drug dealers and other organized (and disorganized) crime networks. Because the underworld now operates largely on a cash basis, illegal business would have a difficult new hurdle to overcome.

I've actually discussed this idea with a number of congresspeople and senators. Most of them agree the idea would work—and probably work very well. But they admit that the main obstacle would be all of the special interest groups that benefit from the current system and would fight to the death against change. So it would require strong and courageous leadership willing to take the risk or enough of the populace understanding the challenge to pressure their legislators to do something that makes sense. If we all start thinking about solutions rather than sitting around complaining and criticizing, we would be much better off as a society.

I have little doubt that some moneyless electronic plan will be the way we eventually do business in this country. With the advent of electronic banking and online bill paying in the last few years, we're already a long ways down that road. It's eventually going to happen—unless we first succumb to a related risk I'd like to point out.

The Do-Nothing Risk

Some issues confronting us seem so big, so overwhelming, that we become paralyzed and unable to respond at all. More often than not, our lack of response is the manifestation of an even bigger societal threat—the risk of complacency.

One example: virtually everybody knows our government and its bureaucratic machinery are being run (or at least regularly and routinely manipulated) by special interests. Our congresspeople are spending more than half their time raising funds just to stay in office. Naturally they are influenced by those who provide those funds, some more easily than others. We all know this. The majority of us agree it's a serious problem that places our democratic ideals at risk, yet most of us just shrug and say, "What can we do? That's just the way it is!"

Yet the more we voice such acquiescence, the greater the risk our words will become a self-fulfilling prophecy. We need to remember that the very foundation and strength of our nation is "we the people." From its very beginning until and including today, *we the people* are the United States of America. It's not *we the government*! The government doesn't exist to rule us; it exists to serve us!

Ultimately, we still hold the power. We hold the purse strings. We all have a vote, and we all have a voice with which to speak, to be heard, to try to make a difference.

We forget that at our own risk.

Playing with Risk

I believe far too many of us are complacent about the devastating impact of gambling on our nation and on so many families and individuals today.

I absolutely abhor gambling. But I'm also a pragmatist who realizes, abhorrent or not, it's not going away anytime soon.

So when I received an invitation to speak at a huge national convention of the gaming industry, I accepted. Then I had to decide what I ought to say to them. I took the risk of leveling with my audience and posing what I knew was something of a wild idea to all those casino owners and operators. After I recounted some of my personal story and talked to them about the amazing potential of the human brain to help us solve problems and deal with the challenges facing us—individually and as a nation—I went on to tell them, "I know you guys like to think what you do is all fun and games, that you are just providing entertainment for people. But if you are really honest about it, you have to realize you are ruining a lot of lives.

"Now, I've met some of you, and I don't think you're the kind of people who *want* to ruin other people's lives. You really do want your customers to be entertained and have fun. So wouldn't it be great if we could find a better, more responsible way to let gamblers have fun? Surely if we devoted our brainpower to this question we could come up with a better, workable way.

"Credit card companies manage risk by offering limited credit to people based on their income. What if you set things up so it could only be possible to gamble with a gambling card, which had a pre-imposed limit based on a person's current level of income? That way nobody could spend the baby's milk money or the family rent money and yet they can still have fun."

Believe it or not, when I finished my speech, that audience gave me a warm response. I don't know if they really liked everything I said, or if they just acted as if they liked it.

But did I really expect to change people's minds, to get them to buy into such a radical idea? Do I think they all went back to Las Vegas or Atlantic City or wherever and started designing gambling cards for their casinos? Of course not. Would I expect an industry that makes billions and billions of dollars every year off of people taking poor risks to do anything that would change the status quo? Not really. But is it possible I got some of the people in my audience that day to begin to think, to at least consider the possibility there could be some better, less harmful way of doing business? I believe the odds on that are quite good.

I always knew that was a long shot at best. In fact, I wasn't at all sure what kind of reaction I would get even raising the subject before such a potentially hostile audience. But I decided it was worth the risk.

I didn't do a formal B/WA before determining what to say. But thinking in basic risk-analysis terms is so habitual now that I do it at least subconsciously.

What is the worst thing that could happen if I challenge leaders of the gambling industry? They might simply ignore what I said or decide never to invite me to speak at a gaming industry convention again. No great loss to me there.

What is the best thing that could happen if I say what I want to say? I could be planting a seed that might at least get some people thinking about what they do.

What is the best thing that could happen if I don't take the risk of saying anything? I could just take their money, make some benign comments at the convention that skirt my convictions, and count it as a plus to turn false-hope gambling money into Carson Scholar money that could offer real hope to young people.

What is the worst thing that could happen if I don't say anything? I'd be making a compromise I couldn't feel good about—by accepting the speaking engagement for the money and passing up the opportunity (maybe even the responsibility) to be true to my convictions.

Thinking about it that way, I realized I was, in gambling terms, playing with house money. I really had nothing to lose. If we're going to have legalized gambling, I think some sort of framework for limiting its damage makes a lot of sense. I don't really expect the gaming industry to voluntarily impose limits on itself. Gambling lobbyists spend millions to buy legislative votes in a day when state-run lotteries have become some of the nation's most popular and exploitative gambling ventures, so I don't expect a gambling-addicted government to push for reform anytime soon either.

But what might happen if "we the people" realized that legalized gambling is already regulated in this country and is subject to both laws and gaming commission regulations? What if enough of us decided not to just sit here and let things keep going the way they are? What if we realized we really do have the ability to intervene?

What are the risks? Given the growing popularity of everything from online gambling to televised celebrity poker tournaments, this probably wouldn't be the most popular topic to talk about. So I suppose there is some risk in raising questions and speaking out on the subject. But in my mind that doesn't compare to the greater risk to society in silently standing by and watching the lives of so many millions of individuals and families being destroyed by foolish risks taken in pursuit of false dreams. If the biggest downside is that the gaming industry might make a few billion less each year, is that a bad thing?

Certainly it's worth the risk to at least talk about.

Nuclear Risks

For more than sixty years now, the inhabitants of our planet have awakened each morning to a nightmarish reality that has included the specter of nuclear destruction. The level of threat has waxed and waned over the past couple of generations as the Cold War played out and new players have entered the current high-stakes game of global risk. But we all know the threat remains, so maybe it's time to do a serious B/WA of what many would consider the ultimate risk facing our world today.

Let's look at the point in time when many historians would argue our world was at greatest risk of nuclear annihilation. No one can know all the thoughts that went through the mind of President Kennedy during the Cuban Missile Crisis, but it seems obvious to me he did his own version of B/WA, which must have gone something like this:

What's the best thing that could happen if we allow Russia to put nuclear missiles in Cuba? We would have to live at the mercy of our biggest enemy.

What's the worst thing that could happen if we allow Russia to carry out its plans? With nuclear missiles aimed at us from ninety miles away, our greatest enemy could destroy America before we even had time to retaliate.

What's the worst that could happen if we try to stop them? It could escalate tensions or even trigger a nuclear war.

What's the best that could happen if we try to stop them? Russia could back down, we could return to the uneasy stalemate we have had before now, and our willingness to stand strong might discourage further threats in the future.

Different people might have answered those questions differently depending on their knowledge of the facts, their understanding of the possibilities, and even their own sense of values. But clearly President Kennedy came to the conclusion that the only acceptable and positive outcome required the United States to take whatever measures were necessary to prevent the deployment of nuclear-armed missiles in Cuba.

Of course, the question of how to do that required many subsequent decisions that would have warranted their own B/WAs. (Do we declare our position publicly to try to bring international pressure to bear? Should we start with back-channel communications to call their bluff and give them a chance to save face and retreat quietly? Do we enforce a naval blockade? And so on.)

We all know what happened in that nuclear stare down. The level of risk did indeed escalate in the short run. But then the Communists blinked, and the imminent threat quickly ebbed to an unsettling, deeper, yet perhaps healthier, understanding of the reality in our two nations' policies of mutually assured destruction.

The nuclear threat our nation faces today is quite different from our two-party standoff with Russia in the early 1960s. But the threat posed by a rabble of nuclear-armed rogue states is every bit as real and perhaps even more dangerously nuanced than a straightforward showdown with an opposing superpower. So a similar risk analysis might serve us well.

Would it be risky for the United States to become "the world policeman" and try to prevent more nations from developing nuclear capability? Of course. But determining whether we should do so ought to require us to ask, *What's the best thing that happens if we take a stand to prevent rogue nations from developing nuclear weapons? What's the worst thing that can happen? What's the best thing that happens if we allow a rogue nation to develop nuclear weapons? What's the worst that can happen?*

Here again, possible answers to these questions may vary depending on people's knowledge and understanding of current circumstances, their reading of historical precedent, their own convictions and beliefs, and so on. But to my thinking, the only question that offers any hope for a positive outcome and would be at all acceptable is the first one. And that brings me to this personal conclusion: if we don't take a stand but rather continue a course of inconsistent responses, we may well exacerbate deteriorating international relationships, which could lead to another world war with an attending threat of atomic annihilation.

When there is no course to take without risk, you have to carefully weigh which risk you prefer to live with. I sometimes find myself getting into arguments, or "intense discussions," about such issues — often with people with significant diplomatic and government experience. Sometimes they will dismiss my arguments by pointing out that I am not trained in international affairs, and since it's not my field of expertise, I therefore couldn't possibly grasp the subtleties of the issue. They suggest that if I only knew what they knew, I wouldn't be making such simplistic suggestions.

Such condescension bothers me because I always tell my patients, or the parents of my patients, that even though a planned neurosurgical procedure will be extremely complex and requires years of study and training to perform, I believe I have failed as a pediatric neurosurgeon if I cannot help them fully understand what we are about to do, the rationale behind it, and all of the risks it presents.

Saying that something is too complex for others to understand is usually a cop-out people use when they don't have a good argument. I believe all things that are logical can be broken down, explained, and understood. Certainly we should expect no less from our government with anything as crucial as our stand on nuclear proliferation. We may not all come to the same conclusions when we do our risk analysis, but we should all agree that an open and thoughtful discussion would benefit, and just might reassure, us all. Maybe we could start with a good B/WA!

The Risk of Silence

There's one more serious risk for America that I want to mention here—the risk we have created by shouting down and shutting up any discussion of faith in the public square. It's as if we've decided expressions or discussions of faith shouldn't qualify as free speech. What's even stranger is the way it has somehow been tied to the concept of separation of church and state, even though that concept has nothing to do with people living by or publicly discussing their faith.

In fact, if you go back and look at the public and private writings of many of our founding fathers, you will find they are riddled with religious thought, biblical values, and spiritual principles. In many cases it was those very thoughts, values, and principles upon which this nation was built. And yet the purveyors of political correctness would have us all believe their revisionist history in which America was founded to provide its citizens "freedom *from* religion" instead of "freedom *of* religion." What a travesty that we've allowed them to muddy and distort the difference!

I have no doubt that the men who laid the foundation of this country would turn over in their graves if they knew that public expression of faith faced the kind of opposition it does today. They would probably say, "Why, this is the very sort of restriction of thoughts and words that we were trying to get away from!"

If you doubt my imagined speculation, consider the actual words of Thomas Jefferson etched upon the stone walls of his monument in our nation's capital:

> Almighty God hath created the mind free. All attempts to influence it by temporal punishments or burthens ... are a departure from the plan of the Holy Author of our religion.... No man shall be compelled to frequent or support any religious worship or ministry or shall otherwise suffer on account of his religious opinions or belief, but all men shall be free to profess and by argument to maintain, their opinions in matters of religion....

> God who gave us life gave us liberty. Can the liberties of a nation be secure when we have removed a conviction that these liberties are the gift of God? Indeed I tremble for my country when I reflect that God is just, that his justice cannot sleep forever.

Does that sound as if Jefferson understood the distinction between freedom *from* religion and freedom *of* religion?

I've been telling audiences for years that this politically incorrect attitude that any public talk about God is not only inappropriate but somehow violates the principles upon which this country was founded is absurd. Our country's Declaration of Independence talks about the inalienable rights our Creator endowed upon us. Our Pledge of Allegiance to our flag says we are "one nation under God." Many courtrooms in our land have on their walls "In God we trust." Every coin in our pockets, every bill in our wallets also reads "In God we trust."

If he is acknowledged in our Constitution, honored in our pledge, and paid tribute to in our courts and on our money, yet we can't talk about God in public, what does that say about the state of our country? In medicine we'd diagnose that as schizophrenia! Wouldn't that designation describe a lot of what's going on in our nation today?

Politically correct paranoia requires us to speak of "winter holidays" rather than "Christmas." How ridiculous is that? Think about it. The last time you signed a check and wrote in the date, you included the year—and the year itself is a reference to Christ. So it makes little sense that we refuse to recognize Christmas as Jesus' birthday when every day and all of history are referenced to his existence. There have been a lot of great people throughout history, but nobody else has seen history divided by his birth.

This too may be changing, however, as a growing number of secular historians and assorted other academic types have redefined *BC* to mean "before the common era" and replaced *AD* with *CE*, for "common era." But this intellectually dishonest sleight-of-hand doesn't change the significance of the one person whose birth triggered the most important turning point in history.

Not only is the current politically correct attitude silly, but limiting the discussion of faith in the public square creates some serious risks for all of society. Let me explain.

Once expressions and discussion of faith are no longer welcome or permitted in the public square, our society and our people will quickly lose touch with the spiritual dimension of life. If we no longer talk freely and openly about faith, we won't understand the language or the significance of faith, we'll misinterpret the religious words and deeds of others, and we'll underestimate the power faith can have in the lives of those deeply committed to their spiritual beliefs. This may present a serious risk to a generation whose most troubling conflicts promise to involve people who are primarily motivated by a very different faith. If we don't understand the faith roots of our American culture, how will we be able to defend it against theirs?

There is also a serious risk to believers when there is no public discussion of faith and the general populace no longer understands the basics of faith. What people don't understand, they tend to fear, and fear triggers anger. You can see evidence of this already in the growing hostility toward believers in so many segments of society.

This is all the more reason I believe accomplished people in particular, who are also people of faith, should be open about what they believe, because there is a pervasive feeling in the intellectual community that faith is only for weak-minded folks. We as Christians need to dispel that notion by articulating what we believe and why. We need to make it clear to people what it means to live by godly principles—loving your fellow man, caring for your neighbor, and living a life of service by developing your God-given talents to the point that you become invaluable to the people around you. We need to remind each other that there is nothing judgmental about having values and principles, and there is nothing wrong with standing for something.

The greatest risk in removing faith from the public square is that we, our society, and our world lose any real sense of right and wrong. The politically correct thinking on this is not only completely illogical, but distortedly dangerous. The attitude seems to be that if only we could remove God from the equation, then everyone would be not only good but better than ever.

The great Russian novelist Fyodor Dostoevsky, a man who witnessed and understood a lot more about human nature than most, knew better. He observed, "If you were to destroy in mankind the belief in immortality, not only love, but every living force maintaining the life of the world would at once be dried up.... [For] if God does not exist, everything is permitted."

Dostoevsky was right. Without faith and values by which to weigh the answers of our B/WAs, there is no way to conduct a valid or meaningful risk analysis. For if there is no right or wrong, there can be no best or worst.

That's a risk none of us should be willing to take.

Conclusion
My Prescription
in a Dangerous World

As boys, whenever my brother, Curtis, or I offered our mother an excuse for failing to accomplish something—whenever we complained about some seemingly insurmountable problem, whenever we grew weary or discouraged by some obstacle in the road of life, or especially whenever we whined about anything—she always offered the same response. She would get a puzzled look on her face and ask, "Do you have a brain?"

The implication was crystal clear: *If you have a brain, use it! It's all you need to overcome any problem!*

My mother instilled in me a deep respect for the potential of the human brain, and that respect has deepened over the years to an attitude I can only describe as *awe*. Every time I open a child's head and see a brain, I marvel at the mystery: *This is what makes every one of us who we are. This is what holds all our memories, all our thoughts, all our dreams. This is what makes us different from each other in millions of ways.* And yet if I could expose my brain and your brain and place them side by side, you wouldn't be able to tell the difference— even though we might be very different people. That still amazes me.

Inside each human brain are billions and billions of complex interconnections, neurons and synapses, which science has only barely begun to understand. When you add to that the mystery of mind and spirit, the human brain becomes a laboratory so vast and intricate you could work in it for a millennium and hardly scratch the surface.

Whenever I speak to audiences, I try to inspire them to consider the power and implications of such potential. I tell them that no computer network on earth can come close to the capacity of the average human brain. This resource that each one of us has is a tremendous gift from God—the most complex organ system in the entire universe. Your brain can take in two million bits of information per second. I tell audiences of several thousand people that if I could bring one person up onstage, have her look out at the crowd for one second, and lead her away, fifty years later I could perform an operation, take off the cranial bone, put in some depth electrodes, and stimulate the appropriate area of her brain, and she could remember not only where everyone was sitting, but what they were wearing.

That's how amazing and complex the human brain is. It's literally mind-boggling.

When I speak to students I sometimes illustrate this further by asking how many of them remember what they had for lunch in the cafeteria that day. (If I'm addressing accountants, I'll ask who remembers the last time they did a sum total of values.) The point is to get them to raise their hands.

Then I run through a rapid-fire riff something like this: "Let's think about what your brain had to do when I asked that question. First, the sound waves had to leave my lips, travel through the air into your external auditory meatus, travel down to your tympanic membrane, and set up a vibratory force that traveled across the ossicles of your middle ear to the oval and round windows, generating a vibratory force in the endolymph, which mechanically distorts the microcilia, converting mechanical energy to electrical energy, which traveled across the cochlear nerve to the cochlear nucleus at the ponto-medullary junction, from there to the superior olivary nucleus, ascending bilaterally up the brain stem through the lateral lemniscus to the inferior colliculus and the medial geniculate nucleus, then across the thalamic radiations to the posterior temporal lobes to begin the auditory processing, from there to the frontal lobes, coming down the tract of Vicq d'Azur, retrieving the memory from the medial hippocampal structures and the mammillary bodies, back to the frontal lobes to start the motor response at the Betz cell level, coming down the cortico-spinal tract, across the internal capsule into the cerebral peduncle, descending to the cervicomedullary decussation into the spinal cord gray matter, synapsing, and going out to the neuromuscular junction, stimulating the nerve and the muscle so you could raise your hand."

Of course, that's the simplified version. If I were to get into all of the inhibitory and coordinating influences, I would be talking for hours about this one thing.

The point is, we can decry the dangers we face or ignore them or even allow ourselves to be paralyzed by fear.

Or we can ask ourselves, *do we have a brain?*

Then let's use this incredible tool God has given us to assess the risks that we face every day. We have the means to analyze risks and decide which are worth taking and which should be avoided.

Do you have a brain? Then use it.

That's the secret.

That's my simple but powerful prescription for life, love, and success in a dangerous world.

Notes

1. John F. Ross, *The Polar Bear Strategy: Reflections on Risk in Modern Life* (New York: Perseus Books, 1999), 7.
2. Peter L. Bernstein, *Against the Gods: The Remarkable Story of Risk* (New York: Wiley and Sons, 1996), 2.
3. Gavin de Becker, *The Gift of Fear* (New York: Dell, 1998), 376.
4. Gregg Lewis and Deborah Shaw Lewis, *Ben Carson* (Grand Rapids: Zonderkidz, 2002).

Think Big

Unleashing Your Potential for Excellence

Ben Carson, MD, with Cecil Murphey

This book is for you if your life is a series of shattered dreams.

This book is for you if you have no dreams at all. It's for you if you've bought the lie that you'll never amount to anything. That's not true. Your life is BIG — far bigger than you've imagined.

Inside these pages lie the keys to recognizing the full potential of your life. You won't necessarily become a millionaire (though you might), but you will attain a life that is rewarding, significant, and more fruitful than you ever thought possible.

The author of this book knows about hardship. Ben Carson grew up in inner-city Detroit. His mother was illiterate. His father had left the family. His grade-school classmates considered Ben stupid. He struggled with a violent temper. In every respect, Ben's harsh circumstances seemed only to point to a harsher future and a bad end. But that's not what happened.

By applying the principles in this book, Ben rose from his tough life to one of amazing accomplishments and international renown. He learned that he had potential, he learned how to unleash it, and he did.

You can too. Put the principles in this book in motion. Things won't change overnight, but they will change. You can transform your life into one you'll love, bigger than you've ever dreamed.

ZONDERVAN®
.com

Gifted Hands

The Ben Carson Story

Ben Carson, MD, with Cecil Murphey

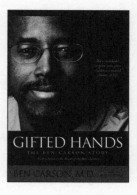

In 1987, Dr. Benjamin Carson gained worldwide recognition for his part in the first successful separation of Siamese twins joined at the back of the head. The extremely complex and delicate operation, five months in the planning and twenty-two hours in the execution, involved a surgical plan that Carson helped initiate. Carson pioneered again in a rare procedure known as hemispherectomy, giving children without hope a second chance at life through a daring operation in which he literally removed one half of their brain. But such breakthroughs aren't unusual for Ben Carson. He's been beating the odds since he was a child. Raised in inner-city Detroit by a mother with a third grade education, Ben lacked motivation. He had terrible grades. And a pathological temper threatened to put him in jail. But Sonya Carson convinced her son that he could make something of his life, even though everything around him said otherwise. Trust in God, a relentless belief in his own capabilities, and sheer determination catapulted Ben from failing grades to the top of his class — and beyond to a Yale scholarship … the University of Michigan Medical School … and finally, at age thirty-three, the directorship of pediatric neurosurgery at Johns Hopkins Hospital in Baltimore, Maryland. Today, Dr. Ben Carson holds twenty honorary doctorates and is the possessor of a long string of honors and awards, including the Horatio Alger Award, induction into the "Great Blacks in Wax" Museum in Baltimore, Maryland, and an invitation as Keynote Speaker at the 1997 President's National Prayer Breakfast. *Gifted Hands* is the riveting story of one man's secret for success, tested against daunting odds and driven by an incredible mindset that dares to take risks. This inspiring autobiography takes you into the operating room to witness surgeries that made headlines around the world — and into the private mind of a compassionate, God-fearing physician who lives to help others. Through it all shines a humility, quick wit, and down-to-earth style that make this book one you won't easily forget.